EDIBLE AND POISONOUS
MUSHROOMS
OF THE WORLD

POISONOUS
MUSHROOMS
OF THE WORLD

IAN R. HALL

STEVEN L. STEPHENSON

PETER K. BUCHANAN

WANG YUN

ANTHONY L. J. COLE

Timber Press
Portland • Cambridge

Published in 2003 by

Timber Press, Inc.
The Haseltine Building
133 S.W. Second Avenue, Suite 450
Portland, Oregon 97204, U.S.A.

Timber Press
2 Station Road
Swavesey
Cambridge CB4 5QJ, U.K.

Printed through Colorcraft Ltd, Hong Kong

Library of Congress Cataloging-in-Publication Data

Edible and poisonous mushrooms of the world / Ian R. Hall ... [et al.].
   p. cm.
  Includes bibliographical references (p.)
  ISBN 0-88192-586-1
     1. Mushrooms, Edible--Identification. 2. Mushrooms, Poisonous--
   Identification. 3. Mushrooms, Edible--Pictorial works. 4. Mush-
   rooms, Poisonous--Pictorial works. I. Hall, Ian R. (Ian Robert), 1946-

QK67.E37 2003
579.6'163--dc21   2002075652

CONTENTS

WARNINGS

Certain poisonous and edible mushrooms are easily confused. Before eating any mushroom, be absolutely sure of its identity and edibility. When it comes to mushrooms that are not illustrated in this book, or that are known to vary in appearance from the illustrations included in this book, it may be necessary to consult other texts listed in the bibliography, or a mushroom specialist. Please note, however, that the edibility of many mushrooms is still unknown. If there is any doubt whatsoever as to the identity and edibility of a mushroom, do not eat it. Even for a mushroom known to be edible, one should eat only a small amount the first time. Moreover, when eating wild mushrooms or new cultivated mushrooms, always place some uncooked ones aside in the refrigerator in case there has been a mistake or there is an allergic reaction to the mushroom. If any illness is experienced after eating a mushroom, consult a doctor immediately.

Reasonable efforts have been made to publish reliable data and information, but the authors and publisher cannot assume responsibility for the validity of all materials or for the consequences of their use. The publishers and the authors can take no responsibility for the misidentification of mushrooms by the users of this book nor any illness that might result from their consumption.

Lưu ý

Một số loại nêm độc rết khó phân biệt với các loại nêm có thể ăn được. Vì vậy trước khi ăn bết cứ loại nêm nào, bạn phải biết chắc chắn về nguồn gốc và tố chết của nó. Bạn cần tra cứu lại danh mục cuốn sách hoặc tham vên các chuyên gia về nêm nếu gặp phải những loại nêm không được mô tả trong cuốn sách này hoặc hình dách của nó khác với những loại được minh họa. Xin lưu ý, chúng ta vẫn chưa biết rõ nguồn gốc và độc tố của một số loại nêm. Vì vậy xin đừng ăn nếu bạn có nghi ngờ về nguồn gốc và độc chết của các loại nêm đó. Khi ăn các loại nêm dại hoặc các giống nêm mới, bạn nên luôn để dành một ít vào tủ lạnh phòng khi bạn bị dị ứng với loài nêm đó. Nếu cảm thêy khó chịu sau khi ăn bạn nên đến xem bác sỹ ngay lập tức. Tác giả và nhà xuết bản đã nỗ lực để mang đến cho bạn những thông tin chính xác đáng tin cậy.

Tuy nhiên chúng tôi sẽ không chịu trách nhiệm về sự chính xác tuyệt đối của các thông tin trên và hậu quả của việc sử dụng nó. Chúng tôi sẽ không chịu trách nhiệm nếu độc giả không phân biệt đúng các loài nấm và những căn bệnh gây ra bởi sử dụng các loài nấm trên.

注意

毒茸か食べられる茸か紛らわしいのがあります。茸を食べる前に、その正体と食用性を、必ずご確認ください。この本に描かれていない茸、またはこの本に含まれている図とその外見が異なっていることが知られている茸については、参考文献に挙げられている他の教本を調べたり、茸の専門家に相談する必要があるかも知れません。しかしながら、食用性がまだ知られていない茸は多いので、初めてその茸をお試しになられる際は常に少量お召し上がりになることをお気に留めください。もしその茸の正体と食用性が少しでも疑わしい場合は、お召し上がりにならないでください。野性の茸や新たに培養された茸をお召し上がりになられる際は、誤りがあった場合やその茸にアレルギー反応があった場合に備えて、料理されていない茸をいくつか別に冷蔵庫に取っておいてください。もし茸を食べた後に何か病状が現われた場合は、直ちに医師にご相談ください。

信頼性のある資料や情報を出版するのにかなりの努力が成されましたが、著者と出版者は全ての資料に関する有効性とまたはその利用法の結果に関して、責任を負えません。著者と出版者は、この本の利用者が茸の正体を間違ったり、茸を食べたことから起こる如何なる病状に関しては責任は取れません。

경고

어떤 독버섯과 식용 버섯은 쉽게 혼동되기도 합니다. 어떠한 버섯이든지 먹기 전에 그 버섯의 정체와 먹을 수 있는지 여부에 대한 절대적인 확신을 가져야 합니다. 이 책에 사진으로 설명되지 않은 버섯이나 또는 이 책의 사진 설명과 모양에 차이가 있는 버섯에 관하여는 참고 서적 목록에 나와 있는 다른 책을 참고하거나 또는 버섯 전문가와 상의하십시오. 하지만 먹을 수 있는 버섯인지 아닌지 아직도 규명되지 않은 것들이 많으며, 따라서 어느 경우라도 처음 먹어보는 버섯인 경우는 아주 조금만 먹어야 합니다. 버섯의 정체나 식용 가능여부가 불확실하면 그 버섯은 먹으면 안됩니다. 야생 버섯이나 인공 재배한 새로운 버섯을 먹을 때는 항상, 실수나 또는 버섯에 대한 알레르기 반응에 대비하여, 요리하지 않은 버섯을 조금 냉장고에 따로 보관해야 합니다. 버섯을 먹은 후 조금이라도 이상한 징후가 나타나면 즉시 의사와 상담해야 합니다.

신뢰할 수 있는 데이터와 정보를 출판하려고 상당한 노력을 기울였지만, 저자와 발행인은 모든 자료의 확실성 또는 이 자료를 사용한 결과에 대하여 책임을 질 수 없습니다. 발행인과 저자는 이 책의 독자가 버섯을 잘못 확인하거나 또는 그 결과로 버섯을 먹어서 생기는 일체의 병에 대하여 책임지지 않습니다.

He Whakatūpato

Kei haere pōhēhē te tangata ki te kato i ngā harore me ngā kōpurawhetū, kei riro mai ko ngā harore paihana i te taha o ngā harore e taea te kai! I mua i te kainga i tētahi harore, kia tino mōhio koe he aha taua harore! Kia tae ki ngā harore kāore i tāia he pikitia i tēnei pukapuka, ki ngā harore rānei he rerekē te āhua i tēnā rā, i tēnā rā, arā, he rerekē i ngā whakaahua i tēnei pukapuka, me tiki rawa ki ngā pukapuka kua oti te whakarārangi i te rārangi pukapuka. Ā, me haere rānei ki te tino tangata pūkenga mō ngā harore katoa. Kia tūpato! Kāore anō ngā tohunga kia mōhio ki te tōtika o ngā harore katoa hei kai. Mehemea kātahi anō koe ka kai i tētahi harore, me whakamātau kau atu, kia iti te kainga. Mehemea kei te rangirua ō whakaaro, kāore koe e mōhio he aha rawa taua harore, kaua e kainga. Kia tae koe ki te kai i ngā harore i tupu noa i te tuawhenua, ki ngā harore hou rānei, nā te tangata i whakatupu, meatia atu ētahi harore mata tonu, (kāore i tunua) ki roto i te pouaka makariri. He mea tēnei mō ngā wā kua pōhēhētia ngā momo harore, mō ngā ohonga pāwera (allergic reaction) rānei o te tangata ki taua harore. Ki te māuiui te tangata i muri i te kainga o tētahi harore, whakapā tika atu ki te tākuta.

I mahi nui mātou ki te tā i ngā mōhiotanga whai tikanga, me ōna whakamārama katoa e tika ana, heoi anō, e kore e taea e te kaiwhakaputa te kī, he pono tūturu ngā whakamārama katoa a te tangata kē i roto i tēnei pukapuka, me ngā āhuatanga ka puta i te haringa hei tino kōrero whai-mana e te tangata. Kāore hoki te kaiwhakaputa me ngā kaituhi e whakaae ka tau te hē ki a rātou mō te whakaingoa pōhēhē a te tangata kē, i ētahi o ngā harore i tēnei pukapuka, me ngā māuiuitanga tērā pea ka pā ki te tangata i te kainga o aua harore.

คำเตือน

เห็ดบางชนิดสามารถนำมารับประทานได้และบางชนิดเป็นเห็ดมีพิษซึ่งสามารถทำให้เกิด
ความสับสนได้เสมอ แต่ก่อนที่จะรับประทานเห็ดชนิดใดก็ตาม ก็จะต้องให้แน่ใจจริงๆว่า
เป็นเห็ดที่เรารู้จักและสามารถรับประทานได้ สำหรับเห็ดใดก็ตามที่มิได้นำมาแสดงไว้
ในหนังสือเล่มนี้ อาจจำเป็นต้องไปค้นคว้าหาความรู้เพิ่มเติมเอาจากหนังสือเล่มอื่น
ตามที่มีรายชื่อปรากฏอยู่ในหน้าบรรณานุกรม หรือไปขอรับคำปรึกษาจากผู้เชี่ยวชาญ
ด้านเห็ด และขอให้โปรดทราบไว้ด้วยว่ายังมีเห็ดอีกเป็นจำนวนมากที่ยังไม่ทราบว่าสามารถ
รับประทานได้หรือไม่ หากต้องรับประทานเห็ดชนิดใดเป็นครั้งแรก ก็ขอให้รับประทาน
เพียงจำนวนเล็กน้อยก่อน เมื่อมีข้อสงสัยว่าเป็นเห็ดชนิดใดและสามารถรับประทาน
ได้หรือไม่ ก็ไม่ควรรับประทานเข้าไป และเมื่อต้องรับประทานเห็ดที่ขึ้นเองหรือ
เห็ดชนิดใหม่ที่ได้มาจากการเพาะเลี้ยง ขอให้นำส่วนที่ยังมิได้ปรุงเป็นอาหาร
จัดเก็บไว้ในตู้เย็นจำนวนหนึ่ง เมื่อมีความผิดพลาดเกิดขึ้นจากการเพาะเลี้ยง หรือมีอาการแพ้
ที่เกิดขึ้นจากเห็ดนั้นๆ ถ้ารับประทานเห็ดเข้าไปแล้วมีอาการไม่สบายขึ้นมา ก็ให้
ไปพบแพทย์ทันที

หนังสือเล่มนี้ได้พยายามที่นำเสนอที่มีรายละเอียดและเนื้อหาที่น่าเชื่อถือ แต่ผู้เขียน
กับผู้พิมพ์โฆษณาไม่สามารถแสดงความรับผิดชอบต่อความสมจริงสมจังของสาระเนื้อหา
หรือสิ่งอื่นใดที่จะเกิดขึ้นตามมาภายหลังจากที่ได้นำไปปฏิบัติ ดังนั้นผู้เขียนและ
ผู้พิมพ์โฆษณาจึงไม่สามารถรับผิดชอบในการที่ผู้อ่านหนังสือเล่มนี้นำไปใช้ระบุชนิดของเห็ด
แล้วเกิดความผิดพลาด หรือต่อความเจ็บป่วยที่เกิดจากการรับประทานเห็ดเหล่านั้น

PREFACE

The past few decades have witnessed a dramatic increase in the diversity of mushrooms gracing the tables of our restaurants and the shelves of our supermarkets. While the increased consumption has consisted primarily of cultivated varieties of Asian origin, there has also been an upsurge of interest in mushrooms that can be obtained only from the wild.

A concern over a lack of knowledge in Australasia, the often prevailing opinion that "if it's natural it must be edible," and some significant incidents of mushroom poisonings prompted the development and ultimate publication of a book on the subject in New Zealand in 1998. The book, written by Ian Hall, Peter Buchanan, Wang Yun, and Tony Cole, covered the most important edible and poisonous mushrooms that Australians and New Zealanders might encounter in the wild, as well as the edible mushrooms that could be purchased in supermarkets. The original authors were joined by Steve Stephenson, a mycologist from the United States, and their combined efforts produced this new book. Whereas the first book mentioned or illustrated about 205 taxa, this book treats about 280 taxa, and many taxa only mentioned or illustrated in the first book are now discussed. The resulting reference is truly international in its coverage and will appeal to enthusiasts from around the world.

Edible and Poisonous Mushrooms of the World is aimed at individuals who are interested in mushrooms and wish to expand their knowledge about the subject, including information on the roles of fungi in nature and how they can be grown and cultivated. The introduction provides essential background information about what mushrooms are, both poisonous and edible, how they are named, and how they fit into the big picture, both as part of the natural world and as part of the world market. The first section, Cultivating Mushrooms, divides its attention between nonmycorrhizal mushrooms, including the eight most popular saprobic mushrooms, and mycorrhizal mushrooms, with an emphasis on the Périgord black truffle. The second section, Collecting Wild Mushrooms, discusses the identification and collection of mushrooms and the rules that should be followed when picking them. It also includes a helpful list of the major poisoning syndromes and the mushrooms known to be associated with each one. The final section, A List of Wild Mushrooms, is the cornerstone of the book, providing details of size, color, habit, and other identifying factors for the world's most common edible wild mushrooms (including those with major international markets), for poisonous species that should be avoided at all costs, and for mushroom curiosities likely to be encountered in nature.

Many hundreds of species of questionable or unknown edibility have been omitted, as have a large number of lesser edible mushrooms that may be important in one country but not in others. For information on these species it would be wise to consult mushroom field guides in the relevant country.

A vast amount of information on mushrooms can be found on various Web sites, a few of which are listed in *Mushroom Cultivation with Special Emphasis on Appropriate Techniques for Developing Countries* (Oei 1996) and related articles in *Mycologist* magazine (Hamlyn 1996, 1997a, 1997b). Simply typing the word "mushroom" into a general search engine will bring up tens of thousands of references. A more useful and orderly search can be obtained by accessing Cornell University's WWW Virtual Library of Mycology. While a good proportion of the information available from the Web is of high quality, much of it is also ephemeral, and this creates major problems for those using it. Web addresses also have a tendency to change when those who created the Web page change employment or move to another server. Consequently, the list of Web addresses at the back of the book includes only those sites expected to be reasonably permanent, such as those run by universities or other major institutions.

Chinese Names of Mushrooms is a helpful list of edible mushrooms at the back of the book. It should be a useful tool for those wanting to purchase mushrooms at Chinese markets. Addresses of organizations and periodicals that might be of interest are also listed, and a glossary is included to familiarize readers with terms used in the book. All amounts of money stated in dollars are United States currency.

ACKNOWLEDGMENTS

We are indebted to designer Jo Smith of the New Zealand Institute for Crop and Food Research at Lincoln for producing the graphics, Lynette Mitchell for patiently making all the many corrections and changes to our text, and Sue Zydenbos, Tracy Williams, and Angela Templeton for their essential editorial work. We are extremely grateful to a number of friends and colleagues who provided photographs for inclusion in this book. Without their contributions it would have been impossible to make this book a comprehensive introduction to the edible and poisonous mushrooms of the world. Particular thanks are extended to Masana Izawa, Emily Johnson, Tony Lyon, and Tian Jinghua. Additional slides were provided by Jim Douglas, Forest Research, Juliet Fowler, Bruce Fuhrer, Don Hemmes, Mario Honrubia, HortResearch, Peter Johnston, Landcare Research, William C. Roody, Jack Squires, and Alessandra Zambonelli. Our thanks also go to Mel Boulton, Ilse and Erhard Jungmayr, Peter Katsaros, Orson K. Miller, Jr., Jean-Marc Moncalvo, Makoto Ogawa, Peng Jin Torng, Shaun Pennycook, Fabio Primavera, Scott Redhead, Geoff Ridley, Barbara Segedin, Walter Sturgeon, Jim Trappe, Georgette Wang, and Wu Chi Guang for their assistance on various aspects of this project. Finally, we are indebted to the Agricultural and Marketing Research and Development Trust and the Foundation for Research, Science, and Technology for their foresight in funding the 1998 book on which this book is founded.

INTRODUCTION

When tree leaves change color, dew rises, and autumn mists descend, mushrooms begin to appear above the soil, and logs, stumps, and fallen branches come alive with "toadstools" and other mysterious protuberances. This is the signal for mushroom collectors to take to the fields and forests. They often do so with the zeal and passion of antique collectors in a flea market, or miners smitten by gold fever—though experienced collectors temper excitement with caution, knowing as they do that an inaccurate identification can be fatal. Others may hunt mushrooms for different reasons, appreciating them as intriguing life forms or marvelous photographic subjects.

This book provides a brief introduction to edible mushrooms for the layperson, while also including warnings about poisonous species. It also introduces mushroom cultivation methods, points the way to additional sources of information for those who would like to try to grow mushrooms, and provides a useful reference to anyone with a scientific interest. The aim, however, is not solely to inform but also to generate interest in the fascinating world of fungi.

Fungi, Mushrooms, Toadstools, and Truffles

Many people grow up thinking fungi are the molds and spots on roses and shower curtains, mushrooms are the things sold in the market or collected in the woods, toadstools include everything else and are probably poisonous, and truffles are expensive chocolates. But there is a lot more to these subjects. Because of their sudden appearance and disappearance, their frequent association with decaying organic matter, their vivid colors, fantastic shapes, and, in some instances, poisonous properties, mushrooms have often been regarded as objects of mystery, and have even at times been associated with the supernatural. In reality, mushrooms are among the most fascinating and beautiful inhabitants of the natural world.

This book adopts a very broad definition of the word "mushroom," using it in its widest sense to encompass not only what the layperson would call mushrooms but also toadstools, truffles, puffballs, stinkhorns, bracket fungi on wood, and various other forms, whether they are edible or not—in other words, any fungus with "a distinctive fruiting body that is large enough to be . . . picked by hand" (Chang and Miles 1992). Such readily visible fruiting bodies (as opposed to the many fungi with microscopic fruiting bodies, such as molds) may include a stalk, cap, and gills, as with the button mushrooms found in the supermarket, or, as with many other fungi, quite bizarre shapes.

All life forms can be segregated into a few kingdoms. The animal kingdom, thanks to the huge numbers of insects, contains the greatest number of species. The fungi are the second largest assemblage of organisms and should be considered quite separate from the plant kingdom, containing several times as many species. Fungi comprise an estimated 1.5 million species of nonphotosynthetic (chlorophyll-free) organisms that absorb their nutrients from dead or living organic matter, have cell walls containing chitin and β-glucans, and reproduce sexually or asexually. Most fungi are placed together in their own group, known as the kingdom Fungi. This is where the mushrooms are found (Alexopoulos et al. 1996, Hudler 1998, Kirk et al. 2001).

The fungi are an exceedingly diverse group of organisms. Because they cannot manufacture their own food, they must obtain nourishment from plants and animals or their products, or even from other fungi. Each day people come into contact with both the harmful and the beneficial effects of fungi, the former including the molds that grow on bread and shoes and those that cause plant and animal diseases. Fungi play a positive role in foods such as beer, bread, and blue cheese, as they do in antibiotics like penicillin (from *Penicillium*), the immunosuppressant cyclosporine (from *Tolypocladium*), which reduces organ rejection after transplant operations, and ergometrine, which is extracted from diseased flowers (ergots) of rye and used in the management of the third stage of labor and the treatment of bleeding after childbirth (Reynolds and Parfitt 1996). However, the most important service provided by fungi has to do with the role they play as decomposers: fungi help rid the earth of huge quantities of plant and animal remains by recycling the nutrients found in dead matter. They also help plants grow through mycorrhizal relationships.

A number of the larger mushrooms are also valuable for their medicinal qualities, some even having been used at one time as styptics to constrict blood vessels and check the flow of blood (Baker 1989). Mushrooms have more obscure uses as well: a beautifully colored timber is produced when oak is infected with beefsteak fungus (*Fistulina hepatica*); a dye used by the New Zealand Maori in tattooing is prepared by grinding steamed and dried caterpillars infected with the vegetable caterpillar fungus (*Cordyceps robertsii*); and the Australian Aborigines use the stalked puffball (*Podaxis pistillaris*) to darken white hair and repel flies (Kalotas 1997, Riley 1994).

Where Do They Come From?

Mushrooms as a group are found all over the world. The individual organism (the "body" of the fungus) consists of an extensive network of very finely branched microscopic threads called hyphae. Collectively, the hyphae making up such a network are referred to as a mycelium. The structure we recognize as a mushroom is in reality just a highly organized system of hyphae, specialized for reproduction, that develops from the otherwise vegetative mycelium inhabiting soil, leaf litter, or decaying wood. The individual hyphae obtain the nutrients and water the fungus needs to grow. After a period of growth, and under favorable conditions of temperature and moisture, the mycelium gives rise to one or more fruiting bodies, or mushrooms. As such, what is thought of as a mushroom performs the same function and is analogous to an apple on an apple tree, since it is the "fruit" of the mycelium. Long-distance dispersal is achieved by the many millions of microscopic spores produced by the fruiting body. These spores can be carried by wind currents to very distant places. While mushrooms are the most visible representatives of the fungi, they form only a minor part of a group that has, in an evolutionary sense, been very successful. Fungi occupy nearly every imaginable type of habitat, including both fresh water and the sea as well as all habitats found on land, and have been said to have twice the collective biomass of all animals on earth.

Although fungi have long been thought of as members of the plant world, their ancestors might actually have been animals. The divergence of the fungi and animal kingdoms must have occurred a very long time ago, since molecular evidence suggests that fungi have been present on the earth for as long as one billion years (Heckman et al. 2001). Regardless of their exact evolutionary affinities, a wealth of fungi now exist, including mushrooms with complex structural organizations. These structures, as already noted, are only the visible fruiting bodies of often very extensive underground networks of hyphal threads. According to recent reports, there is one fungus in the United States that occupies some 600 hectares of forestland, making it the world's largest organism (Brasier 1992). At an estimated age of well over a thousand years, it is also one of the oldest.

A few of the mushrooms seen in one place may have arrived from another part of the world as mushroom spores borne on wind currents. Others may have arrived in a very different way, perhaps on soil adhering to plants, shipping containers, or boots, or even within the bodies of plants carried from one country to another by early settlers. As a result, it can be very difficult to distinguish between a country's native fungi and those that have been introduced or have recently arrived from elsewhere.

Edible Specialty Mushrooms

Everyone is familiar with the white button mushrooms found in plastic containers on supermarket shelves, and many will have ventured to

A mushroom counter in a large supermarket in Hong Kong. (Buchanan)

A wild mushroom collector sells hatsudake (*Lactarius hatsudake*) on a roadside in northern Hunan, China. (Hall)

try the darker, larger, and better-flavored Swiss brown strain button mushrooms, shiitake, and, perhaps without even realizing it, straw mushrooms, which are often used in dishes at Chinese restaurants. For many people, however, experimentation with alternative mushrooms may well have stopped there. In China, where mushrooms have been cultivated for thousands of years, and in continental Europe and many other parts of the world, shops, roadside and market stalls, and supermarkets offer a wide range of mushrooms. To the unenlightened these could be regarded as unappetizing, even dangerous, but in reality they are often a gourmet's delight.

There are many devotees of mycophagy (fungus eating) in Japan, where more than one hundred types of wild mushrooms are popular (Ueda et al. 1992). In Britain the population is not noted for consumption of specialty mushrooms (cultivated mushrooms other than *Agaricus bisporus* and *A. bitorquis*), and keen mycologists have struggled to assemble a similar list, eventually coming up with only twenty commonly eaten wild mushrooms (Legg 1990). Sadly, in countries such as Australia, New Zealand, England, and the United States,

Tremella fuciformis (white jelly fungus), *Lentinula edodes* (shiitake), *Dictyophora indusiata* (bamboo mushroom), and *Auricularia polytricha* (wood ear) in a local market at Wuyi Mountain, Fujian, China. (Buchanan)

TABLE 1. EDIBLE MUSHROOMS PRODUCED IN TWENTY-TWO CHINESE PROVINCES IN 1998 (Chinese Association of Edible Fungi 2000).

Scientific name	Common name	Amount produced (× 1000 tons)
Lentinula edodes	shiitake	1338
Pleurotus spp.	oyster mushroom	1020
Auricularia polytricha	wood ear	432
Agaricus bisporus and *A. bitorquis*	button mushroom	426
Flammulina velutipes	enokitake	189
Tremella fuciformis	white jelly fungus	100
Auricularia auricula	wood ear	59
Volvariella volvacea	straw mushroom	32
Pholiota nameko	nameko	31
Hypsizygus marmoreus	shimeji	22
Grifola frondosa	hen of the woods	10
Boletus spp.	boletes	8.1
Ganoderma spp.	conks	6.7
Lactarius deliciosus	saffron milk cap	6.0
Hericium erinaceus	lion's mane mushroom	2.8
Coprinus comatus	shaggy ink cap	1.8
Dictyophora indusiata	bamboo mushroom	1.1
Pleurotus cornucopiae var. *citrinopileatus*	golden oyster mushroom	0.5
Agaricus blazei	almond portobello	0.1
Others		293.9
TOTAL		**4350**

mushrooms such as the delicious giant puffball (*Calvatia gigantea*) and porcini (*Boletus edulis*) are more likely to receive a swift dispatch with the end of a boot than to be picked as a delicacy.

Identifying and Naming

Most people are familiar with *Homo sapiens*, the scientific Latin binomial name for humans, and perhaps also with names such as *Rosa*, the genus in which roses are placed, *Ficus*, which might be found on a label attached to a rubber tree, and *Amanita muscaria*, commonly known as fly agaric, the red mushroom with white markings often seen in autumn and illustrated in children's books. Though they are sometimes awkward to pronounce, there is really no substitute for these scientific names. The strict rules attached to their usage make confusion over different kinds of fungi unlikely—and confusion is to be avoided, especially when trying to distinguish between edible and poisonous mushrooms. These names are universally accepted and are common to publications on mushrooms in Japanese and Chinese as well as those written in English or the languages of continental Europe. However, they are not always used in China, which is one reason why pinyin names have been included at the back of the book (see Chinese Names of Mushrooms).

That said, even scientific names occasionally cause problems. Thus, to be precise, each scientific name should be followed by the name of the person, called the authority, who first described the fungus in question. Authorities can be found in many books on mushrooms. For the species mentioned in this book, this information appears in the index. Occasionally taxonomists may not be absolutely sure which species they are dealing with. When this happens they will insert "aff." or "cf." between the genus and species names, meaning that it belongs to the genus and is similar to the species. When they are really stumped, they will simply put "sp." after the name of the genus (for example, *Amanita* sp.) to indicate that it is an unidentified species. The abbreviation "spp." simply refers to several species of a genus.

The genus and species are always set in italics, and only the genus is capitalized. Once the name of a species (*Amanita muscaria*, for example) has been used in a text, it is permissible to abbreviate the genus name (*A. muscaria*) for the rest of the paragraph, unless there could be confusion with another genus beginning with the same letter. Genera with similar features (though these are not always obvious to a nonspecialist) are grouped together in families, the names of which almost always end in *-aceae* (as in Agaricaceae, the family that includes the button mushroom). In turn, families are grouped together into what, for the fungi, can be rather artificial groupings, called orders, with names ending in *-ales* (as in Gasteromycetales, the group that includes puffballs). Above that, they are grouped into classes. Mushrooms can be found in the class Basidiomycetes, which contains the majority of mushroom species, and the class Ascomycetes, which includes the truffles (for example, *Tuber*), morels (*Morchella*), false morels (*Gyromitra*), and the cup fungi (for example, *Peziza* and *Paxina*). Members of the Ascomycetes are considered more primitive than those of the Basidiomycetes and usually produce their spores in small sacs called asci.

Common names, like "field mushroom," are very loosely applied and can be used for one species in one particular area and for something quite different in another area. Therefore, it is preferable to use a common name only when it is clearly equated with a scientific name. Many mushrooms have multiple common names. For the purposes of this book, only one common name is given per scientific name. More common names can be found in the multilingual *Elsevier's Dictionary of Edible Mushrooms* (Chandra 1989) and in *An Index of the Common Fungi of North America* (Miller and Farr 1975).

To Eat or Not to Eat

In China, Japan, and parts of Europe, the well-established tradition of eating wild mushrooms is sustained with books filled with color photographs and information on what is edible and what is not. Children in such places—rural France or Italy, for example—might be taken mushroom hunting with their families, from whom they learn about edible and poisonous species. Later, in the kitchen, mouthwatering traditional recipes might be handed down, along with the special preparations a few mushrooms require to render them safe to eat.

In Germany after World War II, in places where food was in short supply, many people collected wild mushrooms from forests and either ate them themselves or sold them in the marketplaces. To limit the number of inevitable poisonings, inspectors were employed to ensure that people were not sold inedible or poisonous species (I. Jungmeyer and E. Jungmeyer, personal communication), and books were distributed containing watercolor paintings of not-so-edible mushrooms and describing the relative merits of edible species (for example, Neuhaus and Neuhaus 1947). A similar book was issued in Britain just after

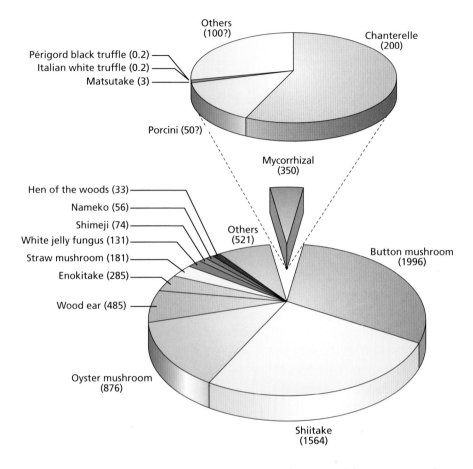

Estimated world consumption of edible mushrooms in 1997 (× 1000 tons) (from Chang 1999).

World War II (Ministry of Agriculture and Fisheries 1945), but no inspectors were employed, which perhaps reflects the level of interest the British then had in wild mushrooms. Mushroom inspectors are still employed in countries such as France and Finland to check the edibility of mushrooms on sale in markets (Ohenoja and Lahti 1978, Renaud 1989). French collectors who are unsure of the edibility of a mushroom can also approach their local pharmacist for advice. During mushroom season it is not uncommon to find pharmacies open on Sunday mornings to cope with the demand for such counsel.

Unfortunately the increased interest in both cultivated and wild mushrooms has led to a mistaken belief by some that anything

TABLE 2. TYPICAL WHOLESALE PRICES FOR THE MAIN CULTIVATED MUSHROOMS (Anonymous 2000a, Chang 1999).

Scientific name	Common name	Typical wholesale prices (per kilogram)
Agaricus bisporus, *A. bitorquis*	button mushroom	$1.76–$3.74, up to $7.70 for portobello
Pleurotus spp.	oyster mushroom	$4.40–$8.36
Lentinula edodes	shiitake	$7.04–$12.47
Auricularia spp.	wood ear	approx. $5.00–$10.00
Volvariella volvacea	straw mushroom	approx. $5.00–$10.00
Flammulina velutipes	enokitake	$4.60–$12.56
Tremella fuciformis	white jelly fungus	approx. $5.00–$10.00
Pholiota nameko	nameko	$4.77–$6.35

To enable comparisons, the following exchange rates are assumed: $1.00 = 14.70 Austrian schillings, 7.00 Chinese yuan, 1.02 European euros, 7.03 French francs, 2.10 German marks, 2072.00 Italian lire, 113.00 Japanese yen, 2.29 New Zealand dollars, 0.67 pounds sterling, 1.72 Singapore dollars.

"natural" must be edible. There are instances of people eating poisonous mushrooms like *Scleroderma* species because "they smell like mushrooms," and the lethal death cap (*Amanita phalloides*) and destroying angel (*A. virosa*) because they resemble edible species. A few mushrooms are deadly poisonous and can be lethal even when only small quantities are consumed. Others are less poisonous but can still produce nausea, stomach upsets, or hallucinations, while some contain compounds that can trigger an allergic reaction months or years after the mushroom was first eaten. A few are only poisonous if consumed with alcohol. Consequently, great care has to be taken to identify a mushroom before it is eaten

TABLE 3. APPROXIMATE WORLD MARKET VALUE AND TYPICAL PRICES FOR MYCORRHIZAL MUSHROOMS.

Scientific name	Common name	Approximate in-season retail market	Approximate wholesale prices (per kilogram, grade one)
Boletus edulis	porcini	> $250 million	$13–$198
Cantharellus cibarius	chanterelle	$1.62 billion	$8–$19
Tricholoma matsutake	matsutake	$500 million	$40–$500
Tuber melanosporum	Périgord black truffle	> $150 million	$250–$1200
Tuber magnatum	Italian white truffle	> $150 million	$1000–$30,000

(Haard and Haard 1980, Lincoff and Mitchel 1977, Scates 1995, Spoerke and Rumack 1994).

There are no rules that make it easy to distinguish between edible and poisonous mushrooms. Forget about a mushroom being edible if it can or cannot be peeled or if it blackens a silver spoon—these are old wives' tales. The only safe practice is to accurately identify a mushroom and then check a good textbook or field guide to determine if it is edible. The golden rule remains the same: if in doubt, throw it out.

Idiosyncratic adverse responses to some mushrooms are not uncommon. When trying a new and confirmed edible mushroom, keep a sample in the refrigerator in case an adverse reaction occurs later on and calls for further identification of the mushroom. It is always best to cook mushrooms before eating them, as some contain poisons that are destroyed by heat; but not all mushroom poisons are so easily destroyed, so be careful.

Many fungi accumulate heavy metals and radioisotopes, some containing one hundred times the levels found in the soil (Benjamin 1995). Avoid eating mushrooms found on roadsides, where lead levels may be high, or from areas where the soil may be rich in elements like cadmium, chromium, and mercury. Likewise, do not eat mushrooms grown where chemical sprays may have been used.

In countries such as Australia and New Zealand there is a general lack of background information on native and introduced mushrooms. This is partly because the native peoples of both countries appear to have used few mushrooms, a fact reflected in the limited literature available on the subject. The Australian Aborigines' native bread (*Laccocephalum mylittae*) and beech strawberry (*Cyttaria gunnii*) are two notable exceptions (Fuhrer 1985, Kalotas 1997). Few of the early European settlers brought information of any use with them, since the species they encountered in Australia and New Zealand were quite different from the species in Europe.

It's a Big Market

It has been estimated that more than six million tons of cultivated mushrooms were consumed worldwide in 1997 (Chang 1999). It is often assumed in Western countries that button mushrooms dominate the market, but in fact they represent only a third of production, with the bulk made up of a dozen or so specialty mushrooms. Assuming a modest average retail price of $5 per kilogram, in United States terms this equates to an annual market of around $30 billion.

However, the real market is larger still. In addition to the cultivated mushrooms that pass through official markets, hundreds of thousands of tons of wild mushrooms are collected from fields and forests, and among these are some of the most expensive foods in the world.

About half of all cultivated mushrooms are produced in China (Chang 1999), where around 2.7 kg of mushrooms are consumed every year by more than a billion people (Chinese Association of Edible Fungi 2000, Sun and Xu 1999). Similar quantities are consumed in the United States, where mushrooms are now the fifth largest crop and are worth around $870 million to approximately three hundred growers (ERS 2002, NASS 2000).

The price paid for each mushroom species tends to reflect the ease or efficiency with which it can be cultivated and, particularly in the case of wild mushrooms, its scarcity and market demand (Anonymous 2000a). For example, the straw mushroom can be grown relatively easily and quickly on almost any cellulosic material, provided the temperature is high enough, and consequently it commands a low price. In contrast, the Périgord black truffle and Italian white truffle, which can take up to twenty years to begin fruiting on their host plants, are in great demand by chefs and gourmets and can command a price equal to that for gold (Hall et al. 1994, Johnston 2000).

CULTIVATING
MUSHROOMS

Depending on how they obtain nutrients, mushrooms are either non-mycorrhizal (saprobic or parasitic) or mycorrhizal. Saprobes gain their nutrition from dead plants and animals. Many can be cultivated, with varying degrees of difficulty (Stamets 2000). Some, like the morels, require very specialized conditions, while others have never been cultivated (Anonymous 1997, Stamets 1993). In contrast to the saprobes, parasitic mushrooms, such as the honey mushroom (*Armillaria mellea*) and some bracket and oyster mushrooms (for example, *Pleurotus eryngii* and *P. ostreatus*), obtain their nutrition from living plants, often causing severe damage to them in the process. Mycorrhizal or symbiotic mushrooms also derive nutrients from living plants, but instead of harming the host plant they assist its growth by stimulating the uptake of nutrients from the soil. Edible examples include the truffles (for example, *Tuber*), matsutake (*Tricholoma matsutake*), porcini (*Boletus edulis*), chanterelle (*Cantharellus cibarius*), and the saffron milk cap (*Lactarius deliciosus*).

NONMYCORRHIZAL MUSHROOMS

About 95 percent of all cultivated mushrooms are saprobic and can be cultivated on various dead organic materials such as straw, wood, and wastepaper. Some saprobes are produced in what are little more than cottage industries, while others are grown in huge, highly efficient factories, their production and sale the basis of multimillion-dollar industries. Certain saprobes, called the sugar fungi, can only use sugars available in the growth medium. Others, including many edible varieties, can break down much more complicated molecules, such as cellulose or other highly resistant compounds found in wood.

Although around fifty saprobic mushrooms are cultivated in China, only eight of these make up the lion's share of the market worldwide: the button mushroom (*Agaricus bisporus* and *A. bitorquis*), shiitake (*Lentinula edodes*), oyster mushroom (*Pleurotus* spp.), wood ear (*Auricularia* spp.), straw mushroom (*Volvariella volvacea*), enokitake (*Flammulina velutipes*), white jelly fungus (*Tremella fuciformis*), and nameko (*Pholiota nameko*). The other cultivated saprobic mushrooms are consumed in relatively small quantities, although locally they can be very important. For example, *Hypsizygus marmoreus*, *Hericium* aff. *erinaceus*, and *Grifola frondosa* are important in East Asian countries, and *Stropharia rugosoannulata* is eaten widely in Germany, Hungary, and Poland. Many other saprobic mushrooms are not cultivated at all, and supplies of many are restricted to what can be collected from nature.

Commercial Considerations

The principles of growing many saprobic mushrooms can be found in scientific literature and other published sources, some of which include descriptions of apparently detailed methods. However, there is a significant difference between producing a few mushrooms in a pilot trial and continuously turning out a consistent, high-quality, high-yielding, disease-free product to be sold to a discerning public. Many important factors are discovered only through experience, and these trade secrets are often jealously guarded. Hygiene and climatic controls are crucial to a successful operation, and failure to prevent and control pests and diseases can jeopardize one or more production cycles. Methods developed in one country are rarely directly applicable to another without first making adjustments. Different growth media, pests, diseases, and ambient climatic conditions will affect the productivity of particular strains.

As previously mentioned, people in Asia are accustomed to eating a wide range of mushrooms, whereas people in Australasia, Europe, and North America have only recently begun to acquire a taste for something more exotic. Therefore, careful market research is required to determine if there is a local demand for a new mushroom and, if so, what quantity the market can absorb—and at what price. If mushrooms are to be exported, it is also necessary to determine whether it is possible to produce mushrooms at a price and quality that will compete with those produced in Asian countries such as China, India, Indonesia, Thailand, and the Philippines, where economies of scale and cheap labor allow production costs to be kept low. It is particularly important to consider the Chinese mushroom industry, which employs ten million people, generates $1 billion in exports, and which increased its production from 0.59 million tons in 1986, 26.8 percent of the world's production, to 4.35 million tons in 1998, more than half of the world's requirements (Sun and Xu 1999).

Quarantine restrictions should also be considered, as some countries prohibit the importation of mushrooms that might have been in contact with contaminated soil. Species with pathogenic traits may also be prohibited imports. For example, *Pleurotus ostreatus*, a common species of oyster mushroom cultivated in many parts of the Northern Hemisphere, cannot be imported into New Zealand because it does not occur there naturally and can pose a risk to plant health (Buchanan 1996).

When it comes to mushrooms as familiar as the button mushroom (*Agaricus bisporus* and *A. bitorquis*), there is a wealth of information available on cultivation. Such subjects as the buildings and equipment required, how to prepare a growing medium, where to get the best strains of mushroom for the climate and growing medium, and what pests and diseases are likely to be encountered have all been widely studied (Penn State Mushroom Laboratory 2002). There are societies and research organizations, such as the American Mushroom Institute and the Mushroom Council, that coordinate market analysis, advertising, and research, and that hold educational conferences, farm visits, and training courses. The Penn State University mushroom industry short course has been given annually in Pennsylvania since 1959. There are seminars on the cultivation of specialty mushrooms as well, such as those run by Paul Stamets, founder and president of Fungi Perfecti.

One essential component in commercial mushroom production is the use of high-quality spawn. Spawn is a culture of a fungus used to inoculate the medium on which the mushroom will grow and fruit, called the substrate. It may be purchased from a spawn company or produced using starter cultures and appropriate equipment. Unfortunately it is rarely possible to simply produce a starter culture from a fresh mushroom and then expect to obtain quality spawn. Not just any spawn will do. It must be one produced from a superior strain, selected from the dozens available, and capable of producing the best-quality mushrooms at the best price for the substrate and ambient climate, a task that usually requires a lot of research. During this preliminary research it is also necessary to find out how much latitude is allowable in the control of environmental conditions and substrate. The methods adopted or developed for the cultivation of the mushroom must also be efficient in terms of staff time, energy costs, and materials.

Button mushrooms (*Agaricus bisporus*) growing in plastic bags filled with substrate. Huon Valley Mushrooms, Australia. **EDIBLE.** (Hall)

A high standard of hygiene is essential when cultures and spawn are being prepared and when the fungus is first introduced into the substrate. Special items of equipment such as a sterilizing autoclave and a lamina flow cabinet or sterile room are needed to do this. Nevertheless, no matter how much care is taken, there still may be a build-up of pests and diseases, and expertise and special methods must then be used to deal with these problems. For some specialty mushrooms there may be only skeletal published information available, with crucial commercial details treated as trade secrets. Finally, before mushrooms are produced in commercial quantities, the grower must have already made contacts in the marketplace. The mushrooms must then be effectively marketed, packaged to enhance shelf life and appeal, and labelled to comply with food regulations as well as to attract, inform, and educate the consumer.

Agaricus bisporus and *Agaricus bitorquis* (Button Mushroom)

The impetus for developing cultivation techniques may be a mushroom's popularity, but the ease and efficiency with which it can be cultivated, the convenience of the product, and its price are very important. It is for these reasons that more button mushrooms are consumed in the Western world than any other type of mushroom.

Button mushrooms are typically cultivated on a composted medium made up of moistened wheat or barley straw, horse and/or chicken manure, and gypsum (calcium sulfate—plaster of Paris). The raw ingredients are mechanically mixed and brought to a suitable moisture content. Composting material is formed into ricks, also known as windrows, 2–3 m wide and high, or may first be formed into piles before preparation of ricks. Piles and ricks are mechanically turned at regular intervals. Supplements to regulate nitrogen content may be added. On a simple concrete pad this Phase I composting will take more than three weeks, but the speed can be increased, aerobic conditions maintained, and the level of unpleasant odors reduced by introducing air into the composting material through pipes and holes in the concrete pad. During composting, the internal temperature should be 65–80°C.

Traditionally Phase I composting occurs outdoors, but increasingly strict environmental restrictions in many countries are encouraging indoor composting in bunkers. Indoor composting reduces odor emissions and allows environmental conditions to be closely monitored and controlled in order to achieve a more consistent product. Successful production of compost is both an art and a science. Parameters

Mechanical assembly of compost materials for button mushroom (*Agaricus bisporus*) cultivation. Prewetted bales of straw are opened, and straw mixed with poultry manure and gypsum is added from the hopper on the right. Meadow Mushrooms, New Zealand. (Buchanan)

Completion of mechanical assembly. The compost mixture will be placed in piles and ricks (in background) for Phase I composting. Meadow Mushrooms, New Zealand. (Buchanan)

Turning button mushroom (*Agaricus bisporus*) compost. Meadow Mushrooms, New Zealand. (Buchanan)

Air pumped through the concrete floor assists in the preparation of the compost. Meadow Mushrooms, New Zealand. (Buchanan)

such as pH, moisture, ammonia, nitrogen, ash, actinomycete concentration, and carbon-nitrogen ratio can be prescribed and measured, but compost quality is often best assessed from experience. This usually involves careful evaluation of odor, appearance, and texture of handfuls extracted from deep within the composted material.

Mushrooms are cultivated on compost in wooden trays, in bags, or on shelves. The compost may be mechanically transferred directly into these containers, followed by pasteurization, or alternatively the compost may be pasteurized and spawned before it is loaded into the growing containers. Pasteurization (also known as Phase II composting) requires temperatures of 50–60°C for five to eight days, during which time an adequate supply of air is essential. In this phase the nutritional status of the substrate is altered to favor growth of the button mushroom and to eliminate potentially contaminating microorganisms and pests.

Spawn is prepared by inoculating sterilized grain with a high-yielding, commercially bred strain of the button mushroom. After cooling the pasteurized compost, spawn is introduced, allowed to colonize for some days, and a layer of casing is applied. A form of spawn known as casing inoculum may be added to the casing layer to improve yield.

In countries where the button mushroom industry is most highly developed, composting, spawn-making, casing, and mushroom production may be performed by separate companies. Compost companies may supply compost ready for pasteurization or compost already spawned. The growing rooms of farms that employ a shelf system, for example, can be rapidly loaded by trucks simultaneously delivering spawned compost and the overlying casing layer. In modern Dutch farms, mechanically harvested mushrooms are grown in large rooms of 1000 sq. m growing surface; smaller rooms with 300 sq. m growing surface are used for hand-harvested mushrooms (J. Janssen, personal communication).

A temperature of 16–20°C with high humidity and low carbon dioxide is required for fruiting, although optimal conditions will vary with each strain used. Mushrooms fruit and are harvested in flushes, six to twelve days apart, with usually three to four flushes per crop. A typical mushroom farm is run on a continuous cycle, with several rooms each at a different stage in the process. Mushrooms are harvested at different stages of maturity to generate products of different appearance (for example, buttons, cups, and flats). Mushrooms to be sold fresh are handpicked, while those to be canned are mechanically

A sophisticated shelving system with automatic watering used for cultivating button mushrooms *(Agaricus bisporus)*. Quality Mushrooms, New Zealand. (Buchanan)

harvested. Selective breeding has produced a range of commercially available strains, including the firmer Swiss brown strain.

Pests and diseases can be a major problem, not just with button mushrooms but with all cultivated species. Bacterial blotch, viruses, and flies can wipe out a producer's commercial venture (Fletcher et al. 1989).

In industrialized countries, most button mushrooms are produced by large, efficient, and highly mechanized companies. This, in addition to the requirement that mushroom growers meet strict environmental pollution standards, means that small new growers may find it difficult to become established. Nevertheless, a number of publications provide a good introduction to the cultivation of button mushrooms. Due to the scale of production in some parts of the world, the disposal of spent mushroom compost presents a major headache for button mushroom growers. In 1994 a conference was held in Philadelphia where the problems were highlighted (Wuest et al. 1994).

Lentinula edodes (Shiitake)

Cultivation of shiitake originated in China about A.D. 1000, but much of its technological development (and the capture of its marketing

The fruiting bodies of the cultivated Swiss brown strain of *Agaricus bisporus*. Parkvale Mushrooms, New Zealand. **EDIBLE.** (Buchanan)

Shiitake (*Lentinula edodes*) sawdust spawn has been placed in holes drilled into bedlogs and then sealed with wax. Tottori Mycological Institute, Japan. (Buchanan)

Bedlogs inoculated with shiitake and stacked under a canopy of bamboo. Tottori Mycological Institute, Japan. (Buchanan)

name) has come from Japan. Although shiitake is primarily consumed as a food, a lot of attention is paid to the medicinal properties of lentinan, a polysaccharide that can be extracted from this fungus (Chang et al. 1993, Mizuno 1995).

The traditional method of growing shiitake—a method that arguably produces the highest-quality product—involves growing it on logs in a shady situation. Just before bud break in spring, logs about 1 m long and 75–150 mm in diameter are cut from trees and carefully dried. Oak (*Quercus*) is traditionally used, but other hardwoods can be substituted. Examples include birch (*Betula*), hornbeams (*Carpinus*), hickory (*Carya*), chickapin (*Castanopsis*), beech (*Fagus* and *Nothofagus*), tanoak (*Lithocarpus*), and poplars (*Populus*) (see also Oei 1996). Once the logs have dried, a netlike pattern of small holes is drilled into the wood. Spawn, prepared by growing the fungus on sawdust or small wooden dowels, is pushed into the holes. These are then sealed over with something like wax to prevent the entry of other fungi and to keep the inoculum from drying out. The inoculated logs are stacked under a forest canopy or in artificial shade, where the temperature is 10–27°C (optimally 20–25°C).

During the six to twelve months following inoculation, the moisture content of the logs is monitored and maintained at 35–55 percent. The fungus grows out from the inoculum and along the log, breaking down the wood and thereby gaining nutrients—a phase called the spawn run. Eventually the fungus forms its fruiting bodies on the sides of the log, but this is usually induced by soaking the logs in cold water. Once the first flush of fruiting bodies has been harvested, the logs are "rested" by maintaining the moisture content at 30–40 percent and the temperature at 15–25°C. When the fungus has accumulated sufficient nutrients, another cycle of fruiting can be induced by again soaking the logs in cold water. Using these techniques, the natural six-month fruiting cycle can be increased in frequency for some strains to four three-month flushes per year. Colonized logs may remain productive for two to five years until decomposition is nearly complete. A maximum yield of about 2 kg of shiitake is possible from a log with an initial fresh weight of about 11 kg (dry weight of 6 kg) (Przybylowicz and Donoghue 1988).

Today most shiitake is produced on sawdust in bags. A typical procedure is to first fill special heat-resistant plastic bags, similar to oven bags, with a mixture of sawdust and supplements (for example, bran). The top of the bag is gathered together and a collar is passed around the outside. The neck is plugged with foam plastic or cotton

Shiitake (*Lentinula edodes*) fruiting on logs that have been artificially inoculated with the fungus. **EDIBLE.** (Buchanan)

wool to allow gaseous exchange. The bag and its contents are then heated to 121°C using steam under pressure in an autoclave. When the bag has cooled down, shiitake spawn is inoculated into it through the neck and the plug is replaced, or the spawn is inoculated through holes cut in the sides of the bag, which are later sealed. This has to be done in very clean conditions such as in a lamina flow cabinet. As with logs, it is essential that a strain of shiitake is used that suits both the climatic conditions and the sawdust mix in the bag. The next step is spawn run: the bags are incubated, preferably at about 25°C, on racks for four to fifteen weeks.

During the spawn run the fungus completely colonizes the sawdust mix, which turns white and is referred to as a "block." The collar is removed from the top of the plastic bag, and the bag is either rolled down the sides of the block or removed completely. The exposed surfaces of the block develop a brown outer layer that functions rather like the bark of a log. At this point the temperature of the blocks is reduced either by plunging them into cold water or lowering the air

Auger bag filler commonly used in China. (Tian)

temperature. Shiitake fruiting bodies then form on the sides of the block. High carbon dioxide levels inhibit fruiting, and so good ventilation is essential. Light is also required to trigger fruiting, which is perhaps a surprising fact since fungi, unlike green plants, do not require light to produce carbohydrates. Once fruiting has been completed, further harvests can be triggered by allowing the blocks to recover for two to four weeks and then again inducing fruiting. Cultivation procedures that use a shelf system, similar to those for growing button mushrooms, have been developed for shiitake, but they are not popular. Year-round fruiting under ambient conditions can be achieved by using strains that have different temperature requirements at different times of the year.

Size, thickness of the cap, taste, texture, moisture content, and the pattern on the cap contribute to the perceived quality of shiitake fruiting bodies. The highest grade, *hua gu* (Chinese) or *donko* (Japanese), has a pattern of cracks that resembles a flower on the surface of the cap and can command much higher prices than the lower grade, *dong gu*

Steel tanks partly filled with water and heated with a wood fire are used in China to pasteurize loose medium or bags of medium. (Tian)

Heat-resistant bags, filled with sterilized medium and plugged with a cotton bung to prevent the entry of contaminating organisms and pests, partly colonized by shiitake (*Lentinula edodes*). (Buchanan)

(Chinese) or *koshin* (Japanese). While it is possible to grow *hua gu* on sawdust blocks, the more usual method is to grow the fungus on logs, using the traditional techniques. Some growers of shiitake on sawdust-based media will scar the surface of the fruiting bodies when they are at the button stage. When these grow to maturity they have the cracked appearance of *hua gu*, although the texture of the caps usually belies their origin.

Once the last flush of mushrooms has been picked, the grower is left with the spent remains of what was once sawdust. The spent material, like spent button mushroom compost, can be used as a garden mulch. However, Forest Foods Company in Christchurch, New Zealand, developed a novel way of growing shiitake on pine sawdust, of which there is a surfeit in New Zealand, and then using the nitrogen-rich spent material as a stock food (Reddish 1995).

Over the past decade there have been major advances in China in minimizing the cost of producing specialty mushrooms like shiitake. The techniques used by Luo Qi Gin in Zhang Jia Jie, Hunan, are typical of those that can be seen throughout China. Mr. Luo's substrate is made from 1000 kg of cotton husks mixed with a suspension

Lentinula edodes (shiitake) fruiting on sawdust blocks. **EDIBLE.** (Buchanan)

of 2 percent calcium hydroxide, 2 percent calcium sulphate, and 2–5 percent ground rock phosphate in water. The mixture is then covered with clear polyethylene and left in the sun until it reaches pasteurization temperature—about five days. The pasteurized materials (2.5 kg) are then placed in polypropylene bags cut from a roll of tubing. The ends of the tubing are passed through 50-mm rings, the bag folded backward over the outside of the ring, and the open neck covered with newspaper. The bags are then inoculated in three positions along the length of each bag, stacked four to five high in rooms, and incubated at approximately 22–27°C for three to four weeks. Remarkably, contamination is not a significant problem. The bags are then removed and the colonized substrate buried horizontally in a field, leaving only the upper 3–5 cm exposed. Fruiting occurs after two weeks and there are a total of five flushes separated by intervals of two weeks. Alternatively the bags may be incubated in rudimentary shelters where, despite a complete lack of hygiene, yields are remarkably high, typically in the order of 1 kg of fresh mushrooms from each kilogram of fresh substrate. A modification of the above technique is to form the sawdust mix into rectangular blocks and incubate these on shelving similar to those used in *Agaricus* mushroom cultivation.

Shiitake-inoculated bags of medium incubating in a simple shade house in China. (Tian)

Simple huts used in China to incubate bags inoculated with various saprobic mushrooms. (Tian)

Lentinula edodes (shiitake) fruiting on slabs of sawdust medium. **EDIBLE.** (Wang)

Yet another method that has gained great favor in China is to raise shiitake in beds of inoculated media between other crops in a field. A sawdust-based mix is first steamed in a steel vessel for five hours and allowed to cool. Channels are then made in the soil between rows of a crop, lined with polyethylene, and filled with the steamed mixture, after which point the spawn inoculum is added. The polyethylene is folded over the bed, and a protective cover of straw supported on wooden hoops is placed over the bed to prevent overheating by the sun. When the mycelium has completely colonized the substrate, the covers and polyethylene are removed and the beds kept moist to ensure fruiting.

Pleurotus Species (Oyster Mushroom)

The common name "oyster mushroom" refers to several species of edible mushrooms all belonging to the genus *Pleurotus*. These are among the most colorful edible mushrooms, ranging from golden yellow (*P. cornucopiae* var. *citrinopileatus*) and pink (*P. djamor*) to gray (*P. pulmonarius*—phoenix mushroom, also widely but incorrectly called *P. sajor-caju*), bluish gray, cream, and brown. Although many

As the first step in the production of shiitake between rows of maize, steamed sawdust medium is used to fill a polyethylene-lined channel cut in the soil. (Tian)

Next the steamed sawdust medium is inoculated and covered with mats made from rice straw. (Tian)

For the third step, the rice straw mats are removed to reveal the fruiting shiitake. (Tian)

The fruiting bodies of *Pleurotus djamor* (pink oyster mushroom) showing the distinctive color of the gills. **EDIBLE.** (Douglas)

Pleurotus pulmonarius (phoenix mushroom) fruiting on horizontally arranged sawdust blocks. Mushroom Developments, New Zealand. **EDIBLE.** (Johnston)

oyster mushrooms are easy to grow, the same factors as those outlined for shiitake must be considered: strain selection, optimal substrate, climatic conditions, and prevention of pests (especially flies) and diseases.

Fruiting bodies of most oyster mushrooms have a characteristic form, with circular to tongue-shaped or shell-like caps developing from a lateral or eccentric stalk and gills that tend to extend partway down the stalk. Like shiitake and most other specialty mushrooms, oyster mushrooms grow naturally as saprobes on dead wood, although a few species, such as *Pleurotus eryngii* (king oyster mushroom), are parasitic.

Oyster mushrooms can be cultivated on a range of waste materials from forestry and agriculture, including hardwood sawdust, paper, cereal, maize, sugar cane bagasse, and banana leaves. This versatility of substrates and relative ease of cultivation, coupled with the number of oyster mushrooms that are edible, have led to rapid increases in production in recent years. As a result, oyster mushrooms are now second only to button mushrooms in terms of volumes produced.

Although oyster mushrooms may be cultivated on hardwood logs, the most common system involves bags and is similar to that used for shiitake. The bags are filled with moist substrate material and addi-

Lower surface of *Pleurotus pulmonarius* (phoenix mushroom) fruiting on a sterilized mixture of sawdust and other ingredients. Mushroom Developments, New Zealand. **EDIBLE.** (Johnston)

tives, and a collar is placed around the neck, which is plugged to prevent entry of contaminating organisms while still allowing for gaseous exchange. After being sterilized in an autoclave, typically at 121°C, the bags are cooled and inoculated with spawn. During the spawn run the substrate becomes paler as it is colonized by the fungus. Fruiting occurs through perforations cut in the bag or over the exposed surface if part or all of the bag is removed. High carbon dioxide concentrations reduce the size of the caps; consequently, adequate ventilation is essential. Each bag often produces three to four flushes of mushrooms. The bags are rested between flushes and successive fruitings are induced by soaking the bags in water.

A simpler process popular among farmers in China involves pasteurizing the bagged substrate instead of sterilizing it. This is usually carried out in a steel vessel about 1.5 × 1.5 × 1.5 m fitted with a grid toward the bottom. Below the grid is a space for water. Several large mesh boxes containing twenty to thirty bags are placed in the vessel, and a fire is lit underneath it. The water eventually boils, raising the temperature of the bagged substrate above 70°C. After several hours the substrate is pasteurized. However, there is a greater risk of contamination using this technique, and as a result, poorer yields are

Pleurotus ostreatus fruiting on a bagged sawdust-based medium. **EDIBLE.** (Hall)

Pleurotus pulmonarius (phoenix mushroom) fruiting through slits made in the side of a large plastic bag filled with substrate. Huon Valley Mushrooms, Australia. **EDIBLE.** (Hall)

achieved. In another technique, pasteurized or sometimes even raw, untreated, or fermented substrate is formed into columns, horizontal or vertical slabs, or loaded into trays and inoculated with the spawn. When the first flush of mushrooms is harvested, the bags or slabs are rested and successive fruitings are induced by soaking them in water. Typically four flushes are harvested.

In contrast to the labor-intensive systems used in China, Japanese production is largely automated and based on unit trays, each containing sixteen wide-mouthed polypropylene bottles fitted with caps containing an air filter. Following sterilization in an autoclave, each bottle is inoculated with spawn inside a clean room. Sterility of the room is ensured by maintaining absolute cleanliness, pumping in filtered air and using ultraviolet germicidal lamps. The bottles are then taken to climatically controlled rooms where they are incubated at a temperature that suits the particular strain being cultivated. *Pleurotus pulmonarius*, for example, typically requires 18–25°C, a high relative humidity (85–95 percent), low carbon dioxide concentration, and moderate light levels. In this species, fruiting is initially induced by dropping the temperature of the bottles to 10–20°C. Species such as *P. ostreatus* and *P. eryngii* fruit best at lower temperatures, typically 15–20°C. Additional details of the cultivation process for several species of oyster mushrooms can be found in the books *Growing Gourmet and Medicinal Mushrooms* (Stamets 2000) and *Mushroom Cultivation with Special Emphasis on Appropriate Techniques for Developing Countries* (Oei 1996), and in a short paper titled "Indoor Cultivation of Paddy Straw Mushroom, *Volvariella volvacea*, in Crates" (Gutierrez Reyes 2000). An extensive literature on oyster mushroom cultivation can also be found in *Edible Mushrooms and Their Cultivation* (Chang and Miles 1989), while details of a simple technique for producing small quantities are described in an article titled "Cultivation of the Oyster Mushroom in Traditional Brick Pots" (Abate 1996).

As some workers may develop an allergic reaction to the massive numbers of airborne spores released by even immature oyster mushrooms, respirators may have to be worn during harvest. Sporeless strains of some species have been developed to reduce this problem.

Oyster mushrooms are sold fresh, canned, or in brine. The shelf life of fresh oyster mushrooms is maximized by picking the mushrooms before they are mature. Most are rather delicate and so are usually prepacked at the factory to prevent damage. Of all species, the robust fruiting bodies of *Pleurotus eryngii* store best. Many believe this species also has the best flavor.

Pleurotus eryngii (king oyster mushroom) fruiting through the necks of plastic bottles filled with a sterilized sawdust medium. **EDIBLE.** (Hall)

Oyster mushrooms are among the most efficient converters of substrate to fungal fruiting bodies among the edible mushrooms. Fresh-weight yields of mushrooms in excess of the dry weight of the substrate can be achieved (expressed as a biological efficiency rating greater than 100 percent). The spent compost is used as an animal feed, as a soil supplement, and as a substrate for the cultivation of other edible fungi such as *Stropharia rugosoannulata*.

Auricularia Species (Wood Ear)

Very different in appearance to a conventional mushroom, the wood ear is thin, rubbery, ear-shaped, and lacks gills. In *Auricularia polytricha* the typically convex upper surface may be covered with whitish hairs, while the concave lower surface, from which spores are produced, is purplish brown. This species has a broad geographic and host range and is commonly seen fruiting on dead wood in the forests of many regions. *Auricularia polytricha* and the related *A. auricula* are widely cultivated, particularly in Asia, and both species have been used in traditional medicine. An aqueous extract (probably adenosine) obtained from *A. polytricha* is thought to have the property of reducing atherosclerosis, while *A. auricula* has been used as a treatment for hemorrhoids.

Spawn for *Auricularia polytricha* is prepared using cereal grains such as millet, rye, and wheat or aged hardwood sawdust amended with rice bran and other supplements. Alternatively, if the mushrooms are to be grown on logs, spawn can be grown on hardwood dowels. Cultivation follows, using a procedure similar to that described for shiitake, with both log and, more recently, bag techniques being common.

Logs 1 m long and about 10–20 cm in diameter of selected hardwood trees, such as *Acacia*, beech (*Fagus*), and mulberry (*Morus*), are cut between late autumn and early spring and inoculated within one week by pushing spawn or dowels into holes drilled into them. The holes are sealed to prevent contamination and to retain moisture. The inoculated logs are then moved to a laying yard, where shade is provided by a natural forest canopy or by artificial shelter. There must be adequate ventilation and a steady temperature. The logs are turned

Auricularia polytricha (wood ear) fruiting on sawdust blocks. **EDIBLE.** (Buchanan)

and watered for thirty to forty days. The logs are then transferred to a shaded cropping yard, where they are placed in an almost upright position. Fruiting is induced by raising the humidity to about 85 percent, sometimes after soaking. The optimum temperatures for fruiting are 23–28°C. Successive crops of mushrooms can be harvested from the logs while the temperatures are high. During winter the logs are covered with straw, and in spring fruiting is induced by heavily watering or soaking the logs.

The procedure for cultivating wood ear in bags is similar to that used for shiitake. Substrates include hardwood sawdust, cotton seed hull, sugar cane, corn, and rice straw. The optimum temperatures are 22–30°C during the spawn run and 20–24°C during the fruiting phase. The bags are stood on end and fruiting is induced by cutting small holes in the sides of the bags and raising the humidity to 90–100 percent. Alternatively, the tops and bottoms of the bags are opened and the bags stacked on their sides to form walls. Although fruiting is quicker on bags of sawdust than on logs, typically only three to four flushes are obtained.

Most wood ear continues to be marketed today in dried form, equating to about 10–12 percent of fresh weight, with simple rehydration prior to cooking. The mushroom is better known for its soft, crunchy, somewhat cartilaginous texture than for any distinctive flavor. It is often added to vegetable and meat dishes in Chinese cooking.

Volvariella volvacea (Straw Mushroom)

The straw mushroom derives its name from the fact that in China this fungus was traditionally cultivated on rice straw. The mushroom is adapted to subtropical and tropical climates, with optimal temperatures of 32–36°C for vegetative growth of the mycelium and 28–30°C for fruiting (Chang and Miles 1989). The cultures must also be stored at high temperatures and will die if stored in conventional low-temperature systems.

Spawn can be prepared on a range of materials, including cereal grains, short lengths of rice straw, and cotton waste. Rice straw is a suitable substrate, but in recent times it has been largely superseded by cotton waste from the textile industry. The highest yields are produced indoors, where climatic conditions can be managed, using pasteurized composted substrates. To create the compost, a mixture of cotton waste, lime, and water is fermented outdoors for three to seven days. The composting pile is turned once and protected from

Volvariella volvacea (straw mushroom) fruiting on a bed of cellulosic waste. **EDIBLE.** (Hall)

rain and cold. The compost is then loaded onto shelves in the growing house and pasteurized with steam for two hours at 62°C, followed by eight to sixteen hours at 50–52°C. This is a very important step because inadequate fermentation of the compost and incomplete pasteurization can result in severe nematode infestations. The pasteurized compost is then cooled to about 36–38°C, spawn is introduced, and the inoculated compost is covered with plastic sheeting. Full colonization occurs in three to four days at 32–34°C. The covers are then removed, and the first primordia appear about the fifth day. The first mushrooms are harvested eight to ten days after spawning. Increased aeration and light levels and a slight reduction in temperature and humidity assist initiation and development of fruiting bodies. Generally there is a large first flush of fruiting bodies followed by a smaller second one.

Straw mushrooms may also be cultivated outdoors when ambient temperatures are high enough to support fruiting. Cultivation beds consist of layers of water-soaked bundles of unfermented rice straw, with each layer spawned as it is laid down. The beds are then covered with a layer of rice straw, followed by a sheet of polyethylene. The sheet

Volvariella volvacea (straw mushroom) sectioned to show the cap and stalk forming inside the egg. **EDIBLE.** (Hall)

is removed after four days, after which time the stacks are watered regularly until fruiting ceases. Further details of cultivation procedures can be found in *Edible Mushrooms and Their Cultivation* (Chang and Miles 1989) and *Mushroom Cultivation with Special Emphasis on Appropriate Techniques for Developing Countries* (Oei 1996).

When mature, the mushrooms have a typical stalked appearance, but they are usually harvested when immature and in what is known as the egg stage, with the cap still inside the volva. When fresh, the mushrooms have a shelf life of only three days, so these mushrooms are often canned. Straw mushrooms are frequently used in Chinese cuisine.

Flammulina velutipes (Enokitake)

Enokitake is a common saprobic wood-decay fungus in the forests of many countries. While the mushroom can be cultivated on a small scale, production in countries such as Japan (where it was first commercialized) and Taiwan is now in the hands of a limited number of very large companies, which have adopted fully automated systems. These farms use sterile circulated air, fully climate-controlled

Flammulina velutipes (enokitake) being harvested and automatically weighed in a factory near Hiroshima. (Hall)

Flammulina velutipes (enokitake) fruiting through the necks of bottles of sawdust and other ingredients. Note the clear plastic collar around the neck of each bottle to maintain high carbon dioxide concentrations. Tan Mushrooms, Tai-chung, Taiwan. **EDIBLE.** (Hall)

Flammulina velutipes (enokitake) fruiting in the light through holes in the side of a bag of substrate. Note the difference in the form of the fruiting bodies with those grown in bottles of sawdust. **EDIBLE.** (Cole)

environments, conveyor transportation, and automated manipulation of the growing containers.

The mushroom is cultivated on a mixture of aged sawdusts amended with rice bran. In Japan, Japanese red cedar (*Cryptomeria*), cypress (*Chamaecyparis*), and pine (*Pinus*) sawdusts are commonly used. Spawn is also prepared on a mixture of sawdust and rice bran. Wide-necked polypropylene bottles are then filled with the substrate, capped, placed in trays, and autoclaved. After cooling, spawn is introduced through the neck of the bottle and the cap is replaced.

The bottles are incubated at about 18–20°C for twenty to twenty-five days. Just before the fungus has colonized all the substrate, the caps are removed and the surface of the sawdust is mechanically scraped to give a flat, even surface or cone-shaped depression. Fruiting body primordia are initiated by dropping the temperature to 10–12°C and adjusting the humidity to 80–85 percent. The temperature is then further reduced to 3–5°C for three to five days, during which time the stalks begin to elongate. When the stalks are about 2 cm high, the temperature is raised to 5–8°C and the mouth of each bottle is surrounded by a tall, paper or plastic, cylindrical collar. This supports the elongating stalks and raises the carbon dioxide concentration, which reduces the size of the cap to little more than a slightly swollen end on the top of the stalk. The humidity is also reduced to 70–80 percent, and overwatering is avoided in order to produce dry fruiting bodies. When the stalks are 13–14 cm high, the collars are removed and the harvested mushrooms are either sold in 5-kg bags for the wholesalers or 100-g packets for the retail trade. The mushrooms can be grown in tall narrow bags instead of bottles, but in this case the bag is only partially filled with substrate and the open extended mouth is used to support the elongating stalks.

Consumers prefer mushrooms with white stalks and caps rather than the golden wild type, and this has resulted in breeding programs, particularly in Japan, for white strains. These strains dominate the market. Enokitake is sold fresh or canned and is a frequent ingredient in Asian soups and stir-fried meat and vegetable dishes.

Tremella fuciformis (White Jelly Fungus)

Members of the genus *Tremella* are common saprobic wood-decay fungi in the forests of many countries, from tropical to temperate regions. Commercially produced fruiting bodies of the white jelly fungus consist of white to pale yellow convoluted folds of gelatinous

Tremella fuciformis (white jelly fungus) fruiting on a sawdust block. **EDIBLE.** (Buchanan)

Tremella fuciformis (white jelly fungus) drying in the sun in Gutian, Fujian Province, China. **EDIBLE.** (Buchanan)

translucent fungal material 8–15 cm across that somewhat resemble a chrysanthemum flower. They were first cultivated on hardwood logs by a method very similar to that used for shiitake, but most are now grown on bagged sawdust or cottonseed hulls.

Unlike the cultivation of other mushrooms, acceptable yields of the white jelly fungus can only be achieved if a companion fungus is grown with it. This fungus degrades the substrate in advance of the white jelly fungus. One companion species that can be used is the ascomycete *Hypoxylon archeri* (Chang and Miles 1989). Spawn production is a specialized procedure. First the slower-growing white jelly fungus is inoculated onto the spawn medium, which consists of sterilized sawdust or bagasse mixed with rice bran, and incubated at 23–25°C. Only when it has become established is the companion fungus introduced. The quality of a spawn is assessed by judging the fruiting bodies that develop on its surface. High-quality spawn is then bulked up for inoculation of the substrate.

Substrates for cultivation include hardwood sawdust (Oei 1996) and cottonseed hulls, along with sources of nitrogen such as corn cobs and wheat bran. These are mixed with gypsum and other ingredients and compressed into long, narrow (perhaps 12 × 55 cm) bags, which are then autoclaved. Spawn is introduced through three to five holes punched in the sides of the bag, which are then resealed with tape. The inoculated bags are incubated at 28–30°C. The temperature is subsequently lowered to 20–25°C and the tape covering the inoculation points lifted to allow gaseous exchange. The first fruiting body primordia appear about sixteen to eighteen days after inoculation. The tape is removed, the inoculation holes enlarged, and the temperature raised to 23–25°C. Once the fruiting bodies have formed, they are covered with newspaper until mature—about thirty-five to forty days after inoculation. In China harvested mushrooms are commonly dried on racks in the sun. Alternatively they can be dried in an oven (first drying the outer surface at about 30°C, followed by higher temperatures to complete the drying process).

Tremella fuciformis has both medicinal and culinary uses. The polysaccharides and steroids it contains reportedly have antitumor and anti-inflammatory properties and also serve as a general tonic. The white jelly fungus can be included in desserts and added to soups and other dishes. Though it has little flavor, the smooth gelatinous texture of this mushroom is appealing to the Asian palate. Other species of *Tremella*, such as the golden ear (*T. aurantia*), are also cultivated in China and used in traditional medicines.

Pholiota nameko (nameko) with caps too mature for Japanese consumers. **EDIBLE.** (Cole)

Pholiota nameko (Nameko)

The small caps of nameko are very popular in Japan. Although the gelatinous surface of the cap sometimes reduces its immediate appeal to Westerners, the slime is not readily apparent once the fruiting body is cooked. The mushroom makes a delicious addition to Japanese soups. Nameko fruits at low temperatures, like enokitake, and is cultivated by a similar procedure (Chang and Miles 1989, Stamets 2000), although Japanese producers usually employ broader-mouthed bottles than those used for enokitake. A range of sawdust substrates has been used, including both hardwood sawdust, such as oak (*Quercus*), and softwoods such as pine (*Pinus*) and Japanese red cedar (*Cryptomeria*), to which is added cereal bran. The fully colonized substrate is subjected to high humidity, low light, and low temperatures (10–15°C) to initiate fruiting. Adequate ventilation is required to lower carbon dioxide concentrations so that the caps develop normally. The production of orange slime on the surface of the substrate often precedes the development of primordia. During maturation of the mushrooms, the temperature is maintained at 13–18°C. In Japan the short-stalked mushrooms are sometimes harvested using scissors as they mature, so that each bottle has to be harvested on more than one occasion. A

Pholiota nameko (nameko) fruiting through wide-necked bottles filled with substrate. Note the partially opened caps required by Japanese consumers. **EDIBLE.** (Buchanan)

second flush can be induced by scraping the substrate surface to expose growing mycelium (Stamets 2000).

Other Species

Several other mushroom species are commercially cultivated in relatively small quantities, often for the production of medicinal products. These include the almond portobello (*Agaricus blazei*), grown as an alternative to button mushrooms (Stamets 2000); several species of *Agrocybe*, which have only recently gained acceptance in the marketplace; bamboo mushroom (*Dictyophora indusiata*), a phalloid mushroom that emerges from an egg and is cultivated mainly in China on bamboo and wood chips outdoors, for both taste and medicinal effects; reishi (*Ganoderma* aff. *lucidum*), a polypore cultivated for its fruiting bodies and their spores; hen of the woods (*Grifola frondosa*), cultivated mainly in Japan; lion's mane mushroom (*Hericium erinaceus*); shimeji (*Hypsizygus marmoreus*), which is popular in Japan and increasingly so in China; *Kuehneromyces mutabilis*, a small, brown, stalked mushroom grown on hardwood pieces in eastern Europe; fat pholiota (*Pholiota adiposa*), cultivated in China; *Pleurotus*

Display of medicinal mushroom products in Hong Kong. (Buchanan)

The fruiting bodies of *Hypsizygus marmoreus* (shimeji) growing in wide-necked plastic bottles. **EDIBLE.** (Buchanan)

Dictyophora indusiata (bamboo mushroom) in its egg stage, fruiting on buried bamboo pieces. **MEDICINAL AND EDIBLE.** (Buchanan)

Mature *Dictyophora indusiata* (bamboo mushroom) fruiting outdoors on buried bamboo pieces. **MEDICINAL AND EDIBLE.** (HortResearch)

Ganoderma aff. *lucidum* (reishi) fruiting on the base of a stump. **MEDICINAL.** (Izawa)

Ganoderma aff. *lucidum* (reishi) cultivation in China on bags of substrate covered with soil. The sheets hanging from the roof are used to collect the more valuable spores. **MEDICINAL.** (Tian)

Ganoderma aff. *lucidum* for sale in Changsha, Hunan, China. **MEDICINAL.** (Hall)

The deformed fruiting bodies of this *Ganoderma* species were produced by growing the mushroom with an elevated level of carbon dioxide. Qi Feng free market, Changsha, Hunan, China. **MEDICINAL.** (Hall)

The large and distinctive fruiting bodies of *Grifola frondosa* (hen of the woods) growing in wide-necked plastic bottles. **EDIBLE.** (Hall)

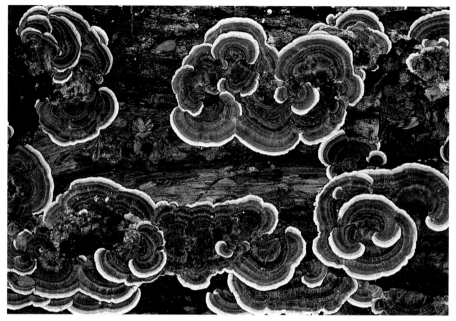

Trametes versicolor (many-colored polypore) is an extremely variable species. Here it grows on a *Nothofagus* species. **MEDICINAL.** (Buchanan)

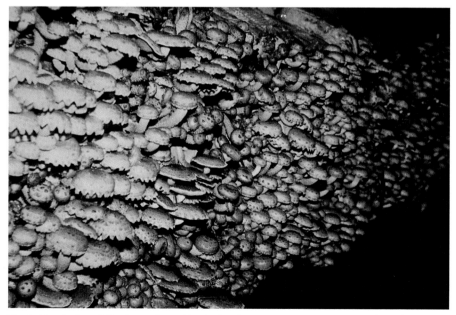

The fruiting bodies of *Pholiota adiposa* (fat pholiota) cultivated in China. **EDIBLE.** (Wang)

The fruiting bodies of a white variety of *Trametes versicolor*, clustered on a decaying trunk. **MEDICINAL.** (Wang)

tuber-regium, a species cultivated not for its fruiting bodies but for the medicinal properties of the sclerotia it produces (Chen and Huang 2001); and many-colored polypore (*Trametes versicolor*), another polypore grown for its medicinal properties.

MYCORRHIZAL MUSHROOMS

Many edible mushrooms are found only in association with the roots of certain trees. In these intimate symbiotic relationships the fungus benefits the growth of the tree by helping with the uptake of essential elements, and the plant provides the fungus with carbohydrates and a place to live. These are the mycorrhizal mushrooms, and among them are some of the most expensive foods in the world.

To understand the high value placed on edible mycorrhizal mushrooms and why attempts to cultivate them have so often proved fruitless, it is useful to understand mycorrhizas and how they function. Many people are surprised to learn that most higher plants, from ferns to flowering plants, do not technically have roots but instead possess mycorrhizas (literally "fungus roots"), the composite structures formed when a mycorrhizal fungus infects the roots of a higher plant (Smith and Read 1997, Mycorrhiza Information Exchange 2002). This relationship generally benefits both the plant and the fungus and is therefore an example of symbiosis. Plants in a few families—the brassicas (Brassicaceae) and nettles (Urticaceae), for example—do not form any type of mycorrhiza, but collectively these amount to only 10–15 percent of all species. Mycorrhizal relationships have existed for a very long time; in fact, mycorrhizas have been reported in 460-million-year-old Ordovician fossils (Redecker et al. 2000, Sanders 2000). Over this long span of time, mycorrhizal fungi have become very specialized so that most cannot survive unless they are in contact with their host plant. Many plants have become equally dependent on mycorrhizal fungi and without them become stunted and yellow—often due to a lack of phosphorus. A lack of these fungi is one reason why some plants, raised in a sterile, soilless potting mix and purchased from a garden center, die when transplanted in the garden (Hall 1988).

The most common mycorrhiza is the vesicular-arbuscular mycorrhiza (VAM), which is formed by almost all agricultural and horticultural plants. In this type, most of the fungus is found inside the root, where the fungus produces small storage organs called vesicles (literally "small bladders") and arbuscules (literally "little trees"), which are

Dichotomously branched ectomycorrhizas formed by *Lactarius deliciosus* (saffron milk cap). The fine external fungal hyphae can be seen between the roots. (Wang)

well adapted to the transfer of nutrients between the host plant and the fungus. These fungi do not produce mushroom fruiting bodies.

Another mycorrhiza is the type known as an ectomycorrhiza. This is the type of particular interest, because some of the fungi that form ectomycorrhizas produce mushrooms, some of which are edible. An ectomycorrhizal fungus forms a layer of fungal material over the surface of small roots, much like the fingers of a glove. This layer is called the mantle. Short fungal threads, called hyphae, extend from the inner surface of the mantle and grow between the outer layers of root cells, producing a three-dimensional structure called the Hartig net. You can get some idea of the structure of the Hartig net if you imagine that it looks like the mortar between the bricks (equivalent to the outer cells of the root) in a brick chimney. From the outer surface of the mantle, hyphae extend out into the soil. There they absorb nutrients such as phosphorus and nitrogen and pass them back down the hyphae to the mantle, eventually reaching the plant via the Hartig net. The fungus obtains carbohydrates from the plant in return, but the loss is more than offset by the increased plant growth made possible by improved access to nutrients.

Host plants for ectomycorrhizal fungi include birches (Betulaceae), oaks and beeches (Fagaceae), eucalypts (Myrtaceae), pines and spruces (Pinaceae), poplars and willows (Salicaceae), rock roses (Cistaceae), and dipterocarps (Dipterocarpaceae) (Becker 1983, Smith and Read 1997). Edible ectomycorrhizal mushrooms are never found associated with, for example, horse chestnuts (Hippocastanaceae), maples (Aceraceae), and apples, apricots, or peaches (Rosaceae), since all of these form vesicular-arbuscular mycorrhizas. Because of the importance of ectomycorrhizal trees in most of the world's forests, it is unusual to find areas where there are no ectomycorrhizal fungi. But there are a few exceptions. For example, all but a handful of New Zealand's native plants form vesicular-arbuscular mycorrhizas. Consequently, ectomycorrhizal fungi, which are dependent on their host plants for survival, are generally restricted to those areas where their southern beech (*Nothofagus*) and tea tree (*Leptospermum* and *Kunzea*) host plants are found (Johnson 1977). Moreover, forests in many areas of the tropics are predominantly composed of vesicular-arbuscular mycorrhizal trees.

Because of the importance of mycorrhizas and the fungi that produce them, more than ten thousand specialist scientific publications deal with the subject. Some of these provide good summaries of the salient points. The Mycorrhiza Information Exchange Web page is a good place to start, while *Mycorrhizal Symbiosis* (Smith and Read 1997) is an excellent book for those wanting a more in-depth treatment.

Commercial Considerations

Mycorrhizal mushrooms are renowned for the flavors they impart to meals, but also for the high prices some of them command—up to $30,000 per kilogram. Compared with their saprobic cousins, the market in dollar terms is disproportionately higher than the relatively small quantities that are harvested. Since only a handful have ever been cultivated commercially, the chef and gourmet have to rely on professional or amateur collectors harvesting the mushrooms from the wild during the few months that they fruit.

Just what quantities are in fact harvested is unknown. Estimates that have been made are very approximate, with official statistics probably containing some gross errors. One reason for this is that many mycorrhizal mushrooms are sold under the counter so that the picker and purchaser can avoid paying taxes. Many more are taken home after a day's collecting without ever passing through a market.

Portia Barnes, one of a small number of competent wild mushroom collectors in Victoria, Australia, with a basket of grade-one *Lactarius deliciosus* (saffron milk cap). **EDIBLE.** (Hall)

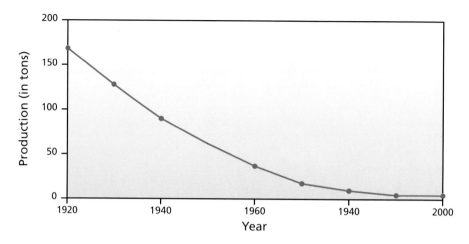

Tuber melanosporum (Périgord black truffle) production in Quercy, France, since 1920 (Fauconnet and Delher 1998).

However, there is mounting concern that the quantities of mycorrhizal mushrooms that can be harvested are declining. While articles with titles like "Disappearing Mushrooms: Another Mass Extinction?" (Cherfas 1991) are somewhat alarmist, it is undeniable that there have been catastrophic declines in the harvest of some mycorrhizal mushrooms over the past hundred years. For example, at the beginning of the twentieth century production of the Périgord black truffle is estimated to have been 1000–2000 tons, but modern production, even in a good year, is often less than 10 percent of this. Forty tons is considered a bad year, 150 tons a good one (Lefevre and Hall 2001, Olivier 2000). The official figures for truffle production for Quercy, France, illustrate this trend well, as do those for matsutake harvests in Japan.

Many suggestions have been advanced to explain the decline. Very likely causes are deforestation and the establishment of plantation forests with trees that are poor hosts or that are planted much closer together than occur in natural forests. Other possibilities include compaction of the soil by hordes of pickers; acid rain that can make a soil too acid for either the mycorrhizal fungus or its host plant; global warming that has gradually made climatic conditions unsuitable for the fungus or host; the loss, during two world wars, of many of the people with knowledge of where and how to harvest mushrooms (particularly so with species such as truffles that fruit underground); the underreporting of harvests by those reluctant to pay taxes; and younger generations being more inclined to spend their

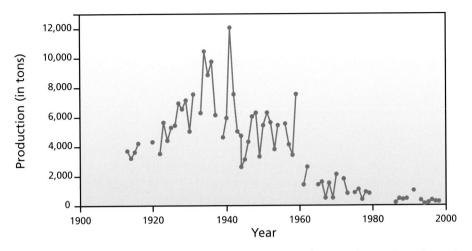

Tricholoma matsutake (matsutake) production in Japan since 1915 (Wang et al. 1997, Japan External Trade Organization 2000a, 2000b).

time behind a computer in an office than wandering around chilly forests at daybreak searching for an unpredictable income (Ciani et al. 1992, Olivier 2000).

Pickers may also be picking mycorrhizal mushrooms when they are still too small, knowing that if they leave them until the following morning to grow to a reasonable size someone else may get there first. An example of what happens when wild mushroom mania strikes comes from Christchurch, New Zealand, in the 1990s. Hagley Park in Christchurch was established in the 1850s with oaks from England that were brought out by some of the first "official" European settlers. It seems likely that around the same time these oaks were introduced porcini (*Boletus edulis*) also arrived, probably on the roots of the same trees. Until 1993 porcini was quietly harvested in Hagley Park by a few Europeans who knew what they were harvesting and did not intend to tell anyone else about it. Across town, on the Canterbury University campus, porcini was meeting a more ignominious fate as periodic mowing delivered shredded porcini to the compost heap. Then in 1993 an observant gardener on the university campus decided to take a couple of the fruiting bodies to Tony Cole for identification. This in turn led to exposure on television and in newspapers and scientific articles, all heralding the find. Since that time there have been dozens of collectors, rather than a few keen amateurs, and the fruiting bodies have been collected almost as soon as they show themselves above the ground. One picker even admitted going out hunting with a torch early in the morning just to make sure he found a few for his breakfast. As a consequence, the weight of porcini now harvested in Christchurch is quite probably lower today than it was in the 1980s.

The edible ectomycorrhizal mushrooms held in the highest regard are the Périgord black truffle (*Tuber melanosporum*), Italian white truffle (*Tuber magnatum*), porcini (*Boletus edulis*), chanterelle (*Cantharellus cibarius*), and matsutake (*Tricholoma matsutake*). However, Caesar's mushroom (*Amanita caesarea*), honshimeji (*Lyophyllum shimeji*), Burgundy truffle (*Tuber uncinatum*), Oregon white truffle (*Tuber gibbosum*), saffron milk cap (*Lactarius deliciosus*), shoro (*Rhizopogon rubescens*), and many other mushrooms are also very popular in some countries.

Because of the general decline in the harvest of many edible mycorrhizal mushrooms, prices have been steadily climbing, particularly since the 1980s. However, the price of the Italian white truffle outshines all others, with retail prices increasing fourfold from around $1000 per kilogram in 1995 to $4000 per kilogram in 1999 (Anonymous 2000a). By 2000, retail prices had jumped to $5680 per kilogram in Milano, with $13,243 per kilogram paid for a 497-g specimen at the Alba Truffle Festival (Johnston 2000). The prices of the next two most expensive species of mycorrhizal mushrooms are trivial by comparison, with Périgord black truffles produced in New Zealand and out of season to the Northern Hemisphere managing only $1450 per kilogram, about twice the 1999–2000 in-season price. It is to be wondered what price Italian white truffles would fetch if they too were produced out of season in New Zealand!

Cultivation Techniques

The earliest cultivation of an edible ectomycorrhizal mushroom was achieved by Joseph Talon in the early 1800s in France (Hall et al. 1994). He found, probably accidentally, that if he transplanted oak seedlings from the rooting zones of trees that produced Périgord black truffles, eventually the transplants would also produce truffles. Despite its lack of sophistication, Talon's technique was widely used for 150 years. A similar technique has been used in Japan to produce plants infected with *Lyophyllum shimeji* (Fujita et al. 1990).

The main drawback with Talon's technique is that seedlings are exposed to infection by all organisms in the rooting zone of the parent tree and, consequently, may become contaminated by pathogenic fungi, nematodes, and insect pests, as well as faster-growing competing ectomycorrhizal fungi that do not produce edible mushrooms. However, in the late 1970s, after much research, French and Italian scientists developed techniques that subsequently led to routine greenhouse practice for infecting plants with various species of truffles. Scientists have also had limited success infecting plants with other types of edible mycorrhizal mushrooms, including Caesar's mushroom (*Amanita caesarea*), porcini (*Boletus edulis*), chanterelle (*Cantharellus cibarius*), saffron milk cap (*Lactarius deliciosus*), dotted-stalk bolete (*Suillus granulatus*), Jersey cow bolete (*Suillus bovinus*), shoro (*Rhizopogon rubescens*), and matsutake (*Tricholoma matsutake*).

Currently only a few species of *Tuber*, including the Périgord black truffle, Italian white truffle, and Burgundy truffle, have been produced in commercial quantities in plantations, although fruiting bodies of saffron milk cap and dotted-stalk bolete have formed in experimental plantations. This situation has partly arisen because effective techniques for infecting plants with many edible ectomycorrhizal mushrooms have yet to be devised. Also, research has not yet identified the climate and soil biological and physiochemical conditions most edible ectomycorrhizal mushrooms require, both to proliferate and fruit. Publications consolidating this type of information have only recently begun to appear.

Tuber melanosporum (Périgord Black Truffle)

Although the cultivation of the Périgord black truffle is still an inexact science, this truffle has been cultivated for much longer than any other ectomycorrhizal fungus. As a result, Périgord black truffle truffières now cover thousands of hectares in Europe (Pacioni and Comandini 2000). The cultivation of this truffle is covered in some detail in books in English, French, Italian, and Spanish, but as it provides such a useful template for other edible mycorrhizal mushrooms, the most important points are included here. Périgord black truffle cultivation is also encouraged by governments in several countries as an alternative source of income to conventional agriculture (Colinas et al. 1999, Olivier 2000).

Production of infected plants
Although Talon's technique is still used by some Périgord black truffle growers, their plants are often heavily contaminated with fast-growing and aggressive contaminants such as *Scleroderma* species

(Hall et al. 1994). Consequently, greenhouse techniques predominate. Many trees will host the Périgord black truffle, but hazel (*Corylus avellana*) is most commonly used because it can be grown relatively easily, it forms many fine roots that are readily converted to mycorrhizas by the fungus (Chevalier 1998), and it commonly produces truffles several years earlier than other host plants (Giovanetti et al. 1994, Hall et al. 1994). Other host plants include Mediterranean hazel (*C. colurna* and *C. heterophylla*), various species of oak (*Quercus*), and hop hornbeam (*Ostya carpinifolia*), which are produced by, among others, Agri Truffe in France and the New Zealand Institute for Crop and Food Research (Chevalier 1998, Craddock 1994, Hall et al. 1994, Lefevre and Hall 2001).

Unfortunately, some producers of infected plants make no distinction between inoculated and infected states. "Inoculated" merely means that the fungus has been introduced to the plant. However, unless the fungus also produces a good infection on the plant's roots, mushroom production will not occur. Completely uninfected plants

Soil-covered *Tuber melanosporum* (Périgord black truffles) for sale in a French marketplace. Bottled truffles are displayed on one side of the table and silver truffle shavers are on the display stand. **EDIBLE.** (Hall)

are rare, but it is not unusual to find the roots of commercially produced plants only partly infected with the Périgord black truffle and the remainder infected with competing ectomycorrhizal fungi. Some commercial producers of truffle-infected plants assume that when their plants are placed in ideal sites any contaminating competing fungi on the roots will eventually die out, but there is little justification for this belief.

Although the inoculation procedure is an important step in producing plants infected with Périgord black truffles, the critical phase is the subsequent six to twenty-four month incubation period. During this time, incorrect watering, air or soil temperatures, light levels, soil pH, nutrient concentrations in the potting medium, and, not least, contaminating ectomycorrhizal fungi, can all upset the infection process. Saprobic fungi may also cause problems, sometimes forming a loose weft of hyphae around the host plant's uninfected root tips, perhaps attracted by sugars leaking out. This presents a significant barrier to infection by the Périgord black truffle. Inoculated plants can also become contaminated with major pathogens. For this reason, plants infected with the Périgord black truffle that are produced in Europe cannot be imported into Australia, North America, New Zealand, or South Africa unless treated with chemicals that render them useless. In some cases infected plants have been smuggled into countries via a back door with no regard to the devastation a major pathogen riding piggyback on the host plants might have on a country's forests and plantation forest industry. Needless to say, the penalties these people face if caught are significant.

Soils and climate

It is critical that infected plants are placed in areas where the ecological conditions suit both the host plant and its fungal partner. In France, Italy, and Spain extensive surveys have determined where the ideal truffle-growing areas are located. These have well-aerated, well-drained, alkaline soils rich in calcium carbonate and with a carbon-nitrogen ratio of about 10:1, and they experience warm summers and cool winters. In Europe these areas are found to the west, south, and east of the Massif Central in France, in the southwest corner of France, northeastern Spain, and northern Italy (Hall et al. 1994). Somewhat surprisingly, of the eight productive Périgord black truffle truffières outside Europe, all but one have been established on naturally acidic soils that have been limed so that the pH is closer to the pH 7.9 optimum for the Périgord black truffle.

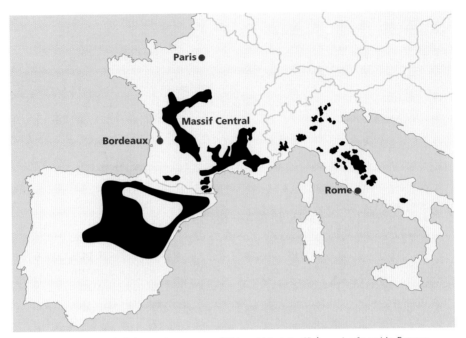

The main areas in which *Tuber melanosporum* (Périgord black truffle) can be found in Europe.

Planting and maintenance

A wide range of planting arrangements has been suggested by researchers (Hall et al. 1994). They usually recommend an alternating arrangement of several species of host plants, as one might be better suited to the ecological conditions than another, and as some species, like hazels, may produce early in the life of a truffière while others, like oaks, may start producing later but continue for longer. Planting two or more host species, such as hazels and oaks, also affords some protection against pathogens, which are unlikely to affect dissimilar species.

While expensive, artificial windbreaks have been used in some truffières. This involves surrounding the young trees with protectors such as Tree Guards, strong plastic tubes 10–15 cm across and 60–100 cm high. These are usually successful in preventing desiccation and damage by wind and browsing animals, at least for the first year or two. After planting, irrigation is often necessary to prevent plant death. Careful aeration of the ground in spring, particularly in areas where the soil has a poor structure, is also important in assisting spread of the truffle fungus and producing large, well-formed truffles (Lefevre and Hall 2001).

A young hazel (*Corylus avellana*) seedling infected with *Tuber melanosporum* (Périgord black truffle) grows in a rendzina soil rich in limestone. The seedling is protected from wind and browsing animals by a Tree Guard protector. (Hall)

Once fruiting starts, perhaps ten years after planting, soil moisture must again be maintained, particularly from midsummer onward, to ensure that young truffles do not die. The trees are usually pruned to a cone shape (with the point downward) to ensure that the soil is heated sufficiently by the sun in spring and autumn and protected from losing too much moisture during the heat of the day in summer. Laying branches on the soil around the trees and adding various mulches have also been used as ways to conserve moisture. The ancient French adage "Water in July, truffles at Christmas" clearly embodies an understanding of the importance of soil moisture.

Plant health is critical to successful truffle growing. In Europe, the pests and diseases of host trees cause major problems, and books have been published offering advice on how to control them (for example, Sourzat 1994). Iron deficiency in plants growing on very alkaline soils can cause yellowing of leaves and, in severe cases, death, with oaks more susceptible than hazels. This condition can be treated by placing chelated iron, such as Ferri-Chel Microgranular, in the rooting zone. Alternatively, a solution of chelated iron, such as Sprint 138, can be sprayed onto the foliage from bud break onward, with repeat sprayings every ten to fourteen days. Weeds around the trees can be treated with various herbicides, but Roundup has been used most frequently. The very poisonous desiccant herbicide Paraquat has also been used in the past, but Buster is a much safer option.

Harvesting

Once the fungus has become well established around its host tree, it kills many of the weeds in the rooting zone, leaving bare areas around the truffle-infected trees. In France this area is called the brûlé, and its development is said to herald the start of truffle production. Prior to the formation of the brûlé, weed control is often done by hand to avoid root damage, but in large truffières machinery or the careful application of herbicides is essential. In France once the brûlé has developed the truffière can be intensively managed with spring tilling, tree pruning, and irrigation, which, in combination, lead to early fruiting. This system is called the Pallier method (Chevalier 1998) and the techniques are similar to those used in New Zealand (Hall et al. 1994). The alternative is the Tanguy method, in which mowing replaces tilling and trees are left unpruned. In France the additional costs associated with the Pallier method have been estimated to be the equivalent of 8 kg of truffle per hectare (Olivier 2000). The cost is likely to be smaller in Southern Hemisphere countries because of the

Two closely planted oaks (*Quercus*) infected with *Tuber melanosporum* (Périgord black truffle). Notice the strong brûlé. (Hall)

Truffle hunters often take their dogs out early in the morning when there are few people about. A thin, long-handled trowel is used to unearth the truffle after the truffle dog has located it. (Hall)

higher returns from the sale of truffles, which are out of season to the Northern Hemisphere harvest.

Unlike most edible mycorrhizal mushrooms that form above the ground, black, rough-walled, potato-like Périgord black truffles are formed just at the soil surface or below ground. Finding them can, therefore, be a bit of a problem. One way is to get down on hands and knees and sniff them out. However, using this method, the owner of even a modest-sized truffière would probably spend more on trousers than could ever be made from collecting truffles. Another technique, developed out of desperation by a dogless New Zealand owner of a productive truffière, was to walk around in bare feet. Because the soil did not contain any stones, she reasoned that a hard spot under the soil surface represented a truffle. She then went down onto her hands and knees and sniffed to confirm whether the truffle was ripe or not before claiming her prize. What is really needed, however, is a more mobile nose—preferably one much more sensitive than that of a human. The traditional solution is a female pig, which has not only a nose even better than a dog's but also a natural yearning for truffles.

To select a pig, simply walk into a litter of piglets with a truffle in your hand, or tucked into your sock, and buy the one that shows the most interest. Train the piglet to walk on a lead. When she finds a truffle, persuade her that a piece of turnip, bread, or cheese is a fair swap—a bargain that may have to be reinforced with a couple of prods with a sharp stick. With piglets this is perhaps not too difficult, but it can pose something of a problem when the piglet grows to twice your own weight and does not discriminate between truffles and fingers. Consequently the majority of truffle hunters now use specially trained dogs, which, incidentally, fit better on the back seat of a car and are a bit less obvious when taken truffle poaching.

Yields

Under ideal conditions Périgord black truffle production can begin three years after inoculated trees are planted (Giovanetti and Fontana 1982), but generally the owner of a truffière will have to wait five to ten years or more before the first, often elusive, truffle is found. In artificial truffières, yields are often considerably higher than the 10 kg per hectare that might be expected from a forest that naturally produces Périgord black truffles. Yields in excess of 40 kg per hectare are infrequent, primarily because contaminating fungi often partially or completely occupy the roots of many of the trees (Chevalier 1998, Hall et al. 1994). However, several eleven- to fourteen-year-old French truffières have produced up to 150 kg per hectare (Chevalier 1998).

A truffle is just an elegant bag of spores, so those not eaten by a pig, dog, or human are not wasted: they eventually rot in the ground, release their spores, and await the arrival of a root from the right host plant. Similarly, the spores in truffles that were eaten by a pig will eventually find their way back to a well-manured patch of soil, probably some distance from the original host, where they may wait, perhaps for years, until conditions are right for germination.

Cultivation outside Europe

In the early 1980s many truffières were established in the United States using plants that were imported from Agri Truffe in France (Picart 1980). While truffles have never been harvested from the vast majority of these truffières and many have now fallen into disrepair, one near Ukiah in northern California began producing Périgord black truffles around 1988 (B. Hatch, personal communication). Truffles were also found in a truffière on Franklin Garland's property near Hillsborough, North Carolina, in 1993, when a group of students was

Oakland Truffière, near Gisborne, New Zealand, where the first Périgord black truffles were harvested in the Southern Hemisphere. Note the strong brûlés around the trees. (Hall)

casually invited to have a look for themselves (F. Garland, personal communication).

The first attempts to produce the Périgord black truffle in the Southern Hemisphere for out-of-season Northern Hemisphere markets began in New Zealand in the mid 1980s when English oak and hazel seedlings were infected with the fungus. Fortunately these experiments were successful, and the first truffières were established in 1987 (Hall et al. 1994). Oakland Truffière, near Gisborne on the east coast of the North Island, produced a few small truffles in 1993, some five years after planting. Disaster then appeared to have struck when *Tuber maculatum* and *T. dryophilum*, two less desirable truffle species, seemed to have taken over the 0.5-hectare truffière and began producing more than 100 kg of their own truffles each year. However, a new management regime was implemented, and between May and August 1997, 9 kg of Périgord black truffles were harvested, some weighing more than 1 kg. This was the first commercial harvest of a cultivated ectomycorrhizal mushroom in the Southern Hemisphere and the successful culmination of more than a decade of research. Since then, harvests have gradually increased, and although the owner of Oakland Truffière is a little reluctant to say just how much of the delicacy he is now harvesting, it is in excess of 40 kg per hectare. In 2000, three other New Zealand truffières and two Tasmanian truffières (Anonymous 2000b) between the latitudes 39°S and 43°S also began producing.

Sources of advice for growers

Throughout France and Italy, truffle societies hold parades during the truffle season and competitions are held to find the best truffle dog, which may later be offered for sale for perhaps more than $1000. Workshops and visits to truffières provide an important forum for the exchange of information between growers and scientists. Helpful periodicals such as *Le Trufficulteur Français* and *Tartufomania* are also available, while articles in popular horticultural and agricultural magazines review important topics such as choice of soil, size of harvests, and marketing (Garcia-Falces and De Miguel Velasco 1995a, Primavera 1995, Urbani 1995). Not surprisingly, elsewhere in the world similar associations are few and far between, although there is the North American Truffling Society, the New Zealand Truffle Association, and the fledgling Australian Truffle Association. Details on periodicals and societies are listed at the back of the book.

Forestry Plantations

The owners of plantation forests receive almost no income during the life of a forestry plantation, apart from the sale of small amounts of timber from thinnings. They must carry the cost of establishing the plantation, plus interest charges, for twenty-five years or more before seeing a return on their investment. In many countries this has meant that only species with relatively short rotations are planted, while species with rotations longer than seventy years have been largely ignored, even though they may produce timber with superior characteristics.

Wild mushrooms are harvested from forests in many countries where their collection and sale are significant industries. For example, in 1992 the forests of Idaho, Oregon, and Washington in the United States yielded $41 million worth of wild mushrooms (Schlosser and Blatner 1995, Thomas and Schumann 1993). The edible mushrooms in these forests are there because they were either in the soil when a plantation was established or were acquired from the nursery soil where seedlings were raised. It is the exploitation of this second possibility that has excited scientists in a number of countries, including

New Zealand (Hall and Wang 1996), Sweden (Danell 1994), and England (Hall and Wang 2000).

Very expensive mycorrhizal mushrooms, like the Périgord black truffle, Italian white truffle, Caesar's mushroom, and matsutake, warrant the expense of establishing plantations dedicated to their production (Hall et al. 1994, Hall, Zambonelli et al. 1998). Because of the high costs and the not inconsiderable risks involved, it is questionable whether there is sufficient economic justification for setting up specialized plantations dedicated to the production of mushrooms with relatively low prices, such as porcini and saffron milk cap. An alternative is to produce these lower-priced mushrooms as secondary crops in plantation forests (Hall and Wang 2000).

Southern Hemisphere

All the main edible ectomycorrhizal mushrooms of commerce are native to the Northern Hemisphere. Only a few of these—for example, porcini (Hall, Lyon et al. 1998, Marais and Kotzé 1977, Van der Westhuizen 1983), saffron milk cap, and shoro—have made the accidental journey to the Southern Hemisphere. This probably occurred on the roots of small deciduous trees that some of the early European settlers of Australia, New Zealand, and South Africa took with them as reminders of the land of their birth. Perhaps if more of the early settlers had been French or Italian instead of British, delicacies like the chanterelle, Périgord black truffle, and Italian white truffle would already be established in these countries.

Because most edible ectomycorrhizal mushrooms of commerce are available fresh only in the Northern Hemisphere for the short periods during the year in which they fruit, the chef, the gourmet, and those who would like to include one of these mushrooms in a favorite dish out of season are reliant on preserved specimens. There is, therefore, a golden opportunity to produce these fungi, such as the Périgord black truffle, in Southern Hemisphere countries in order to satisfy out-of-season demand in Northern Hemisphere markets.

COLLECTING
WILD MUSHROOMS

Throughout continental Europe the arrival of autumn brings with it some unusual sights and seemingly bizarre behavior. For example, in France, Germany, and Italy, lines of empty cars can be seen parked next to what might seem rather unprepossessing areas of woodland. Inside these forests are people with their heads bent down, apparently wandering about aimlessly. Occasionally they pick up a mushroom, carefully inspect and smell it, and then perhaps nibble a corner before either spitting it out and tossing the mushroom aside or consigning it to their basket. People with truffle dogs or truffle pigs are much less likely to be seen. They tend to do their hunting in secret, keeping the location of valuable truffle beds to themselves.

Individuals have a right to pick mushrooms in state-owned forests in many countries, but in Europe and parts of North America and Asia the pursuit is so popular and the number of collectors so great that soil disturbance and compaction have reduced the productivity of some wild mushrooms (Cherfas 1991, Palm and Chapela 1997, Pilz et al. 1999). It is not unusual to see busloads of Italian day-trippers with packed lunches crossing the border to pick mushrooms in the relatively well-stocked Austrian forests, much to the chagrin of many Austrians.

Not every year is a good fruiting year for wild mushrooms. A warm, moist summer followed by a cooler, moist autumn often produces the best fruitings. Some autumns in eastern North America may produce tons of field mushrooms where there were none the year before. Similarly, in New Zealand during a good year it is possible to walk into a forest of Monterey pine (*Pinus radiata*) and see a carpet of slippery jacks and fly agarics. But if a dry autumn follows a hot, dry summer and frosts precede winter rains, most autumn-fruiting mushrooms will not fruit at all, although if the following year is favorable there often seem to be bumper harvests.

When and Where to Look

Learning where a particular mushroom might be expected to appear is the first step to finding it. Each species has its own special ecological niche and occurs only in certain habitats. Knowing what and where these are will eventually save a great deal of futile searching. For example, the fruiting bodies of ectomycorrhizal fungi will only be found associated with those plants that form this type of association, such as beech, birch, fir, oak, pine, spruce, and eucalyptus. Consequently you would not expect to find the fruiting bodies of such fungi as *Amanita* and *Russula* in a forest that does not contain at least some ectomycorrhiza-forming trees.

Fungi are the major group of organisms responsible for wood decay, and the species involved represent a special group. Some of these fungi are generalists and can decompose a wide range of different types of woody substrates, but others are limited to one or a few types. For example, some wood-decay fungi are found only on the wood of conifers, while others are almost invariably associated with wood from broadleaf trees. In the same way, the dead leaves that fall to the forest floor do not continue to pile up year after year because various litter-decomposing fungi break them down. These fungi are not the same species as those found on wood—an unsurprising fact, since the two different types of substrates, wood and litter, are quite dissimilar in terms of their physical and chemical properties.

Another habitat exploited by certain fungi is dung, and many of the species involved are never found anywhere else. Such is the case for a number of species in the genus *Coprinus*. Being aware of such ecological relationships increases the chances of both finding fruiting bodies of the fungus in question and making a positive identification.

In good textbooks on mushrooms, a brief description of each species' habitat is usually provided. The starting point when identifying a mushroom is to take careful note of where it was found, such as on the surface of soil, below ground, or in association with a particular substrate. Noting details of the vegetation, especially of any trees growing nearby, is, particularly relevant for ectomycorrhizal species. The amount of limestone in the soil (seen as white or off-white pebbles or flecks), the elevation, how wet the soil is, and other features of the site may also be important. If a mushroom is found on dead wood or a living tree, make a note of the host plant and on what part of the plant the mushroom is fruiting.

When collecting wild mushrooms, it is best to store them in paper bags or a basket. Mushrooms sweat inside plastic bags and, as a result, decay rapidly. A small cooler containing a few freezer pads wrapped in a towel makes a good temporary refrigerator until you can get the mushrooms home. An article in *The Observer* (Slater 2000) stating that "mushrooms should [be kept] in a bag in the fridge for a day or so, so that they become a bit damp and woodsy" is certainly a risky procedure for wild mushrooms and not to be recommended.

In many parts of the world people have traditionally climbed over a fence to pick mushrooms from a farmer's field. However, this is little different from the same farmer walking into your garden and taking one of your cabbages, so make sure you have the permission of a landowner first. The situation on publicly owned land varies from country to country. In some cases you will have to obtain a permit from a government authority to pick mushrooms, whereas in many European countries the general population has a right to do so.

Identifying Wild Mushrooms

Having recorded details of a mushroom's habitat, the next step is to note its distinguishing features. Key factors include colors, dimensions, and whether the underside of the mushroom is covered with gills, spines, or a system of tubes that makes the underside look like a finely textured sponge. If gills are present, details such as whether they are attached or free from the stalk, or extend down the stalk, their color, and thickness are important. Two very important details are whether the stalk has a ring and a volva. Sometimes the volva is below the soil surface and can easily be missed if the base of the stalk is not carefully excavated. Rings may only be present on very young stalks, so it is important to collect both younger and older fruiting bodies.

The next step is to prepare a spore print. The best way to do this is to get a sheet of smooth black paper and a sheet of white paper, overlapping the two. Cut the stalk off the mushroom and place the cap, gills downward, half on the white paper and half on the black paper. The mushroom should then be covered in order to retain moisture and keep air currents from blowing the spores around. Half a glass petri dish will work well, allowing you to see what is going on inside it (a glass casserole dish lid will work too, but wash it carefully afterward in case the mushrooms are poisonous). After six to twenty-four hours,

A spore print being prepared from the cap of a Swiss brown strain button mushroom (*Agaricus bisporus*). (Hall)

sufficient spores will be released from the cap and deposited on the paper to determine their color. In many cases, placing the mushroom in a small, sealed plastic bag will also work. White and other light-colored spores, of course, show up better on the black paper, while dark-colored spores are better seen on the white paper. Eventually, as experience is gained, either the black or white paper may be omitted.

One way to identify a wild mushroom is to obtain a comprehensive, well-illustrated guide to the mushrooms that grow in your area, something you can flick through to locate the illustration that looks most like your specimen. A word of warning, however: some fungal genera contain mushrooms with very different effects. *Amanita*, for example, includes Caesar's mushroom (*A. caesarea*), which is not only edible but also quite delicious; false death cap (*A. citrina*), which can produce unpleasant vomiting for twenty-four hours after consumption; fly agaric (*A. muscaria*), which causes hallucinogenic effects and often severe nausea; and death cap (*A. phalloides*), which leads to an unpleasant death over several days. Alternatively mushrooms may be identified using printed keys or computer databases (see Percudani et al. 1996), or by speaking with an expert who is well

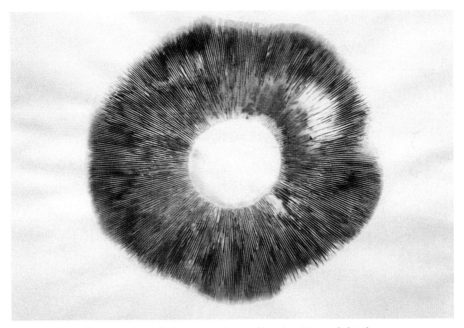

Spore print of a Swiss brown strain button mushroom (*Agaricus bisporus*). (Hall)

acquainted with the mushrooms of the region. Such experts can be difficult to find, although the botany department of the local university or research center might be able to assist.

A key is a device used for identifying organisms, in this case mushrooms, based on their distinguishing features. With printed keys the user is usually presented with lists of questions to which there are two or more answers. Once a question is answered, the user moves on to the next question until eventually the mushroom is identified. For example, a key that separates members of four of the more commonly encountered groups of mushrooms might look like this:

1. Fruiting body with an expanded cap
   supported by a stalk 2
   Fruiting body with or without a cap but
   lacking an obvious stalk 3
2. Fruiting body with gills beneath the cap....................agaric
   Fruiting body with pores beneath the cap ....bolete
3. Fruiting body shelflike or bracket-like ....polypore
   Fruiting body more or less spherical......................puffball

The problems arise when you attempt to identify something not in the key—perhaps one of the few polypores that does have a stalk; or a representative of another group of mushrooms, such as a spherical truffle; or a mushroom that has a stalk and cap but neither gills nor pores, such as a morel. Obviously it is possible to construct a key that gets around these problems, but with mushrooms the questions asked often become rather technical and require some degree of expertise to answer. For many species, distinguishing features are mostly at the microscopic level, and this presents a challenge for all but the most serious amateur mycologists.

A short, easy-to-use key to edible mushrooms of the United Kingdom is provided in *How to Identify Edible Mushrooms* (Harding et al. 1996). After answering a few questions, the reader is referred to an illustration of an edible mushroom, which is followed by illustrations of edible and poisonous look-alikes. A pictorial key helps users identify mushrooms using pictures that illustrate key features. An excellent annotated pictorial key to mushrooms in general that requires a minimum of technical expertise and terminology to work can be found in *The Mushroom Book* (Læssøe and Del Conte 1996), while the *Discover Mushrooms* computer-based key is easy to use for those with a rudimentary knowledge of computers (Samuels 2002). Some simple keys that also rely only on macroscopic features are included in *Mushrooms and Toadstools of Britain and Europe* (Courtecuisse and Duhem 1995).

Good keys to mushroom genera can be found in *A Colour Atlas of Poisonous Fungi* (Bresinsky and Besl 1990) and in the first volume of *How to Identify Mushrooms to Genus* (Largent 1986), but a full knowledge of mushroom terminology is needed to use them. The keys provided in this book, while very rudimentary, are probably an adequate introduction for a beginner.

Trick or Treat

A few mushrooms are deadly poisonous, while others, though not lethal, may produce most unpleasant symptoms if eaten. Consequently, it is important to know how to avoid these "tricksters." There is no simple way to distinguish between those that are poisonous and those that are harmless. There are many myths surrounding the edibility of mushrooms that over the years have taken on the status of rules, but these should all be laid to rest.

Common among the myths: mushrooms that can be peeled are edible; mushrooms that grow in spring or late autumn are edible;

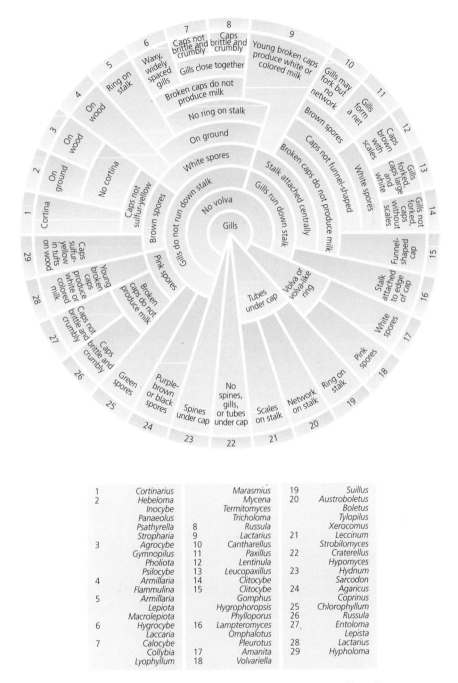

The following labels appear around the wheel diagram (from outer ring inward):

6 Waxy, widely spaced gills
7 Caps not brittle and crumbly
8 Caps brittle and crumbly
Gills close together
Broken caps do not produce milk
9 Young broken caps produce white or colored milk
10 Gills may fork but no network
11 Gills form a net
5 Ring on stalk
No ring on stalk
Brown spores
12 Caps brown with scales
13 Gills forked, caps large and white without scales
14 Gills not forked, caps without scales
4 On wood
On ground
White spores
Stalk attached centrally
Caps not funnel-shaped
White spores
Broken caps do not produce milk
3 On wood
No cortina
Caps not sulfur-yellow
Gills run down stalk
15 Funnel-shaped cap
2 On ground
Brown spores
No volva
Gills
Stalk attached to edge of cap
16
1 Cortina
Gills do not run down stalk
Tubes under cap
Volva or volva-like ring
White spores
17
29 Caps sulfur-yellow in tufts on wood
Young broken caps produce white or colored milk
Pink spores
Broken caps do not produce milk
No spines, gills, or tubes under cap
Ring on stalk
Pink spores
18
28 Caps not brittle and crumbly
Caps brittle and crumbly
Green spores
Purple-brown or black spores
Spines under cap
Scales on stalk
Network on stalk
19
27
26
25
24
23
22
21
20

1	Cortinarius		Marasmius
2	Hebeloma		Mycena
	Inocybe		Termitomyces
	Panaeolus		Tricholoma
	Psathyrella	8	Russula
	Stropharia	9	Lactarius
3	Agrocybe	10	Cantharellus
	Gymnopilus	11	Paxillus
	Pholiota	12	Lentinula
	Psilocybe	13	Leucopaxillus
4	Armillaria	14	Clitocybe
	Flammulina	15	Clitocybe
5	Lepiota		Gomphus
	Macrolepiota		Hygrophoropsis
6	Hygrocybe		Phylloporus
	Laccaria	16	Lampteromyces
7	Calocybe		Omphalotus
	Collybia		Pleurotus
	Lyophyllum	17	Amanita
		18	Volvariella

19	Suillus
20	Austroboletus
	Boletus
	Tylopilus
	Xerocomus
21	Leccinum
	Strobilomyces
22	Craterellus
	Hypomyces
23	Hydnum
	Sarcodon
24	Agaricus
	Coprinus
25	Chlorophyllum
26	Russula
27	Entoloma
	Lepista
28	Lactarius
29	Hypholoma

A key to the main mushroom genera covered in this book that have caps with stalks.

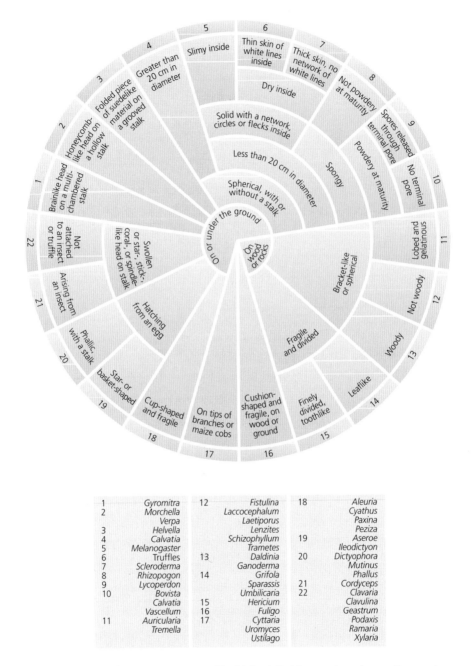

1	*Gyromitra*	12	*Fistulina*	18	*Aleuria*	
2	*Morchella*		*Laccocephalum*		*Cyathus*	
	Verpa		*Laetiporus*		*Paxina*	
3	*Helvella*		*Lenzites*		*Peziza*	
4	*Calvatia*		*Schizophyllum*	19	*Aseroe*	
5	*Melanogaster*		*Trametes*		*Ileodictyon*	
6	Truffles	13	*Daldinia*	20	*Dictyophora*	
7	*Scleroderma*		*Ganoderma*		*Mutinus*	
8	*Rhizopogon*	14	*Grifola*		*Phallus*	
9	*Lycoperdon*		*Sparassis*	21	*Cordyceps*	
10	*Bovista*		*Umbilicaria*	22	*Clavaria*	
	Calvatia	15	*Hericium*		*Clavulina*	
	Vascellum	16	*Fuligo*		*Geastrum*	
11	*Auricularia*	17	*Cyttaria*		*Podaxis*	
	Tremella		*Uromyces*		*Ramaria*	
			Ustilago		*Xylaria*	

A key to the main mushroom genera covered in this book that have various shapes—those not cap-shaped with stalks.

mushrooms that grow on live trees are edible, while those that grow on dead trees are poisonous; mushrooms eaten by snails or other small animals, or that are not poisonous to animals such as squirrels, are edible; violet and viscid mushrooms are poisonous; mushrooms whose flesh changes color on cutting are poisonous; mushrooms that exude latex are poisonous; mushrooms that smell like flour are edible; mushrooms that discolor a silver spoon put into the pot while cooking are poisonous, while those that do not are edible; poisonous mushrooms cause milk or egg white to coagulate, while those that do not are edible; brown-gilled mushrooms are edible, but white-gilled mushrooms are poisonous; mushrooms lose their poison if boiled in water with or without salt or vinegar; mushrooms lose their poison through drying; and those that taste good are safe to eat. None of these statements is true!

The only way to know whether a mushroom is safe to eat is to be sure of what you are eating and to have access to reliable advice on its edibility. To sample the "treats" you must know how to identify and avoid the "tricksters."

Unfortunately, many mushrooms do look alike—especially those growing on your lawn at home, in the nearby woods, or on fallen branches. The common edible field mushroom (*Agaricus campestris*) can be mistaken for numerous brown-gilled species growing in the grass, including poisonous species of *Panaeolus* and *Psilocybe* and toxic species of *Agaricus*. In its button stage the same mushroom, and especially its larger cousin the horse mushroom (*A. arvensis*), can look every bit like some poisonous *Amanita* species in their button stage, especially the fly agaric (*A. muscaria*) and the panther cap (*A. pantherina*). These are white, and the scales on the caps are sometimes not easily discernible. In addition, fruiting bodies at the button stage can create confusion between the highly prized porcini (*Boletus edulis*), other edible boletes, and the button stage of poisonous species of *Amanita*. A number of mushrooms, both edible and poisonous, look just like golf balls in the grass when at their button stage. *Amanita* at a slightly more advanced stage may take on the shape of an inverted pear and can then be confused with some edible puffballs such as *Calvatia* species and *Bovista* species. The common field mushroom and the horse mushroom may also be readily confused with a close relative, yellow stainer (*Agaricus xanthoderma*), which stains yellow quickly on bruising and is renowned for causing stomach disorders.

Within woodlands it is also easy to make mistakes. The honey mushroom (*Armillaria mellea*), a deadly parasite of trees, grows at the base of infected trees or stumps and is considered by some to be good to eat. It can also superficially resemble the big laughing gym (*Gymnopilus junonius*), a psychoactive species, or the sulfur tuft (*Hypholoma fasciculare*), which causes severe gastroenteritis. On dead trees the oyster mushroom *Pleurotus ostreatus* is a particularly desirable species and is widely grown commercially, but in Australia poisoning incidents have been reported when this species has been mistaken for the morphologically very similar *Omphalotus nidiformis*; and in Japan the oyster mushroom has been confused with *Lampteromyces japonicus*. Similarly, the edible and now commercially produced enokitake (*Flammulina velutipes*), which naturally grows on decaying tree stumps, must be carefully identified before eating, since it resembles some species of *Galerina*, which if consumed can prove fatal.

The destroying angel (*Amanita virosa*) is a fungus to avoid at all costs. Its pure white color belies its toxicity, and it must not be confused with other elegant, white mushrooms that occur in similar habitats, such as some species of *Volvariella*. Another group of elegant species are the parasol mushrooms (*Macrolepiota* spp.), which when in their button or juvenile stage are similar to the deadliest of mushrooms: death cap (*Amanita phalloides*). *Tricholoma* is also a difficult genus, containing species with whitish or yellow gills with extremely varied appearances. Not only can choice edible species be confused with poisonous ones within the same genus, but some can be readily confused with the most poisonous species of *Amanita*. Such mistakes are not rare events. In 1996 in the Ukraine ninety-two people died out of eleven hundred who were hospitalized after confusing light-colored *Amanita* species for edible mushrooms (CBC Newsworld 1996), and at the end of the same year nine people in northern California were hospitalized after consuming *Amanita* species (CDC 1997). There are similar examples wherever wild mushrooms are consumed. Around nine thousand mushroom poisonings occur in the United States each year alone (Kidcheck 2002).

Among the most visually appealing mushrooms are the chanterelles (*Cantharellus* spp.), the undersides of their caps covered with blunt, gill-like ridges. Yet here again care needs to be taken so that misidentification does not occur. The highly prized golden chanterelle (*Cantharellus cibarius*) can be mistaken for *Omphalotus olearius* (jack-o'-lantern), the consumption of which promotes the most unpleasant of symptoms, including nausea and vomiting (Lincoff and Mitchel 1977). The poisonous brown roll rim (*Paxillus involutus*) also resembles the chanterelles and the saffron milk cap (*Lactarius deliciosus*) and should not be eaten. Also similar to *P. involutus* is false chanterelle (*Hygrophoropsis aurantiaca*), which is best avoided, since it is known to be hallucinatory.

Some of the most recognizable mushrooms are the morels (*Morchella* spp.), which are said to look like small human brains and are delicious to eat. Unfortunately they can be confused with another brainlike fungus, the false morel (*Gyromitra esculenta*), which has the distinction of containing a chemical compound that is the precursor of methylhydrazine, a rocket propellant used by NASA, and that can have lethal effects. Another species of *Gyromitra*, the hooded false morel (*G. infula*), has a spectacular appearance but is deadly poisonous when eaten raw. Wrinkled thimble cap (*Verpa bohemica*), which closely resembles the cap of the edible half-free morel (*Morchella semilibera*), used to be eaten but is now recognized as poisonous.

Ink caps (*Coprinus* spp.) are another easily recognizable group of edible mushrooms. The common ink cap (*C. atramentarius*) is one such species, though it should never be consumed with alcohol and alcohol should not be taken within one to two days after eating it because severe symptoms will result, including an alarmingly rapid pulse rate and nausea.

Puffballs are easily recognizable, but they also need close examination to distinguish the edible from the nonedible varieties. They should not be eaten without first being cut to ensure there are no gills lurking in the button of a puffball look-alike and to discern the color of the flesh. Young fruiting bodies of the earthballs (*Scleroderma* spp.) have also been mistaken for truffles or puffballs.

Last but certainly not the least is the deceiver (*Laccaria laccata*), which lives up to its name. Though edible, its great variability in form and even color, depending on the environment, allows for misidentification. It may closely resemble a host of poisonous little brown mushrooms (LBMs), such as *Inocybe* species and *Galerina* species.

It is important to remember that there may be large differences in the appearance of the same mushroom in different parts of the world. Even though you may be familiar with and have eaten certain mushrooms in your home country, you cannot assume those of similar appearance in unfamiliar surroundings are edible. Since the edibility of most mushrooms remains unknown, there is plenty of room for error—the look-alike examples given in this section by no means comprise an exhaustive list. Useful generalizations such as being very wary of white-capped and white-gilled mushrooms should be heeded, but also remember that some brown-gilled brown mushrooms are among the deadliest. Err on the side of suspicion and note the old adage, "There are plenty of old mushroom hunters and plenty of bold mushroom hunters, but there are no old, bold mushroom hunters."

Mushroom Toxins

Despite the warnings prominently displayed in books on edible mushrooms, mushroom poisonings are not infrequent for those individuals looking for an out-of-body experience or for bona fide mushroom hunters who have failed to follow the rules. Once these unfortunates get to a hospital, the standard treatment is to feed them with activated carbon, which acts like a chemical sponge, and observe their symptoms. From the particular group of symptoms—or syndromes, as they are called—the toxicologist is often able to determine what type of toxin the patient has consumed and hazard a guess at what follow-up treatments may be necessary (Benjamin 1995). However, the toxicologist may not be able to decide just what has been consumed from the symptoms alone, because several genera and many species may contain the same toxin. For example, amatoxins are found not just in *Amanita* species but also in species of *Conocybe*, *Galerina*, and *Lepiota*.

Detailed descriptions of the syndromes, which toxins are found in which species, treatments used in mushroom poisonings, death rates, and so on, are the subjects of whole books, as with the detailed, though somewhat academic *A Colour Atlas of Poisonous Fungi* (Bresinsky and Besl 1990) and the very entertaining *Mushrooms: Poisons and Panaceas* (Benjamin 1995). Consequently this book is restricted to the following brief descriptions of the syndromes. A list of poisonous mushrooms containing the toxins that cause the syndrome follows each description, and additional symptoms caused by the mushrooms are also provided (primarily from Benjamin 1995, Bessette et al. 1997, Both 1993, Bresinsky and Besl 1990, Dhabolt 1993, Imazeki et al. 1988, Lincoff and Mitchel 1977, Miller 1981, Phillips 1981, 1991, Stamets 1996).

Protoplasmic poisons
Amatoxin (cyclopeptide) syndrome. Symptoms are caused by fungal toxins such as amanitin and amanin, formed of eight amino acids arranged in a ring (cyclopeptides), and develop from six to twenty-four hours after eating the mushrooms. There will be a day or so of violent vomiting, diarrhea, and stomach cramps, followed by lowered blood

pressure, accelerated pulse, and dehydration. By this time it may be too late for some patients as many of the amatoxins in the mushroom will have been absorbed from the intestine and will have begun to damage the liver. After the initial stage there is sometimes an apparent recovery, but two to three days later jaundice and liver and kidney failure develop (Bresinsky and Besl 1990, Freedman 1996, Phillips 1981). Death is not infrequent in severe cases. Complete blood dialysis or a liver transplant have been used to treat severe poisonings; other treatments are listed on the Centers for Disease Control and Prevention (CDC) Web site. Amatoxins are not broken down by boiling.

Amanita bisporigera
Amanita phalloides
Amanita verna
Amanita virosa
Conocybe filaris
Conocybe rugosa
Galerina autumnalis
Galerina fasciculata
Galerina marginata
Galerina sulciceps
Galerina venenata
Hypholoma fasciculare (other symptoms include gastrointestinal
    syndrome, impaired vision, paralysis)
Lepiota brunneoincarnata
Lepiota castanea
Lepiota citrophylla
Lepiota helveola
Lepiota josserandii
Lepiota subincarnata

Gyromitrin syndrome. Symptoms begin two to twenty-four hours after ingestion and can include abdominal pain, diarrhea, vomiting, coma, convulsions, delirium, fever, headache, restlessness, respiratory failure, and liver damage leading to jaundice. Kidney failure may also occur, and death is possible in severe cases. The breakdown products of gyromitrin are hydrazines, which are carcinogenic; however, there is no evidence that these cause cancer in humans.

Cudonia circinans
Gyromitra ambigua

Gyromitra californica
Gyromitra caroliniana
Gyromitra esculenta
Gyromitra fastigiata
Gyromitra gigas
Gyromitra infula
Gyromitra korfii
Gyromitra sphaerospora

Paxillus syndrome (immune hemolytic anemia). In addition to gastrointestinal reactions, *Paxillus involutus* may cause a potentially fatal immune response that leads to a breakdown of red blood cells in those who have eaten the mushroom, possibly for many years, without experiencing symptoms.

Paxillus involutus

Orellanine syndrome (delayed onset renal failure). Symptoms typically develop from thirty-six hours to three weeks after mushroom ingestion and include progressive kidney failure associated with an insatiable thirst and frequent urination, nausea, vomiting, lethargy, headaches, and shivering without fever or liver damage.

Cortinarius gentilis
Cortinarius orellanoides
Cortinarius orellanus
Cortinarius speciosissimus
Cortinarius splendens

Neurotoxins

Muscarine syndrome. The effects of muscarine poisoning—salivation, lacrimation, urination, defecation, gastrointestinal problems, and emesis—have given rise to the acronym SLUDGE. Other symptoms include decreased blood pressure, profuse sweating, and death due to respiratory failure.

Boletus pulcherrimus (other symptoms include gastrointestinal syndrome)
Clitocybe aurantiacum
Clitocybe candicans
Clitocybe dealbata

Clitocybe dilatata
Clitocybe ericetosa
Clitocybe gibba
Clitocybe nebularis
Clitocybe phaeophthalma
Clitocybe phyllophila
Clitocybe rivulosa
Clitocybe truncicola
Entoloma rhodopolium (other symptoms include gastrointestinal
  syndrome)
Inocybe bongardii
Inocybe dulcamara
Inocybe fastigiata
Inocybe geophylla
Inocybe godeyi
Inocybe griseolilacina
Inocybe hirtella
Inocybe lacera
Inocybe maculata
Inocybe napipes
Inocybe patouillardii
Inocybe praetervisa
Inocybe sororia
Mycena pura

Hallucinogenic syndrome. Symptoms, which develop within an hour
and last for up to six hours, are similar to those produced by hallucinogenic chemicals like lysergide. They include vivid hallucinations,
lack of contact with reality, seizures, prolonged reaction time,
increased heart rate, dilation of pupils, and increased blood pressure.

Conocybe cyanopus
Gymnopilus junonius
Inocybe corydalina
Lycoperdon marginatum
Panaeolus ater
Panaeolus campanulatus
Panaeolus foenisecii
Panaeolus papilionaceus
Panaeolus retirugis
Panaeolus sphinctrinus

Panaeolus subbalteatus
Pluteus cyanopus
Pluteus salicinus
Pluteus villosus
Psilocybe argentipes
Psilocybe baeocystis
Psilocybe caerulescens
Psilocybe caerulipes
Psilocybe coprophila
Psilocybe crobula
Psilocybe cubensis
Psilocybe fasciculata
Psilocybe merdaria
Psilocybe subaeruginascens
Stropharia coronilla (other symptoms include gastrointestinal
    syndrome, malaise, headache, ataxia, dizziness)

Pantherine syndrome. There is a rapid onset of symptoms, including
intoxication, ataxia, dizziness, lethargy (but sometimes with periods of
manic behavior), nausea, vomiting, muscle cramps, tremor, seizures,
hallucinations, and dilated or restricted pupils, with the patient finally
moving into a coma-like state.

Amanita cothurnata
Amanita crenulata
Amanita gemmata
Amanita muscaria
Amanita pantherina
Amanita regalis
Amanita solitaria
Tricholoma muscarium

Gastrointestinal irritants

Gastrointestinal syndrome. The main symptoms, which can occur
from a few minutes to a few hours after a meal, include abdominal
pain followed by nausea, profuse sweating, vomiting, and diarrhea.

Agaricus hondensis
Agaricus placomyces
Agaricus praeclaresquamosus
Agaricus xanthoderma

Amanita brunnescens
Amanita chlorinosma
Amanita flavoconia
Amaniata flavorubescens
Amanita frostiana
Amanita parcivolvata
Armillaria mellea
Boletus erythropus
Boletus haematinus
Boletus luridus (other symptoms include coprine syndrome)
Boletus pulcherrimus (other symptoms include muscarine syndrome)
Boletus sensibilis
Bondarzewia berkeleyi
Chlorophyllum molybdites
Clitocybe acromelalga (other symptoms include sharp pains, red swelling of hands and feet one week after ingestion)
Collybia acervata
Collybia dryophila
Cortinarius cinnamomeus
Dermocybe sanguinea
Entoloma rhodopolium (other symptoms include muscarine syndrome)
Entoloma sinuatum
Gomphus bonari
Gomphus floccosus (other symptoms include neurological impairment)
Gomphus fujisanensis
Gomphus kauffmanii (other symptoms include neurological impairment)
Hebeloma crustuliniforme
Hebeloma mesophaeum
Hebeloma sinapizans
Hebeloma vinosophyllum
Hygrocybe conica
Hygrocybe ovina
Hypholoma fasciculare (other symptoms include amatoxin syndrome, impaired vision, paralysis)
Lactarius chrysorheus
Lactarius helvus
Lactarius piperatus

Lactarius pubescens
Lactarius repraesentaneus
Lactarius rufus
Lactarius scrobiculatus
Lactarius torminosus
Lactarius uvidus
Laetiporus sulphureus
Lampteromyces japonicus
Lepiota clypeolaria
Lepiota cristata
Lepiota lutea
Lespista irina (other symptoms include neurological impairment)
Megacollybia platyphylla
Meripilus giganteus
Morganella subincarnatum
Nolanea quadrata
Nolanea verna
Omphalotus illudens
Omphalotus nidiformis
Omphalotus olearius
Paxillus involutus (other symptoms include paxillus syndrome; possibly also a mutagen and carcinogen)
Phaeolepiota aurea
Phaeolus schweinitzii
Pholiota squarrosa (other symptoms include coprine syndrome)
Ramaria formosa
Ramaria gelatinosa
Ramaria pallida
Russula emetica
Russula sardonia
Scleroderma cepa (other symptoms include spasms, tingling sensations, rigidity)
Scleroderma citrinum
Stropharia coronilla (other symptoms include hallucinogenic syndrome, malaise, headache, ataxia, dizziness)
Suillus granulatus
Tricholoma album
Tricholoma inamoenum
Tricholoma pessundatum
Tricholoma pardinum
Tricholoma saponaceum

Tricholoma sejunctum
Tricholoma sulphureum (other symptoms include neurological impairment)
Tricholoma venenata
Tricholoma zelleri
Tricholomopsis platyphylla (other symptoms include muscle cramps)
Verpa bohemica
Verpa conica

Alcohol dehydrogenase inhibition

Coprine (Antabuse) syndrome. Coprine may inhibit the function of alcohol dehydrogenase, an enzyme needed in the conversion of alcohol to acetic acid. The symptoms are similar to those of Antabuse (disulfiram), which is used for the treatment of alcoholism. Symptoms develop soon after ingestion and include severe headaches, rapid pulse, flushed face and chest, sweating, low blood pressure, confusion, nausea, and vomiting.

Boletus luridus (other symptoms include gastrointestinal syndrome)
Clitocybe clavipes
Coprinus africanus
Coprinus atramentarius
Coprinus insignis
Coprinus micaceus
Coprinus quadrifidus
Coprinus variegatus
Pholiota squarrosa (other symptoms include gastrointestinal syndrome)
Tricholoma aurantium

Raw Mushrooms

Many mushrooms, such as *Amanita rubescens, Armillaria mellea, Gyromitra esculenta, Lactarius* spp., *Laetiporus sulphureus, Lepista nuda, Morchella* spp., *Paxillus involutus*, and *Russula* spp., can cause poisoning when eaten raw. In *G. esculenta*, this can lead to death. Therefore, as a general rule it is safer to cook all mushrooms before eating. Only a few mushrooms—traditionally known as salad mushrooms—are safe to eat raw. Examples include button mushrooms (*Agaricus bisporus* and *A. bitorquis*) and *Boletus edulis* (Benjamin

1995, Bresinsky and Besl 1990). In many countries the edibility or toxicity of many indigenous mushrooms is unknown. For this reason, most are best avoided.

Rules for Picking and Eating Mushrooms

There are some simple rules that should be followed when picking wild mushrooms for the table. Each is included here for a very good reason, and, if followed, may one day save you from an unpleasant experience, or even save your life.

Do not eat any mushroom if you have doubts about its identity or edibility. Carefully check every mushroom you are going to eat, first in the field and then when you return to the kitchen. Pick only mushrooms that show no signs of decomposition: worms and insect larvae often found in old mushrooms, as well as the bacteria that follow them, may themselves produce toxins. Cut small puffballs in two vertically to see if there are any structures inside that might suggest they are *Scleroderma* or the button stages of, for example, an *Amanita* species. Do not eat raw mushrooms, which may contain toxins that are destroyed during cooking. Be absolutely certain of the identity of mushrooms with a ring or volva on the stalk, with scales or warts on the surface of the cap, or with white gills.

Unless you really are an expert, do not eat any small *Lepiota*, *Agaricus* that stains yellow, *Lactarius* that does not have red or orange milk, boletes that stain blue when bruised and/or are orange or red on the underside of the cap, brainlike mushrooms (*Gyromitra*), chanterelle-like mushrooms (*Gomphus* and *Hygrophoropsis aurantiaca*), unidentified coral-like mushrooms (*Ramaria*), or little brown mushrooms.

Eat a small quantity of a mushroom the first time you try it, and wait forty-eight hours before eating more of it or another species; if you are allergic to the mushroom, any poisons that might be present may take twenty-four hours to have an effect. Save a couple of uncooked mushrooms in the refrigerator just in case you make a mistake and need medical attention. Do not eat mushrooms from roadsides where lead levels may be high or from areas where the soil may be rich in elements such as cadmium, chromium, and mercury. Similarly, do not pick mushrooms from areas that might have been sprayed with herbicides or pesticides. Never assume a mushroom you have picked in another country is the same species as a similar one you have consumed back home.

Finally, if you have taken all precautions, are sure you have identified a mushroom accurately, and have eaten a hearty meal but have begun to show adverse symptoms, consult a doctor immediately. If you are unable to find a doctor, contact the National Capital Poison Center in the United States (telephone: 800-222-1222; TDD line for the deaf: 202-362-8563) or one of the regional poison centers in the United States or Canada. Do not delay—seek medical attention immediately.

Other countries have similar national poison centers, and the telephone numbers to these are usually prominently displayed in telephone directories. Considerable information is available online—for example, on the Web site provided by the National Capital Poison Center in the United States and in the *Bad Bug Book* from the U.S. Food and Drug Administration—but access to details in the United Kingdom's National Poisons Information Service "Toxbase" is restricted to hospitals and other registered users within the United Kingdom.

A Permanent Record

Once a careful note has been made of a mushroom's habitat, spore prints have been prepared, and features have been noted, it may be worth making a permanent record of the mushroom. One way to do this is to dry the material in a warm dry place, which preserves most microscopic features. Mushrooms can be dried in a small food dehydrator, on a wire screen above a heat source, or in an airing cupboard. A proper thermostatically controlled drying oven set at 40–50°C is best, but a perfectly useful drying chamber can be constructed from a wooden box containing a 100-watt light bulb coupled to a domestic thermostat like those used to control electric heaters. If the mushrooms are particularly important specimens, such as the first collection of a new species for a region or country, they should be deposited in an internationally recognized herbarium (Holmgren et al. 1990). People working in the botany department of a local university or research center should be able to provide guidance on where these herbaria are located.

Photographing Mushrooms

Taking photographs is a good way to record what a mushroom looks like, but because of the size of many mushrooms and the dark places where many are found, a standard point-and-shoot camera will be of little use. Almost any reflex camera will do, provided it has a built-in light meter, a manual exposure override, a cable shutter release, a good range of slow shutter speeds or a timed exposure setting that allows the shutter to stay open as long as a finger is pressed down on the cable release button (usually marked "B" for "Bulb" on the shutter speed setting knob), a set of extension tubes for taking close-ups, and a tripod. A secondhand single-lens reflex camera with extension tubes and a miniature tripod might cost only $100.

A fully automatic camera flash controlled by the camera's light meter is very easy to use and can take almost all the guesswork out of photographing mushrooms against the background of a dark forest floor. With the right kind of flash and camera you can even take photographs at night, though finding mushrooms under such conditions can prove difficult. An automatic ring flash can be used, but it is best to cover up part of the ring; otherwise all the shadows and many details may disappear. This can render a photograph less lifelike and may make it difficult to see certain details, such as pale gills. If you have no flash, a piece of crumpled aluminum foil (about 30 sq. cm) taped to some stiff cardboard can provide that little extra light to highlight one side of a mushroom or illuminate shaded stalks or gills. Many professionals don't like using flash photography, preferring to use a tripod and very long exposure times of thirty seconds or more. If they do use a flash, it might only be to highlight a feature or improve background detail.

In dark places light meters on relatively simple reflex cameras can usually be tricked into giving a reasonably accurate exposure guide. To do this the film speed setting is increased, say from ISO 100 to 3200. A meter reading is then taken at a particular aperture. If it indicates that a one-second exposure should be used, the true exposure is thirty-two times this. Incidentally, don't forget to reset the ISO setting on your camera afterward or you may finish up with a roll of blank film. It is also a good idea to take a few more photographs of the same mushroom with 50 percent and 100 percent longer exposure times, as films tend to behave more slowly than their ISO rating would indicate when given long exposures, something known as the reciprocity effect (Eastman Kodak 1988). The colors may also turn out somewhat different than they really are because the sensitivities of the three color layers of many films are dissimilar with exposure times longer than one twenty-fifth of a second. Fortunately, a few films have been developed that are stable up to a hundred seconds (Barnhart 2000).

When taking close-ups it is very important to mount the camera securely, as it may shake slightly when the shutter opens and closes.

The camera may also shake when the shutter release is pressed, but this can be minimized if a flexible shutter release cable is used in conjunction with a good tripod. Better still are the electronic shutter release mechanisms that can be fitted to many modern cameras. Finally, choose an internationally recognized brand of film to ensure quality results. While fast films give shorter exposures in dark places, they also tend to be more grainy, so in general it is better not to use a film faster than ISO 100. Digital cameras can provide some excellent results, but take care to choose one with a macro facility, automatic flash compatibility, and an image size of at least 1 megapixel.

The Web can provide much valuable information on photographing small objects like mushrooms. Most large photographic companies have good Web sites. Agfa has an especially good photo course.

Photography through a microscope

Spore shapes and other microscopic details are often essential to identify mushroom species. Drawings can be made, but it is also possible to create photographic records (Smith 1990, Thomson and Bradbury 1987). Sophisticated equipment is not absolutely necessary to do this. If certain precautions are taken, good results can be obtained with relatively inexpensive equipment. The simplest equipment would be a student microscope with a vertical eyepiece tube, a single-lens reflex camera with through-the-lens metering or a digital camera, and a microscope adapter. Automatic reflex cameras without a manual override are generally not suitable. More expensive microscopes have triocular heads that permit a camera to be left mounted on the microscope when it is not being used. They usually also have built-in, high-intensity light sources and light-balancing filters, which make taking photomicrographs much easier.

A LIST OF
WILD MUSHROOMS

For some people the collection of wild mushrooms is simply an adjunct to an enjoyable walk in the countryside, but for others their collection and sale are a profitable hobby or even a full-time business. Anyone who eats or intends to eat wild mushrooms must be knowledgeable about species with unpleasant flavors or textures and, more importantly, species that can lead to serious poisoning or even death.

Some mushrooms found growing in the wild are not actually indigenous but have found their way, whether accidentally or intentionally, from another part of the world. For example, porcini (*Boletus edulis*) and saffron milk caps (*Lactarius deliciosus*) found in New Zealand and Australia are certainly not native and have only come to the attention of scientists there within the past few years (Segedin 1987, Segedin and Pennycook 2001, Wang et al. 1995). The same is true of the deadly poisonous *Amanita phalloides*, which seems to have found its way to North America from Europe (R. Tulloss, personal communication). As a result, the mushrooms included in this section are those that might be found in a whole range of countries. This selection concentrates on important poisonous mushrooms and conspicuous edible species, particularly those with sizeable international markets, although the occasional interesting curiosity is also included. The simple keys in Collecting Wild Mushrooms and the photographs of individual species can be used to help identify the edible mushrooms covered and to distinguish them from the poisonous species. As always, however, only eat a mushroom if you are absolutely sure of its identity. See Collecting Wild Mushrooms for more information on symptoms of various poisoning syndromes and a list of toxic mushrooms.

To provide some structure that will allow for easy navigation, mushrooms have been placed into sometimes artificial groups based on their appearance. The following simple key should help to locate the appropriate section.

1. Mushrooms with gills and a more or less centrally placed stalk; white or pale green spore print, rarely with pale pink or other pale-colored spores (page 124)

2. Mushrooms with gills and a more or less centrally placed stalk; pale pink spore print (page 179)

3. Mushrooms with gills and a more or less centrally placed stalk; brown spore print (page 183)

4. Mushrooms with gills and a more or less centrally placed stalk; purple-brown to black spore print (page 195)

5. Mushrooms with ear-shaped or bracket-like fruiting bodies; stalk either absent or poorly developed and attached to the edge of the cap; spores produced on gills, gill-like folds, or directly on the lower undifferentiated surface of the fruiting body (page 209)

6. Mushrooms with more or less funnel-shaped fruiting bodies (or fruiting bodies triangular in cross section), with the spores formed on the outer surface, either on gill-like folds or simply on a rough surface (page 216)

7. Mushrooms with a central, well-developed stalk supporting the cap and no gills but with many tubes present that give the underside of the cap a spongelike appearance—boletes (page 221)

8. Mushrooms with an undersurface devoid of gills or tubes but with minute spines or elongated, toothlike structures (page 236)

9. Mushrooms with a distinct stalk, a conical or spherical honeycomb-like top, or a folded piece of suedelike material on top of a grooved stalk (page 239)

10. Mushrooms with pulvinate to spherical fruiting bodies that are parasitic on living plants (page 252)

11. Mushrooms lacking stalks or whose stalks are rudimentary and attached to one side, with the spores formed in tubes or on the undersurface of the caps (page 255)

12. Mushrooms with fruiting bodies above or below the ground and more or less spherical—puffballs, truffles, and false truffles (page 262)

13. Mushrooms with fruiting bodies consisting of a simple or branched linear structure growing from decaying wood or arising from an adult or larval insect (page 283)

14. Mushrooms with spindle-, coral-, icicle-, or cauliflower-shaped fruiting bodies (page 286)

15. Mushrooms with basket-shaped fruiting bodies or fruiting bodies with tentacle-like arms hatching from an egg (page 292)

16. Mushrooms with spherical fruiting bodies that open out into star-shaped structures, with the spores contained in a central ball that discharges dry spores through a small central pore—earthstars (page 293)

17. Mushrooms with more or less cup-shaped fruiting bodies, with the spores produced inside the cup on a feltlike surface or within small egglike structures (page 293)

18. Mushrooms with cushion-shaped fruiting bodies that are at first outwardly slimy, then rather fragile (page 297)

19. Mushrooms with leaflike fruiting bodies that are dark green or nearly black and closely appressed to vertical rocky surfaces (page 299)

1. Mushrooms with gills and a more or less centrally placed stalk; white or pale green spore print, rarely with pale pink or other pale-colored spores

Amanita Species

The genus *Amanita* contains a few delicious species and, unfortunately, some of the most deadly. Making sure you have the right species before sitting down to dine is therefore absolutely essential. Identification can be rather difficult. Mistaking a poisonous species like *A. pantherina* or *A. virosa* for an edible one has led to the demise of a number of keen amateurs and even an occasional professional mycologist. It is therefore appropriate to begin with those white-spored species that fruit on the ground under trees, with which they very likely form ectomycorrhizal associations.

Amanita jacksonii and *Amanita caesarea* (Caesar's Mushroom)

Caesar's mushroom is so named because it was a favorite of the emperor Claudius and led to his demise when he ate some that had been mixed with poison (Benjamin 1995). It is found throughout eastern North America and the warmer parts of southern Europe in summer and autumn associated with oaks and other deciduous trees. Although the American and European forms of this mushroom are listed under *Amanita caesarea* in many texts, the former is now considered to represent a different species: *A. jacksonii*. The combination of an orange cap up to 18 cm in diameter, orange-tinged stalk up to 15 cm high, orange-tinged ring, distinct volva, and orange gills makes this mushroom unlikely to be confused with any other *Amanita* in North America or Europe, although it is possible that a faded *A. muscaria* might mislead an inexperienced collector, particularly if the scales have been washed off by rain. The very similar species *A. hemibapha* is common in East Asia, where it is also highly regarded.

Amanita citrina (False Death Cap)

Amanita citrina is one of several mushrooms that might be confused with the death cap (*A. phalloides*). Like the death cap, the cap of *A. citrina* may have a greenish tint, and the base of the stalk is conspicuously enlarged. However, *A. phalloides* generally has a cup-shaped volva at the base of the stalk, while *A. citrina* simply has an

Amanita caesarea (Caesar's mushroom) showing the well-formed volva at the base of the stalks.
EDIBLE. (Johnson)

Amanita hemibapha from Japan. Note the prominent cup-shaped volva at the base of the stalks. **EDIBLE.** (Izawa)

Amanita citrina (false death cap) with young caps pushing through the soil surface. In this species the volva is reduced to a bulbous base just below the soil surface. **EDIBILITY UNKNOWN: AVOID.** (Hall)

Amanita citrina (false death cap). Note the downward hanging veil. **EDIBILITY UNKNOWN: AVOID.** (Johnson)

expanded base to the stalk, without a distinct volva. Both have a skirt-like ring on the stalk. Fruiting bodies of *A. citrina* have a cap 4–12 cm in diameter and a stalk 6–13 cm long. Although not nearly as poisonous as *A. phalloides*, the false death cap should not be collected for the table. It is often very common in oak (*Quercus*) forests in eastern North America during the autumn.

Amanita muscaria (Fly Agaric)

No introduction should be required for the fly agaric, which can be found illustrated in a host of children's books and is probably the most photographed of all mushrooms. The orange to red cap with white scales and white gills, stalk, and volva make it almost impossible to mistake. The unopened fruiting bodies can be white but gradually turn orange as they develop. When fully expanded the cap can be up to 20 cm in diameter and the stalk up to 20 cm high and 3 cm in diameter. Some specimens lose their white markings and might then be confused with the edible *Amanita caesarea* (Caesar's mushroom), although the volva of the latter is large and loose, the edge of its cap is striated, and its gills and stalk are a pale orange. In Europe and North America *A. muscaria* forms mycorrhizas primarily with birch (*Betula*), pine (*Pinus*), and spruce (*Picea*), and in countries where European and North American host trees have been introduced, this mushroom has often moved with

Amanita muscaria (fly agaric). Note the white ring on the white stalk. The cup-shaped volva is only just visible on the base of the swollen stalk on the fruiting body at left. **POISONOUS.** (Hall)

Amanita muscaria (fly agaric) that has lost most of the white spots on the surface of its cap. **POISONOUS.** (Hall)

Vertical section of a young fruiting body of *Amanita muscaria* (fly agaric), the cap and stalk forming inside the surrounding veil. **POISONOUS.** (Hall)

The caps of *Amanita phalloides* (death cap) exhibit a large range in colors. In this specimen the cup-shaped volva is visible at the base of the stalk of the larger, colored mushroom. The younger, almost white mushroom has just begun to break free of the volva. **POISONOUS.** (Hall)

Fully mature fruiting bodies of *Amanita phalloides* (death cap). **POISONOUS.** (Hall)

Mature fruiting bodies of *Amanita phalloides* (death cap). **POISONOUS.** (Buchanan)

its hosts. Occasionally this has resulted in the fly agaric jumping onto new indigenous hosts, such as southern beech (*Nothofagus*) in Australia and New Zealand (Johnston and Buchanan 1997).

The common name "fly agaric" probably comes from this mushroom's traditional use as a fly killer (Bresinsky and Besl 1990, Cooke 1980, Phillips 1981). After the mushroom is dried, the dried pieces are placed in a bowl of milk. A compound in the cap (1,3-diolein) attracts flies, who feed on the cap, become intoxicated, and either fall into the milk and drown or die from the toxins they consume. They may not die as quickly as they would from a can of fly spray, but the effect is more ecologically sustainable. *Amanita muscaria* has been used through the ages in religious rites and abused for its hallucinogenic properties, which increase when the cap is dried, due to the conversion of ibotenic acid to muscimol (Benjamin 1995, Bresinsky and Besl 1990, Hobbs 1995). The presence of a number of toxins produces other effects as well, including nausea, vomiting, and diarrhea. Although muscarine was first found in *A. muscaria*, this mushroom actually contains relatively little of this poisonous compound compared with the levels found in some species of *Inocybe* and *Clitocybe*.

Amanita phalloides (Death Cap)

Amanita phalloides accounts for the great majority of deaths from mushroom poisonings worldwide. In the button stage, the fruiting bodies of the death cap are almost white and have a smooth surface that rapidly turns light green to light brown. In this stage they may resemble a puffball, and this resemblance appears to have led to many accidental poisonings (Buchanan 1995, Cole 1993, 1994, Nicholls et al. 1995). As they open, the cap and stalk gradually turn light brown or pale green to greenish brown, becoming yellow with age and sometimes developing a hint of faint radial markings on the surface of the cap. There is also a variety that remains white at maturity. The caps are 4–13 cm in diameter and strongly convex when young, though flat when fully expanded. The stalk is 5–13 cm high and up to 2 cm thick. The white volva is distinct, even on mature fruiting bodies, but can be below ground level and can therefore be missed if care is not taken. Although the spore print is white, the gills can have a faint greenish color at maturity. The smell is sickly sweet and gets stronger after mushrooms have been picked and stored. The western United States has experienced a recent spate of poisonings from death caps, new immigrants from Asia mistaking them for straw mushrooms (*Volvariella volvacea*), which they superficially resemble. The consumption of less than 50 g of the death cap, or about one medium fruiting body, is enough to kill. A smaller dose can cause severe poisoning in adults and can kill a child. Even the spores of the death cap are poisonous, and so edible mushrooms that have been stored in the same collecting bag should always be discarded. If you have been

Amanita pantherina (panther cap). **POISONOUS.** (Lyon)

handling a death cap, do not put your fingers near your mouth, and always wash your hands before eating anything. After eating a death cap there may be a period of six to twenty-four hours before amatoxin syndrome begins.

Amanita pantherina (Panther Cap)

The panther cap is a pale brownish yellow to light brown mushroom. The cap is up to 10 cm in diameter and has white markings on its surface. The white stalk is up to 10 cm high and 2.5 cm wide, with a prominent ring. The volva is prominent and white. The panther cap can be found in summer and autumn (and occasionally spring) associated with deciduous trees, especially beech (*Fagus*) in Europe and eastern North America. The toxins it contains produce delirium and a deep coma-like sleep, and consumption may prove fatal. This species might easily be mistaken for *Amanita rubescens* (the blusher).

Amanita rubescens (The Blusher) and Amanita excelsa

The mature caps of the blusher are 5–15 cm in diameter, brown with a pinkish tinge, and have white to pinkish, irregularly shaped patches

Amanita rubescens (the blusher). **EDIBLE WHEN COOKED.** (Hall)

Amanita excelsa in Hagley Park, Christchurch, New Zealand. **EDIBILITY UNKNOWN: AVOID.** (Hall)

The young fruiting body of *Amanita excelsa* has the superficial appearance of a small puffball. **EDIBILITY UNKNOWN: AVOID.** (Hall)

on the surface. The stalk is 5–14 cm high and white when young, becoming marked with pink patches as it ages. There is a prominent white ring, but the volva, so characteristic of other species of *Amanita*, is usually little more than a ridge at the top of a swollen

Amanita virosa (destroying angel). **POISONOUS.** (Izawa)

base to the stalk. The flesh of the cap and stalk is white when young but gradually becomes pink when cut and exposed to air. *Amanita rubescens* may be eaten, but only if it is first thoroughly cooked. This process renders the mushroom safe to eat, although it can still produce an adverse reaction in some people. Because of the difficulty in distinguishing *A. rubescens* from *A. pantherina* and other poisonous *Amanita* species, many experienced mycologists will not take the risk of eating it. *Amanita excelsa* is similar to *A. rubescens*, and while this mushroom is considered edible in Europe (Phillips 1981), in Japan it is regarded as poisonous (Hongo et al. 1994).

Amanita virosa (Destroying Angel)

The caps of the destroying angel are often bulbous when immature but expand to 5–12 cm in diameter. The stalk is 10–20 cm high, and the volva often occurs just below soil level and is easily missed. The destroying angel fruits from early summer to early autumn in the eastern United States. It is rather uncommon in the United Kingdom (Harding et al. 1996), which is probably why it causes fewer fatalities there than the death cap (Læssøe and Del Conte 1996). This probably also explains why there is some confusion over its habitat, which in different texts is given either as mixed or hardwood forests (Phillips 1981) or conifer forests (Læssøe and Del Conte 1996). The destroying

Amanita vaginata (grisette). **AVOID.** (Izawa)

angel and the white form of the death cap are the most dangerous poisonous mushrooms. This is not because they contain more toxic compounds than other poisonous species but because they can be mistaken for edible white-capped species. Like other species of *Amanita*, the destroying angel can be easily confused with *Volvariella* species. It has a pleasant smell and is reputed to taste quite good. Great care should always be taken when collecting white mushrooms near trees or when picking what appear to be puffballs but which actually may be disguised, unopened caps of an *Amanita*. *Amanita abrupta*, which is common in eastern North America, is another example of a white, highly toxic species (Imazeki et al. 1988).

Amanita vaginata (Grisette)

Some of the names that have been applied to members of the genus *Amanita* are known to refer to a complex of several morphologically very similar species and not just to a single biological entity. This is certainly the case for *A. vaginata*, which occurs throughout temperate regions of the Northern Hemisphere. Unlike the other species of *Amanita* described, *A. vaginata* lacks a ring on the stalk, though it does have a prominent volva. The cap is gray, 5–10 cm in diameter, and has a conspicuously striate margin. The stalk is white, smooth to finely fibrous, 10–20 cm high, and 10–15 mm thick. This mushroom occurs in hardwood as well as coniferous forests. Though not poisonous, it is best avoided because of possible confusion with other deadly species of *Amanita*.

Armillaria mellea (Honey Mushroom)

Over the years taxonomists have come to recognize that *Armillaria mellea* is actually a complex of species that share a similar appearance. The caps of *A. mellea* proper (sensu stricto) are 3–12 cm in diameter and light to dark brown, sometimes tinged olive. The gills are white or off-white. The stalks, which taper slightly toward the base, are up to 15 cm high and paler at the top, though similar in color to the cap at the base. There is a prominent, cottony, thick, off-white ring toward the top of the stalk. These mushrooms can be found from summer to early winter throughout temperate regions of the Northern Hemisphere, where they occur on stumps, logs, at the bases of dead but still standing hardwoods or conifers, or on buried wood around the trunks of trees that have become parasitized by the

Armillaria mellea (honey mushroom). Members of the *Armillaria mellea* sensu lato species complex display a great variability in form. **EDIBLE WHEN COOKED.** (Johnson)

Armillaria mellea (honey mushroom) growing on a rotting stump in northern Italy. **EDIBLE WHEN COOKED.** (Hall)

Armillaria mellea (honey mushroom) from the eastern United States. **EDIBLE WHEN COOKED.** (Johnson)

Armillaria novaezelandiae (bootlace mushroom), a species similar to the more widespread *A. mellea.*
EDIBLE WHEN COOKED. (Hall)

fungus. The fungus spreads from one infected tree to another by long, dark gray to black, shoestring-like hyphae called rhizomorphs (Brasier 1992). *Armillaria mellea* causes gastric upsets when eaten raw or poorly cooked, and for some consumers even after cooking—a feature it shares with several dozen fungi. *Armillaria novaezelandiae* (bootlace mushroom) and *A. tabescens* (ringless honey mushroom) are also edible (Miller 1981, Hood 1992), but it would also be advisable to cook these mushrooms before eating.

Calocybe gambosa (St. George's Mushroom)

The fruiting body of St. George's mushroom has a white to off-white cap and a mealy smell. It can have a cap up to 15 cm in diameter, with a stalk up to 6 cm high and 1–3 cm thick. It is often found fruiting in rings in grasslands, along roadsides, in lawns, and at the edges of woodlands. The caps do not stain red when bruised. The common name for this mushroom stems from the likelihood of first finding its edible fruiting bodies on or about St. George's Day in the Northern Hemisphere (23 April). Its French name, *mousseron*, is probably the

Calocybe gambosa (St. George's mushroom) growing in grasslands in the United Kingdom. **EDIBLE.** (Lyon)

source of the English word "mushroom." This species might be confused with the brown-spored, red-staining *Inocybe patouillardii*, which is very poisonous. St. George's mushroom has white gills, but it has neither volva nor ring, and it fruits in spring rather than autumn. It is therefore unlikely to be confused with any white *Amanita*.

Clitocybe Species

The strongly funnel-shaped edible caps of *Clitocybe geotropa* are up to 20 cm in diameter and have stalks up to 15 cm high and 3 cm thick. The caps are buff when young but turn pale peach with age. The gills are the same color as the caps and extend down the stalk. *Clitocybe gibba* (common funnel cap), a species common in eastern North America, is smaller and has gills that are white to buff. Both species are found in autumn under deciduous trees or in mixed woodlands and consequently are unlikely to be confused with the smaller mushrooms of the deadly poisonous ivory clitocybe (*C. dealbata*) and *C. rivulosa*, which are usually found in grassy areas such as lawns and roadsides. *Clitocybe gibba*, *C. maxima*, and *C. robusta* are all edible

Clitocybe dealbata (ivory clitocybe). **POISONOUS.** (Lyon)

Clitocybe gibba (common funnel cap). **EDIBLE.** (Izawa)

Clitocybe maxima. **EDIBLE.** (Wang)

A *Clitocybe* species of unknown edibility grows beneath a Douglas fir. (Hall)

species eaten widely in China and Japan. The edibility of a number of other species is unknown.

Because the small, white to buff, flat to slightly funnel-shaped fruiting bodies of the ivory clitocybe (*Clitocybe dealbata*) have no ring on the stalk, have gills that extend down the stalk, and are only 4 cm in diameter and 4 cm high, it is unlikely that this species would be confused with field mushrooms growing in the same habitat. However, the ivory clitocybe could easily be confused with the edible fairy ring mushroom (*Marasmius oreades*), with which it is sometimes associated. Great care, therefore, needs to be taken when picking fairy ring mushrooms. Other poisonous *Clitocybe* species such as *C. nebularis* can be found in mossy or grassy areas, on litter in hardwood and conifer forests, or in heathland.

Collybia dryophila (Oak-Loving Collybia)

Few other woodland mushrooms are as common and widespread in North America as *Collybia dryophila*, whose fruiting bodies can be found scattered or in small clusters from late spring through autumn. Although especially common in oak (*Quercus*) forests, the species also

Collybia dryophila (oak-loving collybia). **AVOID.** (Johnson)

occurs in other types of hardwood forests, as well as in those domi-
nated by various conifers. The cap is 1–7 cm in diameter and has a
smooth surface that is dark reddish brown to yellow-brown when
young but soon fades to orange-brown or tan, with the central portion
darker than the margin. The stalk is 3–9 cm high and 2–8 mm thick,
smooth, hollow, and distinctly cartilaginous. The gills are crowded,
white to pale yellow, and produce a white spore print. *Collybia
dryophila* is often confused with *C. butyracea*, though the latter has a
pale pink spore print. Both species resemble the fairy ring mushroom
(*Marasmius oreades*) but differ in that they occur in forests while the
fairy ring mushroom is found in grassy areas. While edible, the thin
caps and tough stalk make *C. dryophila* not worth eating.

Flammulina velutipes (Enokitake)

Fruiting bodies of enokitake growing wild on decaying logs look
nothing like those of the cultivated mushroom. The caps are smooth
and gelatinous, up to 10 cm in diameter, and light tan to light orange-
brown toward the center but with pale yellow edges. The tops of the
stalks are similar in color to the edges of the caps, but the stalks are
dark brown at the base and, unlike the cultivated strains, rarely more
than 4 cm high. The gills do not run down the stalk and are pale
yellow. The common name is Japanese and comes from enokitake's
habit of fruiting on tree species such as Japanese hackberry (*Celtis
sinensis*). It is also known as winter mushroom due to its habit of
fruiting from late autumn to early winter. Enokitake is even capable
of freezing, thawing out, and then continuing to grow (Stamets 2000).

Hygrocybe conica (Witch's Hat)

Hygrocybe conica belongs to a group of small, waxy, brightly colored
mushrooms usually referred to as waxy caps. Members of the group
characteristically have gills that are thick, soft, and waxy in appearance, much like a wax crayon. This is quite unlike the appearance of
the gills in most other gilled fungi. The witch's hat is typical for the
group in that it occurs on the ground in moist places on the forest
floor, usually (but not always) under conifers. The cap is 3–8 cm in
diameter and sharply conic to bell-shaped, often with a prominent
raised center, called an umbo. The surface of the cap is smooth,
slightly sticky when moist, and scarlet-red to red or orange. The stalk
is 2–20 cm long, 0.5–1.5 cm thick, the same color as the cap toward

Flammulina velutipes (enokitake) growing on the stump of a tree has a completely different appearance than the cultivated mushroom. **EDIBLE.** (Hall)

Hygrocybe conica (witch's hat). **EDIBILITY UNKNOWN: AVOID.** (Johnson)

the apex but white toward the base, and appears twisted. When bruised, the flesh of the witch's hat turns black. There is some question as to the edibility of this mushroom. As such, it is best left alone.

Laccaria laccata (The Deceiver)

This edible, highly variable, deceptive mushroom (hence the common name) is often found in clusters under deciduous and coniferous trees in late summer and autumn throughout temperate regions of the Northern Hemisphere. The caps, which are 1.5–6 cm in diameter and have widely spaced gills, are usually reddish brown with peach tones when moist, yellowish brown when dry. The caps are dome-shaped and shiny when young but become flattened with a depression in the center, or funnel-shaped with a wavy edge, as they mature. With age the caps may become dry and dull. The stalks and gills are a similar color to the caps. The stalks are typically 5–10 cm high (though this may be highly variable), 0.5–1 cm thick, and often somewhat compressed or twisted. Moreover, the stalk may have a constant diameter throughout or taper toward either the apex or the base. *Laccaria laccata* sometimes resembles poisonous species.

Laccaria laccata (the deceiver). **EDIBLE.** (Wang)

Laccaria amethystea (Amethyst Laccaria)

The edible and rather common amethyst laccaria is found from late summer to early winter in coniferous or deciduous forests. Its distinctive color, lack of a cortina, and white spores make it unlikely to be confused with a brightly colored poisonous species of, for example, *Cortinarius*. The caps are 1–6 cm in diameter and dome-shaped when young, becoming flattened or depressed in the center as they mature. Like the deceiver, the gills are widely spaced and the stalks are 4–10 cm high, tough, and often twisted.

Lactarius Species

Members of the genus *Lactarius* share many of the same features noted for species of *Russula*, which is not surprising since the two genera are very closely related. In both genera, fruiting bodies have a brittle, granular texture and what could be considered a rather simple overall structure, with no evidence of such features as a ring on the stalk. Moreover, in the majority of species the gills and stalk are white. *Lactarius* and *Russula* are among the more important mycorrhizal

Laccaria amethystea (amethyst laccaria). **EDIBLE.** (Hall)

Lactarius camphoratus (aromatic milky). **EDIBLE.** (Izawa)

mushrooms, forming ectomycorrhizal associations with many different kinds of trees in the forests of the world. The most important difference in the two genera is the presence of a latex in the fruiting bodies of *Lactarius* that is absent in those of *Russula*. The latex, which can be clear, milky, or colored, is exuded when the flesh of either the gills or stalk is bruised or cut.

Lactarius camphoratus (Aromatic Milky)

Lactarius camphoratus can be recognized by the combination of a reddish brown cap, reddish brown gills, and a fragrant odor much like that of sweet clover. The aromatic milky is a relatively small mushroom, with a cap 1.5–5 cm in diameter and a stalk 1.5–6 cm tall and 0.3–1.0 cm thick. The cap is at first convex, becoming depressed with age, often with an umbo at the center. The latex is watery white and does not change color. *Lactarius camphoratus* occurs scattered or in groups, usually under or near conifers, in forests throughout temperate

Young fruiting bodies of *Lactarius deliciosus* (saffron milk cap) display the characteristic darker-colored orange blotches on the stem and cap and the orange latex oozing from the cut on the inverted cap. **EDIBLE.** (Hall)

Lactarius deliciosus (saffron milk cap) fruits prolifically under *Pinus radiata* (Monterey pine) in Victoria, Australia. **EDIBLE.** (Hall)

Young *Lactarius deliciosus* (saffron milk cap), some just showing the green markings that appear on old or damaged caps and stems. **EDIBLE.** (Hall)

regions of the Northern Hemisphere. This is an edible mushroom. When dried and powdered it is used as a flavoring in some parts of Europe (Philips 1981).

Lactarius deliciosus (Saffron Milk Cap)

Young saffron milk caps have a small depression in the center of the cap that gradually deepens so that mature caps become funnel-shaped. Both the caps and stalks are pale orange, with darker orange blotches arranged in concentric rings on the surface of the cap. Similarly colored blotches are also found on the stalk. Green stains develop on the caps and gills as the caps mature or if they are bruised. The gills, which are bright orange in young caps and dull carrot-orange in mature caps, are attached to the stalk and extend a short way down it. All species of *Lactarius* exude a sticky latex when young caps are broken. In the saffron milk cap, the latex is carrot-orange to bright orange. This mushroom is found in late summer and autumn under spruce (*Picea*) and pines (*Pinus*) throughout Europe, Asia, and North America as well as under pines in southern Australia. It is widely eaten in Europe, particularly in Spain, and is one of the few wild mushrooms collected commercially in Australia. The morphologically rather similar hatsudake (*L. hatsudake*) is widely consumed throughout East Asia.

Lactarius indigo (Indigo Milky)

Few other species of *Lactarius* are as distinctive as *L. indigo*. Its fruiting body is dark indigo-blue in fresh specimens, pale gray-blue in older ones. The latex is also dark blue at first but slowly turns green. The indigo milky is a moderately large mushroom, with a cap 5–15 cm in diameter and a stalk 2–8 cm high and 1–2.5 cm thick. This mushroom is found on the ground in oak (*Quercus*) and pine (*Pinus*) forests in eastern North America. It is edible but has been reported to have a slightly bitter taste.

Poisonous *Lactarius* Species

Three poisonous European species—*Lactarius torminosus* (woolly milk cap), *L. chrysorheus*, and *L. zonarius*—might be confused by a novice for the edible *L. deliciosus* (saffron milk cap). However, these other mushrooms do not have the green markings characteristic of the

Lactarius indigo (indigo milky). **EDIBLE.** (Johnson)

Lactarius zonarius. **POISONOUS.** (Hall)

Lactarius blennius. **POISONOUS.** (Hall)

Lactarius pubescens. **POISONOUS.** (Hall)

saffron milk cap, and they have a bitter taste and white latex. As a general rule, it is unwise to eat a *Lactarius* that does not produce red or orange latex immediately after the cap is broken. *Lactarius blennius*, which is commonly found under beech (*Fagus*) in Europe; *L. pubescens*, a species with white latex; and the Australian species *L. piperatus* (Cribb 1987) are all poisonous.

Lepiota, *Macrolepiota*, and *Chlorophyllum* Species

The parasol mushroom (*Macrolepiota procera*) can have caps up to 40 cm in diameter, but it typically reaches only half this size. When young, the caps are egg-shaped, cream to light brown, covered with darker brown scales, and borne on a stout stalk. As the cap opens, it becomes at first umbrella-shaped and then flattened with a raised central portion without scales. The flesh does not change color when bruised. The covering of scales gives the edge of the cap a somewhat irregular appearance. The hollow stalks are up to 30 cm high, have a prominent ring, and are covered with small scales. The gills are free from the stalk and white at first but eventually turn light brown. Although there is often a swollen base to the stalk, there is no volva. In Europe and eastern North America, parasol mushrooms are found in late summer and autumn on the edges of woods and in grasslands. These mushrooms have a sweet and pleasant taste, are widespread, and are ranked very highly by some.

The shaggy parasol (*Macrolepiota rachodes*) has many features in common with the parasol mushroom, but the scales on the cap are chestnut-colored and the cap turns orange-red when cut. Some people develop intestinal problems after eating the shaggy parasol (Southcott 1974). *Chlorophyllum molybdites* can closely resemble the edible *M. rachodes* since it has a similar shape and size, white gills when young, a ring on the stalk, distinct scales on the cap, and no volva. It can, however, be distinguished by its pale green to lime-green spore print and the green color of the gills in mature fruiting bodies. Poisoning from this mushroom begins one to three hours after eating, with severe abdominal pain that progresses to vomiting, diarrhea, and dehydration. It can be fatal.

Like *Macrolepiota*, species of *Lepiota* typically have rings on the stalk, white gills and spores, gills not attached to the stalk, and no volva. Some species like *L. cristata* are poisonous, with symptoms similar to those caused by *Amanita* (Southcott 1997), and consuming *L. brunneoincarnata* may be fatal. However, these species have a quite

Macrolepiota procera (parasol mushroom). **EDIBLE.** (Buchanan)

Macrolepiota rachodes (shaggy parasol). **EDIBLE.** (Hall)

Chlorophyllum molybdites. **POISONOUS.** (Roody)

Lepiota cristata. **POISONOUS.** (Lyon)

different appearance from the edible species *M. procera* and *M. rachodes* and are unlikely to be confused with them. Good illustrations of the suspect and poisonous species can be found in a number of books (see Læssøe and Del Conte 1996, Lincoff and Nehring 1995, Phillips 1981).

Leucopaxillus giganteus (Giant Clitocybe)

As with the giant puffball, the most obvious feature of the giant clitocybe is size: mature funnel-shaped caps can be up to 40 cm in diameter with stalks 4–15 cm high and 4 cm thick. The caps and gills are creamy white, but the caps can develop light brown stains as they age. The cream gills are tightly packed together and extend down the stalk. When young, the edges of the caps are rolled downward. The giant clitocybe often forms very large fairy rings in pastures but can also be found in other grassy areas such as along roadsides. The smell and taste of this mushroom can be mild and pleasant but is sometimes truly disgusting. Occasionally consumption results in stomach cramps and diarrhea.

Leucopaxillus giganteus. **EDIBLE.** (Wang)

Lyophyllum shimeji (Honshimeji)

Honshimeji is a mycorrhizal mushroom that grows in association with various hardwood trees in Japan and other parts of eastern Asia. The caps resemble those of a *Russula* and are 2–8 cm in diameter and buff to light brown or occasionally mid brown. They are strongly convex when young, becoming flattened with age, occasionally with a small depression in the center. The stalks are white to off-white, 2–7 cm high, and somewhat swollen at the base when young. The gills are white to slightly pastel pink or brown. This mushroom is very highly regarded in Japan, where it commands high prices. Researchers there have recently selected a strain of *Lyophyllum shimeji* that is capable of growing saprobically (Fujita et al. 1990, Ohta 1994). This development may eventually result in commercial cultivation of honshimeji.

Marasmius oreades (Fairy Ring Mushroom)

This small fairy ring mushroom has light brown caps that are 2–5 cm in diameter, often with a raised, more darkly colored center portion.

Lyophyllum shimeji (honshimeji). **EDIBLE.** (Izawa)

When fully opened the edges of the caps turn up, revealing widely spaced white, cream, or light brown gills. The tough, fibrous stalks are 2–10 cm high and white at first but turning off-white. The smell is characteristically that of fresh sawdust.

Marasmius oreades can be found in grassy areas such as lawns and pastures from late spring to late autumn. As the fungus grows through the soil it releases nutrients that stimulate the growth of the plants above the ground, often causing them to be a deeper green. As the fungus continues to grow through the soil, nutrients become depleted, toxins are released by the fungus, and the soil becomes somewhat water-repellent, so that plant growth is reduced. However, the fungus only occupies the soil while the nutrients it requires to grow are present; eventually the fungal hyphae die and plant growth returns to normal. Other species that grow in grassy areas and can produce fairy rings include *Agaricus arvensis*, *A. campestris*, *Clitocybe dealbata*, and *Hygrocybe pratensis*, although only the latter two have white spores.

Marasmius oreades (fairy ring mushroom). **EDIBLE.** (Hall)

Marasmius siccus (orange pinwheel). **EDIBILITY UNKNOWN: AVOID.** (Johnson)

Although the fairy ring mushroom has a pleasant flavor that can make a useful addition to soups and stews, it can also be confused with the deadly poisonous *Clitocybe dealbata* and *C. nebularis*, which are often found growing with it.

Marasmius siccus (Orange Pinwheel)

The fruiting bodies of most species of *Marasmius* are smaller than those produced by *M. oreades* and occur in situations where they are less likely to be as easily noticed. Most members of the genus are associated with decaying leaves, pine needles, twigs, and various other smaller bits of plant debris found on forest floors. The fruiting body of a typical species of *Marasmius* is unusual in that it can dry out and become shriveled but then revive and regain the appearance of a fresh specimen when adequate moisture becomes available. *Marasmius siccus* is one of the most colorful and distinctive species in the genus. The rust-orange to rose-colored cap, which looks like a miniature parasol, is pleated, bell-shaped to convex, and 0.3–3 cm in diameter. The flesh is very thin, and the widely spaced gills are white. The stalk, which is white to blackish brown, is very thin (0.2–1.0 mm thick) and relatively long in relation to the size of the cap. *Marasmius rotula* (horsehair mushroom) has a smaller, white cap and a long, shiny black stalk. Moreover, it is more likely to be found on dead twigs and small roots than on dead leaves, the usual habitat for *M. siccus*. Though not known to be poisonous, the fruiting bodies of these and other species of *Marasmius* are much too small to be considered for the table.

Mycena haematopus (Bleeding Mycena)

One of the more distinctive members of the genus *Mycena* is *M. haematopus*, the bleeding mycena. This mushroom is so named because the stalk exudes a deep blood-red latex when broken. Found throughout North America and Europe, the bleeding mycena is common on well-decayed wood, where it occurs in small clusters. The cap is red-brown at the center and reddish gray toward the margin, conical to bell-shaped, and 1–5 cm in diameter. The stalk is 4–10 cm high, 2–3 mm thick, hollow, and typically hairy to strigose at the base. *Mycena haematopus* is edible but hardly worth collecting because of its small size.

Mycena haematopus (bleeding mycena). **EDIBILITY UNKNOWN: AVOID.** (Johnson)

Mycena leaiana (orange mycena). **EDIBILITY UNKNOWN: AVOID.** (Johnson)

Mycena leaiana (Orange Mycena)

Mycena is a large genus that contains a diverse assemblage of mostly relatively small, largely nondescript mushrooms. Only a few species are large enough to be easily noticed or to be considered for the table. One prominent example is *M. leaiana*, which occurs in dense clusters on the decaying wood of various hardwoods throughout central and eastern North America. It is particularly common on beech (*Fagus*). The caps are bell-shaped, 1–5 cm in diameter, smooth, and slightly slimy. A conspicuous bright reddish orange when young, the caps become more yellow as they mature. The gills are crowded, relatively thick, and yellow to pink with bright red-orange edges. The stalk is 3–7 cm high, 1–3 mm thick, and tough, with a base covered in dense, coarse hairs. The edibility of most species of *Mycena* is not known. Although *M. leaiana* is probably not poisonous, there would seem to be little food value in this small species.

Russula aeruginea (Green Russula)

Species of *Russula* are some of the easiest mushrooms to identify, as they have a granular texture when broken, regularly arranged brittle

Russula aeruginea (green russula). **EDIBILITY UNKNOWN: AVOID.** (Johnson)

gills, and usually brightly colored caps. When young the caps are dome-shaped, usually with a small depression in the top. As they mature they flatten out and the depression in the cap deepens. The stalks have a constant diameter throughout and are often rounded at the base. There is no ring on the stalk and no volva. All species of *Russula* form mycorrhizal associations with hardwoods or conifers.

Though the fruiting bodies of fungi come in an assortment of colors, some colors are much less common than others. For example, there are relatively few green mushrooms. One prominent member of this underrepresented group is *Russula aeruginea*, rather appropriately called the green russula. Widely distributed in both North America and Europe, *R. aeruginea* typically occurs under oak (*Quercus*), aspen (*Populus*), and birch (*Betula*). The dull green to dark green cap is 3–9 cm in diameter and convex at first but becomes flattened or slightly depressed in mature specimens. The surface of the cap is smooth and slightly sticky when moist. The stalk is 4–8 cm high, 1–2 cm thick, and white or faintly yellow. The green russula is regarded as edible by some authors but probably is best avoided (Arora 1986). Edible species of *Russula* include the wine-colored *R. vinosa*, yellow *R. violeipes*, and greenish *R. virescens*.

Russula emetica (the sickener). **POISONOUS.** (Hall)

Poisonous *Russula* Species

The poisonous Northern Hemisphere species *Russula emetica* (the sickener), *R. mairei* (beechwood sickener), and *R. luteotacta* have red or faded red caps along with white stalks and gills. It is highly unlikely that these would be confused with *Amanita caesarea* (Caesar's mushroom), particularly as the latter has a prominent volva at the base of the stalk. The Japanese species—*R. foetens*, *R. japonica*, *R. omiensis*, *R. senecis*, and *R. subnigricans*—are also toxic (Imazeki et al. 1988). Unless you know a *Russula* species to be edible, do not eat it. Do not eat red, pink, or pink-tinged varieties such as *R. atropurpurea* or those with a hot, bitter, or peppery taste when raw.

A number of species of *Russula* are extremely variable in appearance. To correctly identify these requires careful examination of the color of the spore print, colors of the cap, details of the cap edge, taste, smell, whether the surface layers of the cap can be peeled away, the reaction of the flesh of the fruiting body to various chemicals, and certain microscopic details.

Russula atropurpurea. **EDIBILITY UNKNOWN: AVOID.** (Hall)

The fruiting bodies of *Termitomyces eurrhizus* (termite mushroom) grow from the fungal garden tended by the worker termites. **EDIBLE.** (Izawa)

Termitomyces eurrhizus (Termite Mushroom)

Most termites, which feed on dead plant material such as wood and leaf litter, are only able to digest cellulose and lignin because they have symbiotic protozoa and bacteria living in their intestine. However, the most advanced species in the Macrotermitinae found in Africa, Madagascar, India, and much of Southeast Asia do not have these symbiotic protozoa and bacteria. Instead they rely on their food being processed by one of two dozen mushroom species in the genus *Termitomyces* (Wood and Thomas 1989). These termites forage for food and then deposit fecal pellets on a spongelike "garden" of *Termitomyces* that may be up to 50 cm in diameter. These gardens, which are tended by the worker termites, are inside mounds up to 6 m high and 3 m across and are equipped with air shafts that keep them aerated and cool. Clusters of fungal spores, called sporodochia, develop on the fungal garden and are eaten by the workers, with the king, queen, soldiers, and nymphs living off the salivary secretions of the workers.

When rainfall exceeds about 2 cm per day, *Termitomyces* produces long-stalked, edible mushrooms above the ground that are considered a delicacy. They are widely used as food throughout much of Africa (Rammeloo and Walleyn 1993). Although it is possible to grow *Termitomyces* in culture, all attempts to cultivate these mushrooms commercially have been unsuccessful.

Tricholoma flavovirens (Canary Tricholoma)

The distinguishing feature of the canary tricholoma is the pale yellow to sulfur-yellow color of the cap, gills, and stalk. The caps are usually 5–10 cm in diameter and the stalk is 3–7 cm high. This species can be found as solitary fruiting bodies or in clusters on the ground under conifers and in mixed forests throughout temperate regions of North America and Europe. It typically fruits in late summer and autumn. *Tricholoma flavovirens* is often listed as edible. However, some people develop an upset stomach after eating it, and a few cases of poisoning have been reported. For this reason, it should be avoided.

Tricholoma matsutake (Matsutake)

When young and unopened, the fruiting bodies of matsutake (literally "pine mushroom") are somewhat club-shaped and 10–30 cm long. They are creamy white with a light brown top and brown

Tricholoma flavovirens (canary tricholoma). **EDIBILITY UNKNOWN: AVOID.** (Johnson)

Grade-one fruiting bodies of *Tricholoma matsutake* (matsutake), the most important edible mushroom in Japan. **EDIBLE.** (Hall)

blotches along the sides. At this immature stage the mushrooms are mostly below ground, with perhaps only the tops showing through cracks in the soil surface. As they open, the fruiting bodies take on a more conventional mushroom shape. When fully expanded, the caps

Grade-three fruiting bodies of *Tricholoma matsutake* (matsutake) are at the stage of growth just before the cap opens. **EDIBLE.** (Hall)

are creamy brown with prominent brown markings and can be 10–30 cm in diameter. The stalks are typically 10–20 cm high and have a ring toward the top and coloring similar to that of the caps.

In Japan matsutake is primarily associated with *Pinus densiflora* (Japanese red pine), an early colonizer of bare or disturbed soil, although it is also associated with a range of other conifers. This mushroom forms distinctive white, compact fungal colonies in the soil, called the shiro. These occur just below the litter layer and can be up to 25 cm thick. Volatile antibiotics produced in the shiro elim-inate most soil microorganisms (Ogawa 1977, Ohara and Hamada 1967). Fruiting normally begins when the host trees are about twenty years old and 4–5 m high. Production peaks in forty- to fifty-year-old forests and can reach 100 kg per hectare. It then gradually declines over the following thirty to forty years as the litter layer builds up and Japanese red pine is replaced by other trees such as deciduous oaks.

Matsutake is more than just a food in Japan: it is a symbol of autumn and a special part of Japanese culture. Such is the status of this mushroom that many presentation packs of matsutake are never eaten but are instead kept as symbols of autumn and friendship. It is quite an expensive mushroom too, however, and so many people succumb to the temptation of trying it in their favorite dish. Thinly slicing the fruiting bodies lengthwise and then cooking slivers in

Roasting *Tricholoma matsutake* (matsutake) over a charcoal fire, Yamagata Mura, Japan. (Hall)

A typical *Tricholoma matsutake* (matsutake) forest in Japan with about 75 percent canopy cover and limited understory plants. The positions of previously collected matsutake have been marked by colored flags and show the approximate extent of the shiro. (Hall)

A small tunnel house, called a "Hiroshima tunnel," is used to stimulate the fruiting of *Tricholoma matsutake* (matsutake) in Japan. (Hall)

miso soup is one way to enjoy matsutake. One of Ian Hall's most memorable experiences in Japan was eating this mushroom in a thatched cottage in Yamagata Mura at the northern end of Honshu. There, surrounded by good company and lubricated with more than adequate quantities of sake, matsutake was simply roasted over a charcoal fire.

If you are invited to a Japanese home for dinner during autumn, a suitable present would be a small presentation pack of unopened grade-one matsutake. But beware: Because of the shape of unopened fruiting bodies, in past times the word "matsutake" became synonymous with the male organ. Consequently, in polite company the word was dropped in favor of "the take." When Ian visited a wholesaler near Hiroshima, a packer went into a fit of giggles when asked to bring out specimens of grade-one matsutake, and his interpreter showed distinct discomfort when asked to hold one while he took a photograph. As previously mentioned, this is a pricey mushroom, so when you go out to buy your presentation package take plenty of money. At the start of the fruiting season, in late August, prices for unopened grade-one matsutake can be up to 160,000 yen ($1250) per kilogram, with prices reflecting grade, quality, origin, and availability.

In the early 1940s about 12,000 tons of matsutake were harvested each year in Japan, but since then production has gradually fallen to about 1000 tons (Wang et al. 1997). Another 2000 tons of matsutake, white matsutake (*Tricholoma magnivelare*), and European matsutake (*T. caligatum*) are imported from Canada, China, Korea, Morocco, Taiwan, and the United States, but demand still exceeds supply, which is why matsutake commands very high prices. The estimated annual retail market for matsutake in Japan is worth $250 to $500 million.

All attempts to produce matsutake-infected plants and establish new matsutake forests have failed. However, considerable progress has been made in Japan in developing methods to maximize production in forests where matsutake occurs naturally (Ogawa and Ito 1989). Surveys show that production is greatest when the canopy provides only 75 percent cover, the shrub layer is relatively sparse, the soil is moist but not wet, and the litter layer is about 3 cm deep. It has also been found that production can be increased by raking the litter layer to reduce the depth to 3 cm, and by removing some of the shrubs and large trees to ensure adequate aeration and to allow sufficient sunlight onto the forest floor (Ogawa and Ito 1989). Modifying the soil humidity and temperature by erecting irrigated tunnels over shiros, the so-called Hiroshima method, has also been found to stimulate

Tricholoma magnivelare (white matsutake) is slowly gaining favor in Japan. It can fruit in Canada right up to the first snowfall. **EDIBLE.** (Hall)

fruiting (Iwase et al. 1988, Tominaga 1975, Tominaga and Komeyama 1987). In South Korea plastic tunnels have been replaced with small plastic hoods or caps to cover shiros or individual fruiting bodies.

Tricholoma terreum

Tricholoma terreum is fairly common throughout temperate regions of the Northern Hemisphere, where it can be found fruiting in late summer and autumn. The caps are light to dark gray, often with a slight violet hue when young, and 4–10 cm in diameter. The gills and stalks are white. The stalk is up to 8 cm high and has no ring. The gills are attached to the stalk but do not extend down it. The taste of this mushroom is pleasant but not outstanding.

Other *Tricholoma* Species

Like *Lepiota*, some species of *Tricholoma* are either suspect or known to be poisonous. Tiger tricholoma (*T. pardinum*) causes severe intestinal symptoms and in the early 1900s was responsible for about 20 percent of all poisonings in Switzerland (Bresinsky and Besl 1990).

Tricholoma terreum. **EDIBLE.** (Hall)

Tricholoma ustale (burnt tricholoma). **POISONOUS.** (Izawa)

The fruiting bodies of *Tricholoma pessundatum* under *Pinus radiata* (Monterey pine). **POISONOUS.** (Wang)

Tricholoma ustale (burnt tricholoma) is a common cause of poisoning in Japan, presumably because of its similarity to *T. bakamatsutake* and *T. matsutake*.

While *Tricholoma pessundatum* has been consumed by some without ill effects, others have experienced twenty-four hours of moderate stomach upsets. It is possible, however, that the ill effects were caused by the presence of bacteria in old, decaying mushrooms rather than by the mushrooms themselves. Symptoms of diarrhea, sweating, difficulty in focusing, and restriction of the pupils have also been reported after ingestion of an unidentified species of *Tricholoma* (Southcott 1997).

Hypomyces lactifluorum (Lobster Mushroom)

Hypomyces lactifluorum is a parasitic fungus that infects species of *Lactarius* and *Russula*. The infection of the mushroom by this fungus distorts the shape of the fruiting body, producing a funnel-shaped structure 10–15 cm wide and 7–15 cm high with a stalk 5–10 cm thick. The infected mushrooms are characteristically bright orange. They can be found from midsummer to midautumn and are very popular in North America, where they are frequently available in markets and featured widely on restaurant menus.

Hypomyces lactifluorum (lobster mushroom). **EDIBLE.** (Hall)

2. Mushrooms with gills and a more or less centrally placed stalk; pale pink spore print

Entoloma Species

The fruiting bodies of *Entoloma* species can be confused with those of edible *Lepista* species because they have pink spores and pale lilac to buff to lilac-brown gills that are attached to the stalk. Some species of *Entoloma* are edible; others, such as *E. rhodopolium*, are poisonous. The novice would be wise to avoid species in this genus.

Lepista Species

Species of *Lepista* produce a pale pink spore print. When the spores are observed under a microscope they are found to be elliptical and covered with minute spines, particularly if stained with cotton blue, a dye commonly used by mycologists. It is very important to make a spore print when identifying species of this genus, as it is possible to

Entoloma rhodopolium. **POISONOUS.** (Izawa)

Lepista nuda. **EDIBLE WHEN COOKED.** (Lyon)

Lepista aff. *luscina.* **EDIBLE WHEN COOKED.** (Hall)

mistake some for brown-spored species of *Cortinarius*, which may be poisonous. Many species of *Lepista* have the odor of a sweet perfume and the general shape of a *Tricholoma*. No species of *Lepista* appears to be toxic, provided it is cooked first (Benjamin 1995).

Lepista nuda has lilac-tinged gills when young, but these turn pale pinkish brown as the mushroom ages. The caps are at first conical, later becoming flattened with a raised portion in the center, and are 6–12 cm in diameter. The stalks are 5–9 cm high, sometimes with a bulbous portion at the base. This mushroom has a very powerful, attractive smell. In Europe and North America it is found in woodlands, hedgerows, and gardens in late summer to autumn and occasionally throughout winter. Techniques have been developed in France for cultivating *L. nuda* (Guinberteau et al. 1989), so it is now available in European markets. Other edible species in the genus include *L. irina*, *L. luscina*, and *L. personata*.

Pluteus atricapillus (Deer Mushroom)

Another group of pink-spored mushrooms is represented by members of the genus *Pluteus*. These small to medium mushrooms occur on decaying wood and wood debris, most often from broadleaf trees. Perhaps the most commonly encountered species is *P. atricapillus*,

Pluteus atricapillus (deer mushroom). **EDIBLE.** (Johnson)

The fruiting bodies of *Volvariella speciosa* showing the distinctive volva at the base of the stem. **EDIBLE.** (Wang)

also known as *P. cervinus*, which can be quite common in forests throughout North America and Europe from late spring until early autumn. The dark brown to drab brown cap is 5–14 cm in diameter, smooth to fibrous, and convex to somewhat flattened. The gills are white when young but become pink as the spores mature. The stalk is white, 5–12 cm high, 6–16 mm thick (becoming enlarged toward the base), and streaked with tiny grayish brown hairs. *Pluteus atricapillus* is edible, but the flesh of this mushroom is soft and quickly spoils in warm weather. As a result, specimens must be refrigerated or prepared for the table as soon as possible after being collected.

Volvariella Species

Like *Amanita*, the fruiting body of *Volvariella* develops within a cup-shaped volva, the remains of which can be seen at the base of the stalk of mature fruiting bodies. While *Volvariella* has no ring on the stalk, this is not a reliable characteristic for distinguishing this genus from *Amanita* because rings are not found on all *Amanita* mushrooms. However, the two genera are relatively easy to distinguish from the

Volvariella volvacea (straw mushroom) fruiting on plant debris in the wild. **EDIBLE.** (Izawa)

spore print—*Volvariella* has a pink spore, whereas that of *Amanita* is white. The cultivated *V. volvacea* can be found fruiting in tropical countries, while other species, such as *V. speciosa*, are common in temperate countries on ground containing considerable organic matter, such as stable manure and compost heaps.

---

3. Mushrooms with gills and a more or less centrally placed stalk; brown spore print

---

Agrocybe Species

The brown-spored *Agrocybe* species can be confused with *Agaricus* species, but they have a prominent, though thin, sometimes membranous ring on the stalk. The gills are a little paler than those found in *Agaricus* species and are attached to the stalk. In some species of *Agrocybe*, the gills may extend down the stalk a short distance. Many species are edible. The edible *Agrocybe praecox* is often found in pastures rich in animal waste, where its fruiting bodies might be confused with those of *Agaricus* species. Many species of *Agrocybe* occur on

Agrocybe parasitica. **EDIBILITY UNKNOWN: AVOID.** (Fowler)

wood, and some are parasites. *Agrocybe parasitica*, for example, is a parasite on trees and can often be found fruiting on decaying stumps. A few species of this genus have been cultivated and are becoming popular in parts of China.

Cortinarius Species

The many species in this genus have rust-brown spores and a cortina, which extends between the edge of the cap and the stalk on immature fruiting bodies. The remains of the cortina may be found on the stalk or along the margin of the cap on older fruiting bodies. Species of *Cortinarius* also often have a distinct bulb at the bottom of the stalk. Many have yellowish, orange-red, purplish, violet, or greenish stalks and flesh. Some species are edible, but *C. orellanus* is deadly poisonous, and the toxicity of many other species is unknown. The genus is therefore best avoided by the novice. Members of this group of mushrooms are ecologically important because they form ectomycorrhizal associations with their host trees. At times, especially in some high-latitude spruce (*Picea*) forests of the Northern Hemisphere, the fruiting bodies of *Cortinarius* are exceedingly common.

Young fruiting bodies of *Cortinarius*, with the cortina covering the gills of the cap on the left. **EDIBILITY UNKNOWN: AVOID.** (Hall)

Unidentified *Cortinarius* species. The discolored markings on the stalk of the largest mushroom represent all that remains of the cortina. **EDIBILITY UNKNOWN: AVOID.** (Hall)

Many species of *Cortinarius* are vividly colored. **EDIBILITY UNKNOWN: AVOID.** (Hall)

Galerina Species

Members of the genus *Galerina* have brownish, relatively small caps up to 7 cm in diameter, and brown spores. There can be a ring on the stalk, which tends to be scaly below the ring. *Galerina mutabilis* is considered edible and good (Phillips 1981). However, *G. autumnalis* contains amatoxins and is considered deadly poisonous. *A Colour Atlas of Poisonous Fungi* (Bresinsky and Besl 1990) lists a number of poisonous species of this genus, including *G. marginata* ("Dangerously poisonous fungus! Can be fatal!"). Of the three species listed in *The Audubon Society Field Guide to North American Mushrooms* (Lincoff and Nehring 1995), two are considered deadly. Some poisonous species have been confused with *Armillaria mellea* and other edible species. Because some poisonous species of *Galerina*, such as *G. unicolor*, are often found in damp grassy or mossy areas and a number of these can have a raised peak in the center of the cap, it is perhaps not surprising that they have been mistaken for species of *Psilocybe*.

Gymnopilus junonius (Big Laughing Gym)

The pale orange to orange-brown fruiting bodies of the big laughing gym can be found in late summer and early autumn in spectacular

Galerina fasciculata. **POISONOUS.** (Izawa)

Gymnopilus junonius (big laughing gym). **POISONOUS.** (Hall)

Hebeloma crustuliniforme (poison pie). **POISONOUS.** (Hall)

clusters on stumps and on soil containing rotting wood. The caps are up to 18 cm in diameter with a surface that is suedelike or covered with tiny scales. The gills are brown and often covered with a dusting of rusty brown spores. The stalks are somewhat lighter in color than the cap and are up to 20 cm high and 3 cm thick. There may be a ragged ring on the stalk or merely a darker zone where the veil was attached. The smell of this mushroom is not unpleasant, but it has a very bitter taste and so is unlikely to be consumed for its psilocybin content. Consumption may result in uncontrollable laughter, nausea, abdominal pain, convulsions, or death (Benjamin 1995, Craw 1995).

Hebeloma and *Inocybe* Species

Mushrooms belonging to the genera *Hebeloma* and *Inocybe* have ochre to brown spores, and most have no ring on the stalk. *Hebeloma crustuliniforme* (poison pie) and *H. sinapizans* have tan caps, light brown gills, whitish stalks, and are found associated with hardwoods and conifers in late summer and autumn. Both species smell strongly of radish and have a bitter taste. Many species of *Inocybe* have a small brown cap with a raised center and a variety of strange smells,

Inocybe fastigiata, one of the little brown mushrooms. **POISONOUS.** (Izawa)

including that of semen. The gills are grayish beige when young, turning darker brown with age. Although most are associated with hardwoods and conifers, some can be found in the grassy margins of paths and trails. Many *Hebeloma* and *Inocybe* species, including those referred to in *The Audubon Society Field Guide to North American Mushrooms* (Lincoff and Nehring 1995), are of unknown

Inocybe geophylla. **POISONOUS.** (Izawa)

An unidentified species of *Inocybe*. **POISONOUS.** (Hall)

edibility or are toxic due to their muscarine content. No European species are considered edible (Phillips 1981), many are poisonous, and *I. patouillardii* (red-staining inocybe) is potentially deadly.

Paxillus involutus (Brown Roll Rim)

Found in the Northern Hemisphere on deciduous trees such as beech (*Fagus*) and birch (*Betula*) in late summer and autumn, the brown roll rim has caps 5–12 cm in diameter on stalks up to 8 cm high. It can be identified by the strongly inward-rolled edge to the yellowish brown to mid brown cap, the concave often slimy center of the surface of the cap, the gills extending down the stalk, and the brown spores.

In many parts of the world the brown roll rim is considered safe to eat, although if not cooked properly it may cause severe gastric upsets within one or two hours of eating. It is suspected that people who have eaten the mushroom in the past without any apparent harmful effects may develop an allergy to it, which only shows up perhaps several years later (Bresinsky and Besl 1990). Because poisoning is an acquired allergic response to the brown roll rim, others who have eaten it at the same meal often appear to be completely unaffected.

Paxillus involutus (brown roll rim). **POISONOUS.** (Hall)

Symptoms include abdominal pain, vomiting, diarrhea, pain in the region of the kidneys, and kidney failure. Consumption of raw or poorly cooked brown roll rim can also lead to direct gastrointestinal symptoms (Southcott 1997). *Paxillus involutus* (brown roll rim) has been confused with *Lactarius deliciosus* (saffron milk cap). The other species in the genus are either not edible or are of unknown edibility. Consumption of *Paxillus* species is therefore best avoided.

Pholiota Species

Species of *Pholiota* are found in summer to late autumn at the bases of trees or on rotting stumps or logs, occasionally on living trees, or on burnt ground. The yellowish to light brown to brown caps, which can be up to 12 cm in diameter, may be very gelatinous, but many species have conspicuous scales on the edge or surface of the cap and/or stalk. Some species are very slimy, as with *P. nameko* (nameko). It is this textural characteristic, in addition to flavor, that makes nameko a favorite in Japan and other East Asian countries. While nameko is one of the ten most important cultivated mushrooms in the world, its characteristic sliminess also makes it unattractive to some in the West. While *P. adiposa* and a number of other species are eaten in

Pholiota adiposa (fat pholiota) displays the scaly cap and stalk characteristic of some members of the genus. **EDIBILITY UNKNOWN: AVOID.** (Hall)

China (Ying et al. 1988) and Japan (Imazeki et al. 1988), Roger Phillips (1981), author of *Mushrooms and Other Fungi of Great Britain and Europe*, variously lists the European species he illustrates as "edibility unknown," "not edible," or "edible—not worthwhile." *Pholiota high-landensis, P. limonella,* and *P. terrestris* are mildly toxic and may cause mild to moderate stomach upsets (Benjamin 1995, Imazeki et al. 1988).

Pholiota squarrosa (Scaly Pholiota)

One of the most distinctive and easily identified species in the genus *Pholiota* is *P. squarrosa*. Both the surface of the cap and the stalk are covered in coarse, red-brown or yellow-brown, down-turned scales. The convex to somewhat flattened cap is dry, yellow-brown, 2.5–10 cm in diameter, and has an incurved margin that usually contains fragments of the partial veil. The very similar species *P. squarrosoides* can be distinguished from *P. squarrosa* by virtue of having a cap with a sticky surface and more erect, pointed scales. The stalk of the scaly pholiota is 5–10 cm tall and 0.3–1.5 cm thick, tapering slightly toward the base. Like most other species of *Pholiota*, the scaly pholiota occurs on wood, from both broadleaf trees and conifers. The species is widely distributed throughout temperate regions of the Northern Hemisphere. *Pholiota squarrosa* has been regarded as edible by some people but can cause severe gastrointestinal discomfort and should therefore be avoided.

The clustered habit of *Pholiota squarrosa* (scaly pholiota) is characteristic of many species in this genus. **AVOID.** (Hall)

4. Mushrooms with gills and a more or less centrally placed stalk; purple-brown to black spore print

Agaricus arvensis (Horse Mushroom)

The large, excellent-tasting horse mushrooms, with caps 6–20 cm in diameter, are commonly found in pastures from late summer to late autumn, usually in clusters but sometimes in huge fairy rings. At first the mushrooms are white with a fine suedelike surface, and they have a shape similar to the button mushroom, although they are larger. As the caps open they become gently convex and creamy white, sometimes with yellowish patches. The stalks are up to 10 cm high and 3 cm thick, with a ring formed of two thin layers. The gills are pale grayish brown at first, turning pinkish brown and then chocolate-brown.

Agaricus campestris (Field Mushroom)

Field mushrooms are smaller than horse mushrooms, rarely reaching more than 10 cm in diameter, and have a smoother surface. They are common in pastures, as their name suggests, and are never associated

A fairy ring formed by *Agaricus arvensis* (horse mushroom). **EDIBLE.** (Hall)

Agaricus arvensis (horse mushroom). **EDIBLE.** (Wang)

with trees. The gills are pink both before and after the caps open, only turning brown when the caps are fully expanded. While the stalks may be slightly yellow toward the base, they do not stain chrome-yellow like the poisonous *Agaricus xanthoderma*.

Agaricus xanthoderma (Yellow Stainer) and *Agaricus pilatianus*

Agaricus xanthoderma and *A. pilatianus* have relatively large caps, up to 15 cm in diameter, with prominent rings on the stalks. The gills are white when young, becoming brownish with age. They therefore superficially resemble the common field mushroom (*A. campestris*), but both species are poisonous and should not be eaten. *Agaricus xanthoderma* can be easily distinguished because it stains bright yellow when bruised or cut, while *A. pilatianus* stains yellow only when young. Because both *A. xanthoderma* and *A. pilatianus* are similar to the edible species of *Agaricus*, they are a common cause of poisonings. The genus *Agaricus* contains a number of other toxic species, including the deadly poisonous *A. aurantioviolaceus*, which is found in tropical Africa (Walleyn and Rammeloo 1994).

Agaricus campestris (field mushroom) fruiting in a well-tended lawn. **EDIBLE.** (Hall)

Agaricus xanthoderma (yellow stainer). **POISONOUS.** (Hall)

Coprinus atramentarius (Common Ink Cap)

The light brown caps of the common ink cap are larger than those of the non-inky coprinus (*Coprinus disseminatus*); they are typically 3–7 cm high and 4–7 cm in diameter. The caps are borne on a white stalk 7–17 cm high, which can have the remains of a ring close to the base. This species is often found growing in unlikely places such as along roadsides and in waste areas where there is rotting wood in the soil. It also occurs in lawns. The caps are edible but must be cooked within a few hours of picking as they rapidly turn black and release the spores in a black liquid (which, incidentally, was used in the past as a substitute for ink). If consumed with alcohol or within twenty-four hours of having had any alcohol, the common ink cap will cause a period of extreme nausea, stomach cramps, and palpitations. These symptoms are so unpleasant that the mushroom has been used to cure alcoholics. In North America the scaly ink cap (*C. variegatus*) has similar effects if eaten with alcohol (Fischer and Bessette 1992), as does *C. africanus*, a species normally found growing on dung in tropical Africa (Walleyn and Rammeloo 1994).

Coprinus atramentarius (common ink cap) is unlikely to be confused with the shaggy ink cap. **DO NOT CONSUME WITH ALCOHOL.** (Lyon)

Coprinus comatus (Shaggy Ink Cap)

The shaggy ink cap is much larger than the common ink cap, occasionally reaching as much as 40 cm in height. The caps are cylindrical at first but eventually become bell-shaped. The gills are initially white, soon turning pink and then black. Once the gills are black, the bottom edge of the cap begins to drip a black liquid that contains the spores. Shaggy ink caps are usually found in waste areas and along roadsides during late summer to late autumn. Old caps do not look very appetizing but do have a good flavor, though they must be cooked within a few hours of picking. This mushroom is very widely distributed throughout the world, in part because it has been introduced into regions where it is not indigenous.

Coprinus disseminatus (Non-Inky Coprinus)

Most members of the genus *Coprinus* are characterized by fruiting bodies with gills that dissolve, producing an inky fluid, when the spores are mature. This process, called deliquescence, accounts for

Coprinus comatus (shaggy ink cap) just before the release of spores. **EDIBLE.** (Buchanan)

Coprinus comatus (shaggy ink cap) releasing spores in a black ink. **EDIBLE.** (Hall)

Coprinus disseminatus (non-inky coprinus). **EDIBLE.** (Izawa)

the name "ink cap." *Coprinus disseminatus* is an exception to this rule, as its gills do not become inky. The fruiting bodies occur in large groups (often several hundred in a single fruiting) on well-decayed stumps and other wood debris from broadleaf trees. The rather delicate pale buff to brownish gray caps are 0.5–1.5 cm in diameter, have a deeply grooved margin, and are ovoid at first but expand to become bell-shaped to convex. The stalk is 15–40 mm high and 1–3 mm thick. This mushroom is edible but not worth eating because of its small size.

Hypholoma fasciculare (Sulfur Tuft)

The bright yellow fruiting bodies of the sulfur tuft can be found throughout the year on fallen logs or stumps of deciduous trees. The caps are 2–8 cm in diameter, the stalks up to 10 cm high. The gills are sulfur yellow when young, becoming olive and finally brown. The remnants of the veil often remain attached to the edge of the cap. Although the sulfur tuft has a mushroomy smell, the taste is bitter. Symptoms of poisoning begin up to nine hours after consumption and include nausea, vomiting, and abdominal pain. Fatalities have been reported in Japan and Europe (Fischer and Bessette 1992), though the mushroom is described in *Mushrooms and Other Fungi of Great Britain and Europe* (Phillips 1981) as merely inedible.

Panaeolus foenisecii (Haymaker's Mushroom)

The fruiting bodies of *Panaeolus foenisecii* occur scattered or in small groups in lawns and other grassy areas. The species is often very common, especially in the Northern Hemisphere, and can be found from late spring to early autumn. The cap is 1–3 cm in diameter and occurs on a stalk that is 2.5–10 cm high and 1.5–3.0 mm thick, with no hint of a ring. More or less bell-shaped when young, the cap expands and becomes almost flat in fully mature fruiting bodies. The cap is at first reddish brown to grayish brown, usually fading to grayish tan, often with a dark band apparent near the margin. The gills are thin and grayish brown to tan, the spore print deep brown or purple-brown. Though small and thus easily overlooked, the haymaker's mushroom is potentially poisonous to a small child who is at the stage in which everything goes into the mouth. Instances have been reported of dogs consuming this fungus and showing evidence of its hallucinogenic properties.

Coprinus disseminatus (non-inky coprinus). **EDIBLE.** (Johnson)

Clustered fruiting bodies of *Hypholoma fasciculare* (sulfur tuft) at the base of a stump. **POISONOUS.** (Izawa)

Panaeolus foenisecii (haymaker's mushroom). **POISONOUS.** (Johnson)

Psathyrella candolleana (common psathyrella). **AVOID.** (Hall)

Psathyrella candolleana (Common Psathyrella)

Psathyrella is a large genus containing several hundred species, most of which are quite small and of unknown edibility. *Psathyrella candolleana* is often found in lawns or in areas where there is an abundance of decaying wood debris, such as under trees or on or near rotting stumps. The caps are 2–7 cm in diameter, the stalks 4–10 cm high. While some consider *P. candolleana* edible, its thin caps and fragile stalks might easily be confused with small, poisonous, dark brown-spored mushroom species, which makes its collection and consumption not worth the risk.

Psilocybe Species

The small, almost insignificant species of *Psilocybe* are perhaps as well recognized as *Amanita muscaria*. This is not because of their food value, which must be trivial, but because of the hallucinogenic LSD-like effects produced by eating them. These effects are caused by the tryptamine derivatives psilocybin and psilocin, which begin to take effect fifteen minutes to two hours after consumption and last for up to five

Psilocybe argentipes, one of the many hallucinogenic species in the genus. **POISONOUS.** (Izawa)

hours. Most species grow in grasslands or on rotting wood, dung, and compost where there is abundant organic matter (Stamets 1996).

Species of *Psilocybe* are little brown mushrooms. Consequently the novice in search of a hallucinogenic experience runs a very real danger of consuming other poisonous or possibly deadly little brown mushrooms of the genera *Clitocybe*, *Conocybe*, *Galerina*, and *Inocybe*, which occur in similar habitats. There are large amounts of popular literature available on hallucinogenic mushrooms—Web sites such as Psylocybe Fanaticus and The Vaults of Erowid, for example, and the book *Psilocybin Mushrooms of the World* (Stamets 1996)—but users should be aware of a country's laws governing their collection and use. Other hallucinogenic mushrooms containing tryptamine derivatives include *Copelandia cyanescens*, *Gymnopilus*

Psilocybe fasciata. **POISONOUS.** (Izawa)

The fruiting bodies of *Psilocybe semilanceata* (liberty cap) display the characteristic long stalks. **POISONOUS.** (Lyon)

The fruiting bodies of *Psilocybe subaeruginosa* (little blues), another member of the little brown mushrooms. **POISONOUS.** (Johnston)

The slimy caps and stems of *Stropharia aeruginosa* (blue-green stropharia) are characteristic of the genus. **POISONOUS.** (Hall)

junonius, *Panaeolus foenisecii* and other *Panaeolus* species, and some species of *Mycena*, *Psathyrella*, and *Stropharia* (Allen et al. 1991, Benjamin 1995, Beug 1999, Bresinsky and Besl 1990).

Stropharia aeruginosa (Blue-Green Stropharia)

Like most members of the genus, *Stropharia aeruginosa* has caps that are slimy when wet. These are blue-green, 2–8 cm in diameter, and dome-shaped when young, becoming flattened with age. The gills are white to begin with but turn purple or chocolate-brown. The stalks are 3–8 cm high, up to 1 cm thick, and may have a fragile ring that often disappears with age. This species is found during spring, summer, and early winter in a wide variety of habitats, including forests and pastures, particularly where there is abundant woody debris in the soil. While some species in the genus are edible, *S. aeruginosa* is poisonous.

---

5. Mushrooms with ear-shaped or bracket-like fruiting bodies; stalk either absent or poorly developed and attached to the edge of the cap; spores produced on gills, gill-like folds, or directly on the lower undifferentiated surface of the fruiting body

---

Lampteromyces japonicus

The fruiting bodies of *Lampteromyces japonicus* have caps very similar in appearance to those of shiitake (*Lentinula edodes*), but the former has a laterally attached stalk and the cap is rose-pink. Both species are found growing on decaying tree trunks. Along with *Entoloma rhodopolium* and *Tricholoma ustale* (burnt tricholoma), *Lampteromyces japonicus* shares the distinction of being one of the three most common causes of mushroom poisoning in Japan (Benjamin 1995, Imazeki et al. 1988). Like *Omphalotus*, the fruiting bodies are bioluminescent.

Omphalotus Species

Members of the genus *Omphalotus* share a most unusual feature not found among many other mushrooms: their gills glow in the dark. However, this bioluminescence can only be observed in fresh specimens in which the spores are still forming. The species found in Europe (*O. olearius*), North America (*O. olivascens* and *O. illudens*), and

Lampteromyces japonicus. **POISONOUS.** (Izawa)

The gills of the bioluminescent *Lampteromyces japonicus* glow in the dark. **POISONOUS.** (Buchanan)

Australia (*O. nidiformis*) all have gills that glow in the dark and share a common characteristic of fruiting in late summer and autumn. *Omphalotus olearius* is found on the roots of trees, particularly chestnut (*Castanea*), oak (*Quercus*), and olive (*Olea*), while *O. olivascens* and *O. illudens* typically occur on the dead stumps of hardwood trees or buried wood. In Australia *O. nidiformis* is common on *Eucalyptus* and other native trees as well as on stumps of exotic pines (*Pinus*).

 Omphalotus illudens, *O. olearius*, and *O. olivascens* (the jack-o'-lanterns) are sometimes confused with the honey mushroom (*Armillaria mellea*), which also occurs on dead stumps of hardwood trees. The cap of *O. illudens*, found in eastern North America, is 7–18 cm in diameter, and its gills extend down the upper portion of the stalk, which is 5–18 cm high. Because of their color and size, the jack-o'-lanterns are easily noticed in the forests in which they occur—a fact that undoubtedly increases the odds that an unsuspecting person will collect these mushrooms to eat. Poisoning from *Omphalotus* causes intestinal problems that begin a few hours after eating and that can last for up to two days.

Omphalotus nidiformis under *Pinus radiata* (Monterey pine) in Victoria, Australia. **POISONOUS.** (Fuhrer)

Omphalotus illudens (jack-o'-lantern). **POISONOUS.** (Johnson)

The fruiting bodies of *Omphalotus illudens*, *O. nidiformis*, *O. olearius*, and *O. olivascens* are shades of yellow or orange and are therefore somewhat suggestive of chanterelles. However, they all have clearly distinct gills and white or cream spores. The similarity of *O. nidiformis* to the edible *Pleurotus ostreatus* (oyster mushroom) has resulted in a number of poisonings, although the presence of bioluminescence in *Omphalotus* is a useful distinguishing feature (Southcott 1997).

Pleurotus ostreatus and Similar Species (Oyster Mushroom)

The fruiting bodies of *Pleurotus* are usually flattened, with the stalks attached either eccentrically or to one edge of the cap. They are found on dead or moribund trees or logs, usually in autumn, although *P. ostreatus* can be found at any time of the year. The spores can be lilac, gray, or white. Several species of *Pleurotus* are widely cultivated, with colors including white, gray, yellow, and pink, although cultivated mushrooms generally look rather different from their wild cousins.

Pleurotus cornucopiae var. *citrinopileatus* (golden oyster mushroom) fruiting in the wild. **EDIBLE.** (Wang)

Pleurotus ostreatus (oyster mushroom) fruiting in the wild. **EDIBLE.** (Lyon)

Schizophyllum commune (Common Split Gill)

The most distinctive characteristic of the common split gill, and the basis for its common name, is the presence of longitudinally split or grooved gills on the lower side of the cap. The white to gray cap is without a stalk, fan- or shell-shaped, 1–4 cm wide, and has an upper surface that is densely hairy. This mushroom typically occurs in small groups or rows on dead branches of various deciduous trees. It is one of the most widely distributed of all fungi and is found throughout the world. Unlike most other small shelflike or bracket-like fungi, which would seem too tough to be of any value as food, *Schizophyllum commune* is collected for human consumption over large areas of the African and Asian tropics. The fruiting bodies are often chewed uncooked or used in soups (Rammeloo and Walleyn 1993). This mushroom has also been reported to cure leukorrhea, to serve as a general tonic, and to have antitumor properties.

Pleurotus opuntiae (white oyster mushroom) fruiting on a dead cabbage tree (*Cordyline australis*).
EDIBLE. (Buchanan)

Schizophyllum commune (common split gill). **EDIBILITY UNKNOWN: AVOID.** (Izawa)

---

6. Mushrooms with more or less funnel-shaped fruiting bodies (or fruiting bodies triangular in cross section), with the spores formed on the outer surface, either on gill-like folds or simply on a rough surface

---

Cantharellus cibarius (Chanterelle)

The bright yellowish orange caps of the chanterelle are 2–10 cm in diameter and are borne on a tapered stalk 2–8 cm high and up to 3 cm thick at the top. At first the caps are dome-shaped with the margins rolled downward, but a depression develops in the center of the caps as they mature, and they eventually become funnel-shaped with a wavy margin. The gill-like folds are narrow, forked, egg-yellow, about 2 mm deep, and extend down the stalk some distance. The spores are buff to pale yellow.

Cantharellus cibarius is found throughout the temperate zones of Europe, North America, and Asia, from mid August to October beneath conifers and deciduous trees, in moist, shady situations, and often among mosses. It is not found in the Southern Hemisphere,

Cantharellus cibarius (chanterelle). **EDIBLE.** (Hall)

though there are similar species in South American and Australasian native forests. The bright color, characteristic shape, and apricot-like smell of the chanterelle make it difficult to mistake. However, the false chanterelle (*Hygrophoropsis aurantiaca*) might confuse a novice.

The chanterelle's smell, peppery taste, and excellent keeping qualities give it a popularity rivaled only by porcini (*Boletus edulis*). Although it can be bottled and canned, much of its flavor and firm texture is lost as a result of these procedures. If dried using a kitchen desiccator or threaded onto a piece of string and hung up to dry, its flavor is retained and concentrated. Like porcini, it can then be used to flavor soups and stews during the winter months.

The chanterelle is currently the mycorrhizal mushroom most in demand in Europe and North America. During July and August chanterelles are imported from North America, but later in the year they are imported from Europe. While fresh chanterelles are preferred by the retail market and by the manufacturer because they make a "slightly better product," the demand for convenient, prepared, cooked foods (for example, chanterelle pizzas) means that there is a steady demand for cheaper chanterelles that are dried or pickled in brine. In Scotland and Northern England an experienced picker can earn about $3000 per week collecting chanterelles at the height of the fruiting season.

The volume of chanterelles consumed is difficult to estimate, again because of the large quantities consumed or traded outside markets where official records are kept. However, it has been estimated that world consumption is about 200,000 tons per year, which would be worth $1.62 billion (Baker 1997). Typical wholesale prices in the United States are $30 to $38 per kilogram (Anonymous 2000a), while in 1996 at the Markthalle in Innsbruck, Austria, fully expanded broken chanterelles sold for 160 to 190 Austrian schillings ($9 to $12) per kilogram. In previous years in Europe prices were much higher when demand exceeded supply.

Although the chanterelle has never been cultivated, recent work in Sweden and the United States (Danell 1994, Danell and Camacho 1997) has resulted in a technique for infecting plants with the fungus. Small numbers of fruiting bodies have been produced on experimental plants in greenhouses. Whether or not this technique can be scaled up is not yet known. If it can, plantations will be established with infected trees, making it possible to produce chanterelles where they cannot be produced at the moment, such as in Southern Hemisphere countries for out-of-season Northern Hemisphere markets.

Hygrophoropsis aurantiaca (false chanterelle). **POISONOUS.** (Izawa)

Hygrophoropsis aurantiaca (False Chanterelle)

Like the chanterelle, the false chanterelle is funnel-shaped and yellow to orange, with yellow to yellowish brown gills that extend down the stalk. The cap is 2–8 cm in diameter, and the stalk is 3–5 cm high and up to 1 cm thick. The false chanterelle can be distinguished from the chanterelle by the strongly in-rolled margin of its cap, which is similar to that of *Paxillus involutus*, combined with its lack of the chanterelle's characteristic apricot-like smell, its lack of flavor, and its white spores. Although the false chanterelle is said to be edible, some people experience hallucinations after eating it (Phillips 1981).

Gomphus floccosus (Scaly Vase Chanterelle)

A native of North America, the scaly vase chanterelle differs from the true chanterelle in having quite distinctive scales on the surface of its funnel-shaped, orange cap. This mushroom is found fruiting in hardwood and conifer forests from early summer to autumn. It is 5–13 cm in diameter and 5–18 cm high. Although some can eat this mushroom without ill effects, others suffer intestinal pain, nausea, and diarrhea.

Gomphus floccosus (scaly vase chanterelle). **POISONOUS.** (Izawa)

Craterellus cornucopioides (Horn of Plenty)

In France the horn of plenty is known as *trompette de la mort* ("the trumpet of death"). But though its dry, dark brown, funnel-shaped caps look anything but appetizing, this mushroom is simply an edible delicacy in disguise. The dark color of the caps also makes the horn of plenty particularly difficult to see against a background of decaying leaves on the forest floor. The caps are 2–8 cm in diameter and 4–12 cm high. These mushrooms are often found growing in clusters under hardwoods and conifers from late summer to early winter. The white spores are formed on the outside of the funnel, and, unlike many other basidiomycetes, there are no gills, spines, or tubes. At first the outer surface of the funnel is black, but it becomes grayish as the spores begin to form. *Craterellus fallax*, a very similar species found in eastern North America, has spores that are pale yellow to salmon.

Craterellus cornucopioides (horn of plenty). **EDIBLE.** (Izawa)

7. Mushrooms with a central, well-developed stalk supporting the cap and no gills but with many tubes present that give the underside of the cap a spongelike appearance—boletes

As a group, the boletes are usually rather easy to recognize because of the spongelike appearance of the lower surface of the cap, which is due to the presence of numerous pores that make up the mouths of tubes. The spores are produced on the inner walls of these tubes.

Austroboletus betula (Shaggy-Stalked Bolete)

One bolete that is unlikely to be confused with any other species is the shaggy-stalked bolete, *Austroboletus betula*. This very distinctive mushroom is easily recognized by the combination of a smooth, somewhat slimy, apricot-yellow cap and a long, shaggy, yellow to reddish yellow stalk. The convex cap is 3–9 cm in diameter, and the pore surface is yellow to greenish yellow. The stalk is 10–20 cm long, 0.5–2.0 cm thick, and has a coarsely reticulate to shaggy surface with

Austroboletus betula (shaggy-stalked bolete). **EDIBLE.** (Johnson)

raised yellow ridges that may redden with age. Solitary to scattered fruiting bodies of the shaggy-stalked bolete occur on the ground in mixed oak and pine (*Quercus* and *Pinus*) forests and beech (*Fagus*) forests throughout eastern North America (Bessette et al. 2000). This mushroom is considered edible.

Boletus edulis (Porcini)

The characteristic features of the five or so species that make up the *Boletus edulis* species complex are a spongelike covering (consisting of many tiny tubes) instead of gills on the lower side of the cap; a very fat stalk that, when young, can be wider than the cap itself; a raised network covering the stalk; and an absence of the black scales that are characteristic of the birch boletes and other species of *Leccinum*. Some fungal taxonomists divide *B. edulis* into a number of subspecies or separate taxa including *B. aereus*, *B. aestivalis*, *B. edulis*, *B. pinicola*, and *B. reticulatus*. None of these can readily be confused with any poisonous species, but care should still be taken when identifying porcini. When the cap opens out, it can be as much as 20 cm in diameter. However, an illustration in *The Mycologist* shows a 3.2-kg

Young *Boletus edulis* (porcini) from Christchurch, New Zealand. **EDIBLE.** (Hall)

The network on the stalk of *Boletus edulis* (porcini) is a characteristic feature of *Boletus* species.
(Hall)

Old *Boletus edulis* (porcini), each weighing about 500 g. **EDIBLE.** (Hall)

monster collected in the United Kingdom in 1995 with a cap 42 cm in diameter and a stalk 18 cm high and 14 cm across (Kozikowski 1996).

Porcini is found throughout North America up to 3500 m in the Rocky Mountains, continental Europe, Asia, and from the coolest parts of Scandinavia to as far south as Mexico and Morocco. It is also one of the few edible mycorrhizal mushrooms to reach the Southern Hemisphere, where it is found growing on various species of pine in the Southern Natal Midlands of South Africa (Eicker 1990, Marais and Kotzé 1977) and on oak (*Quercus*), beech (*Fagus*), birch (*Betula*), and lime (*Tilia*) trees around Christchurch, New Zealand (Wang et al. 1995). Almost all boletes form ectomycorrhizal associations with host trees.

What makes porcini so popular is its powerful mushroomy taste, which is retained even after drying. It can be picked in autumn and, if necessary, sliced or cubed, dried, and stored to flavor dishes in winter. A few reconstituted slices can enliven any dish of store-bought mushrooms. Its flavor is also retained after cooking at high temperatures in pressure cookers and during bottling or canning. Porcini is therefore in great demand by soup and stew manufacturers. It is very difficult to make reliable estimates of how much porcini is consumed around the world, but official figures for 1988 show that about 3000 tons passed

Boletus subvelutipes (red-mouth bolete) stained blue where the cap has been cut. **POISONOUS.**

through the marketplaces of France, Italy, and Germany. Nevertheless, actual consumption is much, much higher than this because of informal trade and consumption by collectors. It has been estimated that between 20,000 and 100,000 tons are eaten (Hall, Lyon et al. 1998) annually worldwide. During autumn in the Northern Hemisphere prices range from $20 to $80 per kilogram. However, in New York during 1997 rare fruiting bodies harvested in spring had a wholesale price of $218 to $231 per kilogram (Anonymous 2000a).

Many species of *Boletus* are edible—or if not edible, they have an unpleasant flavor and are not dangerous. However, a dozen or so species are poisonous, and *B. satanas* (devil's bolete) is possibly lethal. It is therefore necessary to learn the characteristics of edible species and how these differ from poisonous ones.

Poisonous *Boletus* Species

Boletus calopus, B. haematinus, B. legaliae, B. luridus, B. pulcherrimus, B. pulverulentus, B. purpureus, B. rhodoxanthus, B. satanas, B. satanoides, B. sensibilis, and *B. subvelutipes* are all poisonous boletes, *B. satanas* (devil's bolete) being possibly deadly (Benjamin

1995, Imazeki et al. 1988, Lincoff and Nehring 1995, Phillips 1981). While it would be difficult to confuse these species with the edible boletes, care is still needed. These poisonous species are orange or red on the underside of the cap and/or stain blue when bruised or cut. Boletes with these characteristics should not be eaten.

Red-mouth bolete (*Boletus subvelutipes*) is a typical member of the group of poisonous boletes. It is fairly common in eastern and central North America, where it occurs in hardwood as well as in coniferous forests (Bessette et al. 2000). Fruiting bodies have a cap that is 6–13 cm in diameter and yellowish brown to brown or reddish brown. The stalk is 3–10 cm high and 1–2 cm thick, and mature specimens often have short, thick, dark red hairs at the base.

Boletus pseudosensibilis

Boletus pseudosensibilis is an edible bolete that might be confused with the poisonous species because its fruiting body stains blue when bruised or cut, a feature of many poisonous boletes. However, the underside of the cap in this mushroom is yellow to ochre-yellow when young and olive-ochre in mature specimens, not the orange or red

These *Boletus pseudosensibilis* exhibit blue stains, a characteristic of poisonous species in the genus. **AVOID.** (Johnson)

associated with most of the poisonous boletes. Nevertheless, *B. pseudosensibilis*, which appears to be most common in northeastern North America (Bessette et al. 2000), is best considered unfit for human consumption in order to avoid any chance of an unfortunate mistake.

Leccinum scabrum (Brown Birch Bolete)

As the common name implies, the brown birch bolete forms mycorrhizal associations with birch and can be found from midsummer to late autumn. The caps are 5–10 cm in diameter, pale to dark gray-brown, suedelike when dry, and somewhat sticky when wet. The tubes on the underside of the caps are off-white to pale gray and turn brown when bruised. The stalk is 6–12 cm high, white to off-white, covered with small black scales, and tapers toward the attachment to the cap. Although the smell of the brown birch bolete is pleasant, it is described in *Mushrooms and Other Fungi of Great Britain and Europe* (Phillips 1981) as edible but not worthwhile—an opinion not shared by all. Despite this, the brown birch bolete is not as good as porcini (*Boletus edulis*), although a number of inexperienced chefs have confused the two species.

The dark scales on the stalk of *Leccinum scabrum* (brown birch bolete) readily distinguish it from *Boletus edulis*. **EDIBLE.** (Hall)

Leccinum versipelle (orange birch bolete) with the typical dark scales on the stalk. **EDIBLE.** (Izawa)

Leccinum versipelle (Orange Birch Bolete)

The easily detected dull orange fruiting bodies of the orange birch bolete are common in summer and autumn throughout Europe under birch (*Betula*) or in mixed woodlands containing birch. The caps are 8–20 cm in diameter, dry at the surface, and, when young, slightly downy. The stalks are up to 20 cm high, up to 4 cm thick, usually swollen toward the base, white to grayish, and instead of having a raised network on the stalk like some species of *Boletus*, are covered in almost black scales. The tubes are small and off-white when young, becoming gray, while the spores are brown. When cut, the flesh is at first white to off-white and gradually turns gray-blue, particularly toward the base of the stalk.

Leccinum aurantiacum (Orange-Capped Bolete)

Leccinum aurantiacum, a species common in North America, is rather similar in appearance to *L. versipelle*, but the flesh turns burgundy and then changes to gray or purplish black. The rusty red to orange-red caps of *L. aurantiacum* are 5–20 cm in diameter and

Leccinum aurantiacum (orange-capped bolete). **EDIBLE.** (Roody)

rounded to broadly convex at first but flattened in older specimens. The stalk is 10–16 cm high and 2–3 cm thick, with the base slightly larger than the apex. This mushroom occurs scattered or in clusters under aspen (*Populus*) and pine (*Pinus*) throughout central and northern North America. While no species of *Leccinum* are outstandingly flavorsome, this species is among the best. There are apparently no references to poisonous species in this genus.

Phylloporus rhodoxanthus (Gilled Bolete)

In some boletes the pores are arranged in rows that radiate outward from the stalk, thus giving the lower surface of the cap a somewhat gill-like appearance. The most extreme expression of this condition is found in the genus *Phylloporus*, in which the greatly elongated pores are truly gill-like (in fact the name of the genus literally means "gill-like pores") (Bissette et al. 2000). *Phylloporus rhodoxanthus* occurs throughout eastern North America as scattered fruiting bodies or in groups on the ground in broadleaf forests under beech (*Fagus*) and oak (*Quercus*). The cap is 2.5–10 cm wide, obtuse to convex at first but becoming flattened, and ranges from dark red to reddish brown

Phylloporus rhodoxanthus (gilled bolete). **EDIBLE.** (Izawa)

or olive-green. The stalk is 3–9 cm high, 3–14 mm thick, and widest at the apex, tapering slightly toward the base. This is an edible mushroom and is considered good by some (Miller 1981).

Strobilomyces floccopus (Old Man of the Woods)

One of the more distinctive mushrooms you are likely to encounter in the forests of eastern North America is *Strobilomyces floccopus*, the old man of the woods. In this species both the cap and stalk are woolly to scaly. The cushion-shaped to somewhat flattened cap, which is 4–15 cm in diameter, is grayish black and has a ragged margin. The stalk, which is similar in color to the cap, is 5–12 cm high and 1.5–2.5 cm thick, sometimes with a slightly enlarged base. The old man of the woods is found in hardwood and mixed hardwood and pine (*Pinus*) forests. It is edible when young but not particularly flavorsome. One unusual feature of this mushroom is that it does not decay as readily as most other mushrooms, and old fruiting bodies can be found well beyond the usual fruiting season. *Strobilomyces confusus* is a morphologically very similar species also found in eastern North America. Fruiting bodies are slightly smaller than those of *S. floccopus*, and the warts and scales on the surface of the cap are firm and erect. In *S. floccopus*, the warts and scales feel soft and woolly.

Suillus grevillei (Larch Bolete)

The shiny or slimy orange to bright yellow fruiting bodies of the larch bolete can be found under larch (*Larix*) from midsummer to late autumn. The caps are 3–12 cm in diameter, and the stalks are 4–8 cm high and up to 2 cm thick. As with most species of *Suillus*, a ring is present on the stalk. The tubes are pale yellow and narrow. The larch bolete is edible, but the slimy surface of the cap should be peeled off before cooking.

Suillus luteus (Slippery Jack)

Fruiting in autumn, particularly under pines (*Pinus*), slippery jack is difficult to confuse with any other mushrooms. The caps are 6–15 cm in diameter, chestnut-brown to dark brown, and very slimy when wet. On drying they become shiny. The stalks are 4–10 cm high and each has a prominent ring. The portion of the stalk above the ring is rough. At first the portion of stalk below the ring is white or creamy white to

Strobilomyces floccopus (old man of the woods). **EDIBLE.** (Izawa)

Suillus grevillei (larch bolete). **EDIBLE.** (Hall

Suillus luteus (slippery jack). **EDIBLE.** (Hall)

light brown, but this soon becomes stained mid to dark brown. There are no references to poisonous species of *Suillus*, but it is known that some contain laxatives (Benjamin 1995). A Russian chef once told Ian Hall that slippery jack is very popular in Russia and quite good to eat with lemon and garlic, though the texture is rather slimy. When asked what it tastes like, the chef replied, "Lemon and garlic." If this mushroom is to be eaten, many say it is better to remove the tubes first.

Tylopilus felleus (Bitter Bolete)

Tylopilus felleus is occasionally confused with *Boletus edulis*, but the reticulation on the stalk is brown in the bitter bolete and white in porcini. In addition, the underside of the cap of the bitter bolete is pink when mature. As its common name suggests, *T. felleus* has a very bitter taste even after cooking. The cap of this mushroom is 5–30 cm in diameter and rounded to convex at first but becoming broadly convex to flat. The cap is pinkish to reddish purple when young but turns brown, buff, or tan with age. The stalks are 4–20 cm high, 1–3 cm thick, and the lower portion becomes somewhat enlarged, although not to the extent

The brown network on the stalk of *Tylopilus felleus* (bitter bolete) distinguishes it from *Boletus edulis* (figure 180). **EDIBILITY UNKNOWN: AVOID.** (Johnson)

found in porcini. Fruiting bodies of the bitter bolete can be found from early summer until autumn throughout eastern North America. The species typically occurs in forests with at least some conifers present. Although not poisonous, this mushroom is best considered inedible because of its bitter taste.

Xerocomus badius (Bay Bolete)

The fruiting bodies of the bay bolete have the smell of button mushrooms (*Agaricus bisporus*). They are found in autumn, and the cap is about the color of a horse chestnut seed. The caps are 4–15 cm in diameter and have a soft suedelike surface when young, but the mature caps are sticky when wet and shiny when dry. The stalks are 5–13 cm high and have a downy patterned surface rather than a raised network like some species of *Boletus*. There is no ring. The tubes are pale cream at first, becoming pale lemon-yellow, and will rapidly bruise a dark blue-green. Great care needs to be taken to distinguish the edible bay bolete from toxic boletes that also stain blue-green when bruised, although these usually have red caps or tubes.

Xerocomus chrysenteron (Red-Cracked Bolete)

Red-cracked bolete is found associated with hardwood trees, particularly oak (*Quercus*), in autumn. Caps are 4–12 cm in diameter and are

Xerocomus badius (bay bolete). **EDIBLE.** (Lyon)

Xerocomus chrysenteron (red-cracked bolete). **EDIBLE.** (Hall)

a dull brown or sepia. When young the surface of the cap has a suede-like feel, but eventually it becomes cracked and stained red within the cracks. The stalk is 4–8 cm high, lemon-yellow at the top and red below, and often has a light brown base. The tubes are large and angular, lemon-yellow when young but becoming tinged slightly green with age, and bruise bluish green. While edible, red-cracked bolete has a poor flavor and a rather mushy texture after cooking. Care needs to be taken to ensure that this mushroom is not confused with poisonous boletes that have red tubes or that stain blue when bruised.

8. Mushrooms with an undersurface devoid of gills or tubes but with minute spines or elongated, toothlike structures

Hydnum repandum (Hedgehog Mushroom)

The hedgehog mushroom is easily recognized by the small spines that hang vertically from the lower side of the creamy or creamy yellow caps. Fruiting bodies are found on the ground, associated with both hardwoods and conifers, in late summer and autumn. The stalks are short and stout, 3–8 cm high and up to 4 cm thick. The caps are 3–17 cm in diameter with off-white to cream to salmon-pink spines.

Hydnum repandum (hedgehog mushroom). **EDIBLE.** (Izawa)

The caps have a pleasant smell, and although the taste of older specimens is somewhat bitter, the hedgehog mushroom is considered an
excellent edible mushroom in Europe. The French name for this species
is particularly descriptive: *pied de mouton*, meaning "sheep's foot."

Sarcodon imbricatum (Scaly Tooth)

As with *Hydnum repandum*, the large, cracked, conspicuously scaly,
mottled brown caps of the scaly tooth have spines hanging vertically
from their lower surface. At first the spines are off-white, but they
gradually turn brown with age. The caps are 5–20 cm in diameter, the
stalks 5–8 cm high and up to 5 cm thick. The scaly tooth is found
under conifers in autumn and is considered edible, though it can have
a slightly bitter taste.

Hericium Species

Lion's mane (*Hericium erinaceus*), coral tooth (*H. coralloides*), and
comb tooth (*H. ramosum*) mushrooms occur on both the dead wood
and living trunks of broadleaf trees, whereas the conifer coral tooth
mushroom (*H. abietis*) is found on conifers. These are among the
most distinctive of all mushrooms and are not likely to be confused

Sarcodon imbricatum (scaly tooth) growing under conifers in the Austrian Alps. **EDIBLE.** (Hall)

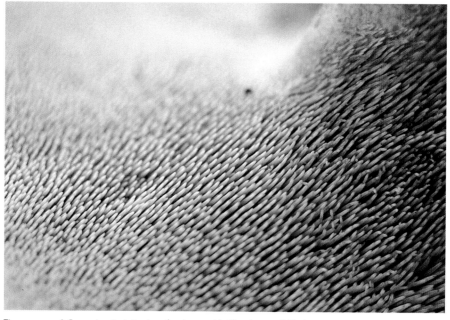

The spores of *Sarcodon imbricatum* (scaly tooth), like those of *Hydnum repandum*, are formed on fine spines that cover the undersurface of the cap. **EDIBLE.** (Hall)

Hericium clathroides (fungus icicles). **EDIBLE.** (Izawa)

with members of any other group. All are very good to eat. *Hericium clathroides* (fungus icicles) is a species very similar to *H. abietis*.

---

9. Mushrooms with a distinct stalk, a conical or spherical honeycomb-like top, or a folded piece of suedelike material on top of a grooved stalk

---

Morchella Species (Morels)

Mushroom connoisseurs consider morels to be among the finest of edible mushrooms, and in certain parts of the world they are much sought after in spring when they appear. They have been likened to a "sponge on a stalk," but this belies their gastronomic delights. In North America, morels may be found in great abundance, especially in the first spring following a forest fire. They can be found in grassy areas, gravel bars along rivers, woodlands, gardens, even the ashes of a barbecue pit (Chang and Hayes 1978). Morels are sporadic and unpredictable—Ian Hall saw his first morels in the 1960s but has not seen them in the same area since.

Morchella esculenta, a yellow morel. **EDIBLE.** (Wang)

Morels are always found on the ground, either alone or in small groups. Unlike most edible mushrooms, morels (as well as truffles) belong to the Ascomycetes. Their reproductive spores, called ascospores, are contained in asci lining the hollows of the sculptured, coarsely honeycomb-like caps of the fruiting body. The fruiting body is hollow from the base of the stalk to the top of the cap, and the spore print, which can be difficult to obtain because of the shape of the caps, is white, cream, or pale yellow.

The fruiting bodies of *Morchella esculenta*, a yellow morel, are some 6–20 cm in height and have a round to oval cap. The cap is yellowish cream to light brown and consists of deep, irregular, angular pits bordered by acute ridges. The base of the cap is joined to a whitish to cream stalk that is generally smooth but may be slightly grooved. The base of the stalk is usually slightly swollen at soil level.

Morchella elata and *M. conica*, two of the black morels, grow to about 10 cm high and have caps that are at first sooty brown but become dark, almost black, with age. The caps are more conical than those of *M. esculenta* and have ridges aligned vertically that tend to be more or less parallel. The cap is supported by a hollow white to cream stalk that is unevenly ribbed and coated with small wartlike

Morchella semilibera (half-free morel), a black morel. **EDIBLE.** (Cole)

granules. Like the yellow morels, the black morels are a highly variable group, and it is often difficult to distinguish species.

Although there is evidence to suggest that some morels may form mycorrhizal associations (Buscot and Kotte 1990), in the mid 1980s the Neogen Foundation in the United States developed a technique to cultivate them (Anonymous 1997, Beauséjour 2000, Ower 1988, Stamets 1993). The current owner of the technique plans to increase production to meet the huge demand for morels. However, it has been reported that these cultivated morels are not as pleasant to eat as their wild cousins (Coombs 1994).

Of the morels, *Morchella esculenta* would take the prize in terms of edibility, but all are considered good eating. If you are so lucky as to find a profusion of fruiting bodies and it is your first encounter, go easy on the amount eaten, as there is always the possibility that you might prove to be allergic. The black morel has also been accused of causing stomach distress when consumed with alcohol (Benjamin 1995, Harding et al. 1996). It is said that morels should not be eaten raw, and blanching for a minute or two before cooking is also recommended. Old morels showing signs of decay should not be eaten, as they may be poisonous (Harding et al. 1996). Because these mushrooms are easy to recognize, the danger of picking a poisonous look-alike is not great. Care, however, should be taken to avoid picking the poisonous false morel (*Gyromitra esculenta*), which at first sight could be mistaken for a true morel.

Morels dry well. The method traditionally used involves threading the caps onto string and hanging them in the sun. As with porcini, the flavor is concentrated in the process. Typical wholesale prices for fresh morels in spring in the Northern Hemisphere are $5 to $20 per kilogram (Anonymous 1997, Rowe 1997). Dried morels can command a price of $600 per kilogram or more in Swiss retail stores.

Verpa bohemica (Wrinkled Thimble Cap)

The fruiting body of the wrinkled thimble cap has a shape similar to that of a morel (*Morchella*). However, the cap of the former is attached to the stalk only at the very top, whereas in morels more than just the top of the cap is attached. In North America the wrinkled thimble cap fruits in mixed and hardwood forests during spring, often appearing before the true morels. The cap is 1–5 cm in diameter and 1–5 cm high, thimble- to bell-shaped, and pale to dark yellow-brown or tan, becoming darker with age. The stalk is 6–15 cm high

Verpa bohemica (wrinkled thimble cap). **POISONOUS.** (Johnson)

and 0.8–3 cm thick. Like *Gyromitra*, specimens of the wrinkled thimble cap must be boiled and the water discarded before eating. Some people tolerate this mushroom, but it is poisonous to others, producing intestinal upsets and uncoordinated movement. As such, it is hardly worth considering for the table.

Gyromitra esculenta (False Morel)

Like the true morels (*Morchella* spp.), the false morel is an ascomycete and can be found in spring in coniferous forests. The cap is more brainlike than that of a morel. It has wrinkles and folds, is not honeycomb-like, and lacks true pits. If you slice the cap of a false morel from top to bottom, you will find it to be multichambered, unlike the true morel, which has a single hollow chamber continuous with the stalk. Some false morels (*Gyromitra* spp.) do not resemble true morels as much as *G. esculenta*. For example, the hooded false morel (*G. infula*), which is common throughout North America, derives another common name, saddle-shaped false morel, from its characteristic saddle-shaped to three-lobed cap.

Gyromitra esculenta (false morel). **POISONOUS.** (Buchanan)

Gyromitra infula (hooded false morel) showing the characteristic cap. **POISONOUS.** (Cole)

The fruiting body of *Dictyophora duplicata* (netted stinkhorn) hatches from an egg. The base of the bell-shaped cap is encircled by a white, skirtlike, netted veil. **MEDICINAL.** (Johnson)

Despite its name (*esculenta* means "edible"), the false morel is deadly poisonous unless cooked and causes poisoning in some individuals even after cooking. Even so, it remains a popular mushroom in parts of Europe, with about 100 tons passing through the Finnish markets each year (Bresinsky and Besl 1990). Cooking involves boiling the mushrooms twice, discarding the water after each boil, before incorporating them into a dish. However, care must be taken when cooking, because the toxins are volatile and it is possible to be poisoned by breathing the fumes produced during boiling.

Dictyophora duplicata (Netted Stinkhorn)

The fruiting bodies of the netted stinkhorn (*Dictyophora duplicata*) and the bamboo mushroom (*D. indusiata*) have the same general form as those of the common stinkhorn (*Phallus impudicus*), but the base of the bell-shaped cap in both *Dictyophora* species is encircled by a white, netlike, flaring veil.

When mature, with the veil fully expanded, the netted stinkhorn is not likely to be confused with any other mushroom. A mature fruiting body is 15–25 cm high, with the cap, usually 3–4 wide and 4–5 cm long, representing approximately a third of the total height. The netted stinkhorn is occasionally found fruiting on the ground under hardwoods in the forests of eastern North America. However, most species of *Dictyophora* are limited to the tropics, and members of the group are not uncommon in tropical forests such as those of Central and South America. Fruiting bodies typically occur on areas of the forest floor rich in humus or with accumulations of well-decayed wood, and are most likely to be encountered during periods of rainy weather. Although these mushrooms are not poisonous, most people would not consider them suitable for the table. However, *D. duplicata* and *D. indusiata* are sometimes consumed for medicinal reasons: both contain an active agent that is reputed to lower blood pressure and reduce body fat.

Mutinus caninus (Dog Stinkhorn)

Unlike the common stinkhorn (*Phallus impudicus*) and the netted stinkhorn (*Dictyophora duplicata*), the dog stinkhorn (*Mutinus caninus*) does not have a clearly defined head (as the caps of stinkhorns are usually called). Instead, the mature fruiting body consists of a single white to pale yellow-buff to orange-red stalklike structure that

Mutinus caninus (dog stinkhorn). **EDIBILITY UNKNOWN: AVOID.** (Johnson)

Immature fruiting bodies of the dog stinkhorn (*Mutinus caninus*) inside the eggs. **EDIBILITY UNKNOWN: AVOID.** (Johnson)

extends upward from a white pouch (the ruptured egg) and tapers almost to a point at its apex. The entire structure is 10–18 cm high and 1.5–2.5 cm thick, the upper portion covered with the slimy, olive-brown, foul-smelling spore mass. The dog stinkhorn is encountered occasionally in forests, gardens, and waste areas in eastern North America and Europe. *Mutinus elegans* is a very similar species but can be distinguished by its taller fruiting body, which has a relatively larger area covered by the spore mass. Moreover, the portion of the fruiting body below the spore mass is pitted in *M. caninus* and pebbly in *M. elegans*. Both *M. caninus* and *M. elegans* are apparently nonpoisonous, but few people would have the stomach to eat them.

Phallus impudicus (Common Stinkhorn)

A pleasant summer stroll through a forest in Europe or eastern North America can be quickly interrupted if you come across a group of stinkhorns: the smell is truly disgusting. When fully expanded, the fruiting bodies are up to 25 cm tall and 6 cm thick. The entire fruiting body expands out of an egg 4–6 cm in diameter and is in this respect similar to the basket fungus (*Ileodictyon cibarium*). The upper portion of the fruiting body is represented by a clearly defined head

Mature fruiting bodies of *Phallus impudicus* (common stinkhorn), with the remains of the egg from which they have emerged just showing above the ground. **EDIBILITY UNKNOWN: AVOID.** (Wang)

that is covered with a fetid, slimy, olive-green spore mass. While the common stinkhorn is edible before it has expanded out of the egg stage, disassociating the mild taste from the smell of a mature fruiting body would presumably take some effort. Flies, however, are attracted by the smell and sometimes cover the fruiting bodies. Spores then adhere to the flies and are carried away with them, which aids in the dispersal of the fungus. While the stinkhorns superficially resemble morels (*Morchella* spp.), the smell of a stinkhorn would make confusing the two virtually impossible.

Podaxis pistillaris (Stalked Puffball)

The stalked puffball is not uncommon in the Hawaiian Islands and Australia, where it can be found in drier, disturbed areas such as along roadsides. The common name might suggest this species is related to the giant puffball (*Calvatia gigantea*), but it is actually more closely related to the shaggy ink cap (*Coprinus comatus*) (Hopple and Vilgalys 1994). The edibility of the stalked puffball is unknown, but the fact that it is used by Australian Aborigines to dye white hair and ward off flies suggests it might be less than palatable.

Podaxis pistillaris (stalked puffball). **EDIBILITY UNKNOWN: AVOID.** (Hemmes)

Helvella crispa (white helvella). **EDIBLE.** (Lyon)

Helvella Species

Species of *Helvella* have a fruiting body that somewhat resembles a crumpled sheet of velvet on top of a grooved stalk. Like the true and false morels (*Morchella* spp. and *Gyromitra* spp.), they are ascomycetes, with spores produced on the velvet-like surface of the cap. The white *H. crispa* and black *H. lacunosa* are edible, but the edibility of some species is unknown. Although it is possible to confuse fruiting bodies of *Helvella* with those of the false morel, species of *Helvella* normally fruit in autumn, while the morels and false morels fruit in spring. They are usually found in wooded areas.

10. Mushrooms with pulvinate to spherical fruiting bodies that are parasitic on living plants

Cyttaria Species

Cyttaria is a genus of mushrooms that are parasitic on certain species of *Nothofagus* (the southern beeches of, for example, southern South America, Australia, and New Zealand). These fungi attack the fine

Cyttaria gunnii (beech strawberry), a parasite of the fine branches of a southern beech (*Nothofagus menziesii*). **EDIBLE.** (Forest Research, New Zealand)

branches of beech trees, eventually producing galls of deformed host tissue upon which clusters of fruiting bodies develop. The fruiting bodies are soft, yellowish orange, spherical, 1–3 cm in diameter, and superficially similar to the cap of a morel. *Cyttaria espinosae* is eaten in South America, where the production of fruiting bodies in suitable areas has been estimated to be 80–90 kg per hectare (Gamundí 1991, Gamundí and Horak 1995). *Cyttaria gunnii* (beech strawberry) is a traditional food of Australian Aborigines in southern Victoria and Tasmania (Kalotas 1997) and may have been eaten by Maori in New Zealand.

Uromyces digitatus

Most rusts form the powdery yellow, brown, or reddish lesions often found on cereals and other grasses. Some species, however, such as *Uromyces digitatus*, form galls on the ends of branches. Although formation of the gall is triggered by the fungus, most of the internal tissue is of plant origin.

Uromyces digitatus forming a gall on a wattle (*Acacia*). **EDIBILITY UNKNOWN: AVOID.** (Hall)

Ustilago maydis (Corn Smut)

Corn smut is a pathogenic fungus found virtually everywhere corn is grown. Ears of corn infected by the fungus exhibit tumor-like growths that are as much as 2 cm long or wide and have the general appearance of grossly overgrown corn kernels. Although they might not appear to be particularly appetizing, these maize mushrooms, as the growths are sometimes called, are considered a great delicacy in Mexico and the southwestern United States. Indeed, although the

Ustilago maydis (corn smut). **EDIBLE.** (Johnson)

economic losses worldwide from *Ustilago maydis* are considerable, Mexican farmers welcome its appearance in their cornfields because infected ears of corn command a higher price than those that remain healthy (Arora 1991). At first almost white, the growths soon darken to gray. They are considered suitable for consumption when gray on the outside and black and juicy or slightly grainy on the inside. The Spanish name for the maize mushroom is *cuitlacoche*.

---

11. Mushrooms lacking stalks or whose stalks are rudimentary and attached to one side, with the spores formed in tubes or on the undersurface of the caps

---

Anyone who has ever taken a stroll through a forest has certainly noticed the bracket-like or shelflike growths that occur, often in great profusion, on logs, stumps, dead branches, and even living trees. Most of these growths are tough, leathery, or woody, but a few are soft and fleshy, at least when young. The vast majority are the fruiting bodies of a very large and exceedingly diverse assemblage of wood-rotting fungi. Several different taxonomic groups are represented in this assemblage, but the polypores are easily the most important. The polypores (literally "many pores") are so named because they produce fruiting bodies with small tubes on the underside of the cap, and the opening at the end of each tube is called a pore. Each fruiting body has numerous pores, which in most instances are more or less cylindrical.

Although most polypores are too tough and woody to be considered for the table, some have been used in traditional medicine. The reputed medical benefits of *Ganoderma* aff. *lucidum* (reishi) are particularly noteworthy in this regard. Products derived from this mushroom have been championed as cures for everything from venereal diseases to cancer. The mycelial mats produced by *Fomitopsis officinalis* in decayed wood were once used by American lumberjacks to stop bleeding caused by ax wounds (Gilbertson 1980), and the agaric acid obtained from the fruiting bodies of this mushroom has been used as a purgative. Antibiotics have been isolated from the fruiting bodies of a number of polypores (Quack et al. 1978), and examples such as *Trametes versicolor* (many-colored polypore) and *Wolfiporia cocos* contain polysaccharides and steroids reported to have antitumor properties. *Pycnoporus sanguineus* is reputed to be useful in treating mouth ailments, while substances extracted from some species of *Phellinus* have been used to treat sore throats, respiratory conditions, and diarrhea. In addition to their uses in traditional medicine, fruiting bodies of polypores have been used as sources of dyes for fabrics, as tinder for starting fires, as razor strops, and as currycombs for horses (Alexopoulos et al. 1996).

Fistulina hepatica (Beefsteak Fungus)

The beefsteak fungus forms a fairly firm bracket up to 20 cm across and 2–7 cm thick on the trunks of chestnuts (*Castanea*) and oaks (*Quercus*) that it parasitizes. Fruiting bodies are pink or orange to begin with but change to red or purplish brown with age. When cut they exude a blood-red sap from the dark pink flesh, which looks a little like uncooked meat. The lower surface of the bracket is covered with a system of fine pores, each of which is less than 0.5 mm in diameter. The reddish brown timber from trees parasitized by the beefsteak fungus is highly sought after by cabinet makers. The fungus itself is edible.

Laccocephalum mylittae (Native Bread)

The fruiting body of the polypore *Laccocephalum mylittae* is stalked, mushroom-shaped, and inedible. However, it arises from a sclerotium

Fistulina hepatica (beefsteak fungus). **EDIBLE.** (Izawa)

An excavated fruiting body of *Laccocephalum mylittae* (native bread) growing on buried wood. **EDIBLE.** (Fuhrer)

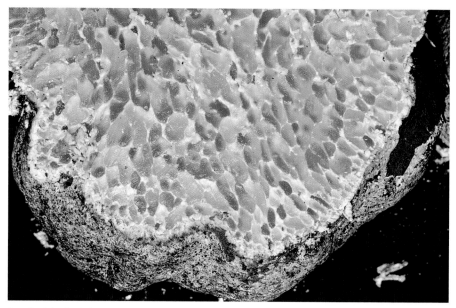

Detail of the buried portion of *Laccocephalum mylittae* (native bread). **EDIBLE.** (Fuhrer)

that can be as large as a football and weigh several kilograms. This is a traditional food eaten cooked or raw and a valuable source of water for the Aborigines in the central arid regions of Australia (Kalotas 1997). The fruiting bodies also appear to have some medical uses, since they contain proteinases that have been reported to kill parasitic worms and help relieve indigestion.

Laetiporus sulphureus (Chicken of the Woods)

The bracket-like fruiting bodies of the chicken of the woods can be found on dead wood, stumps, or living trees such as oaks, chestnuts, and willows from spring to autumn. They can be up to 40 cm across and are, when young, bright orange above and sulfur-yellow below, drying to a very pale yellowish brown. Chicken of the woods has a strong mushroomy smell, while the taste is not unpleasant. It is a very popular mushroom in the United States, Germany, and east European countries, but there is evidence of severe allergic reactions in some people, especially when consumed with alcohol (Evans 1996, Jordan 1996).

The fruiting bodies of *Laetiporus sulphureus* (chicken of the woods) growing from the base of a dead tree. **EDIBLE WHEN COOKED.** (Lyon)

Lenzites betulina (gilled polypore). **EDIBILITY UNKNOWN: AVOID.** (Johnson)

Lenzites betulina (Gilled Polypore)

In *Lenzites betulina*, the lower surface of the cap is conspicuously gill-like, and only near the margins are there more or less typical pores present. The fruiting bodies of this mushroom occur scattered or more often in overlapping clusters on the decaying logs and stumps of various hardwoods throughout temperate regions of the Northern Hemisphere. The individual caps are stalkless, 3–10 cm wide, semicircular to kidney-shaped, and nearly flat. The surface of the cap is velvety to hairy, with distinct concentric multicolored zones that range from white to gray to brown, sometimes with pink, orange, or yellow tints. *Lenzites betulina* is much too tough to be considered edible.

Auricularia Species (Wood Ear)

The wood ears are classified with the jelly fungi, like *Tremella*, and do not produce their spores in tubes like the bracket fungi. This group is included here simply because on first glance a bracket-like wood ear might be mistaken for a bracket mushroom. When young, the brown to purplish brown ear-shaped fruiting bodies of wood ears are gelatinous, with a smooth, shiny, spore-producing lower surface, and, in

Auricularia polytricha (wood ear) on the trunk of a dead tree. **EDIBLE.** (Buchanan)

one species (*Auricularia polytricha*), a downy, sterile upper surface. When old, the fruiting bodies remain attached to the host log or stump and become shrunken, dry, and tough. Wild wood ears can reach 10 cm in diameter, although, like cultivated wood ears, they are sometimes much larger.

---

12. Mushrooms with fruiting bodies above or below the ground and more or less spherical—puffballs, truffles, and false truffles

---

While specialists have always had problems identifying particular species of truffles and false truffles (Trappe 1979), poisonings suggest that nonspecialists also have difficulty distinguishing edible truffles from false truffles, puffballs, and unopened fruiting bodies of, for example, *Amanita*. The truffles fall into two groups: the true truffles, which are ascomycetes, and the false truffles, which are basidiomycetes. The latter are generally agreed to have evolved from a typical mushroom through reduction and the adoption of an underground fruiting habit. This seems to be the case, for example, in genera such as *Melanogaster* and *Rhizopogon*. Puffballs are also basidiomycetes.

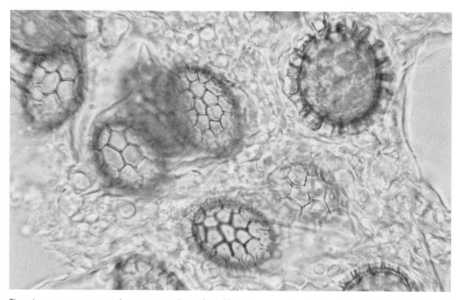

The shape, structure, and ornamentation of truffle spores are key features in the identification of species. Pictured are spores of *Tuber maculatum*, a species with little commercial value. (Hall)

When a true truffle is cut in two with a sharp knife, a system of white lines can be seen radiating through a matrix that, depending on the species, is off-white, cream, light to dark brown, black or occasionally gray, gray-blue, or even blue (Astier 1998). The false truffles appear quite different inside and are often somewhat spongy. Other characteristics used to separate the genera and species of truffles include the surface appearance of the fruiting bodies and the shape, size, and ornamentation of the spores (visible under a microscope) found on the inside.

Tuber melanosporum (Périgord Black Truffle)

Périgord black truffles range from little more than the size of a fingernail to larger than a tennis ball, sometimes weighing more than 200 g. The surface is covered in small diamond-shaped facets and is a dark ruddy brown when young, turning black at maturity. When cut in two, the interior of a young truffle is cream to light coffee-colored and traversed by a system of fine, pure white lines. As the truffle matures, the interior turns black, but the pure white lines are retained. Immature Périgord black truffles have little odor, but as the number of mature spores increases inside, so too does the aroma. Once the truffle is fully mature, the smell is almost overpowering, so that even a small truffle is enough to scent an entire room. The Périgord black truffle is found from just at the soil surface to 30 cm below and is associated mostly with hardwood trees, including oaks and hazels. As with many other expensive foods, this truffle has a reputation for being an aphrodisiac (Hall et al. 1994).

The Périgord black truffle was exported from France to North America in the late 1970s, to New Zealand in 1985, and to Tasmania around 1993. Since then, plants infected with it have been established in truffières in various localities. It can be expected that the fungus will eventually escape from these truffières, perhaps inside a pig, and become established on appropriate host plants growing in other areas with suitable conditions.

Wholesale prices of Périgord black truffles in season can range from $200 to $800 per kilogram, although retail prices as high as $10,000 per kilogram have been reported in Japan. As a result a number of other truffles are often substituted for the Périgord black truffle. These include the winter truffle (*Tuber brumale*), Burgundy truffle (*T. uncinatum*), and various Asiatic truffles, including *T. himalayense*, *T. indicum*, and *T. sinense*.

Very immature *Tuber melanosporum* (Périgord black truffles) with a light brown interior traversed by a network of pure white lines. **EDIBLE.** (Hall)

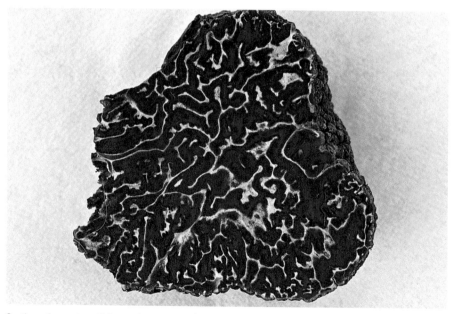

Section of a mature *Tuber melanosporum* (Périgord black truffle) with the black tissue crossed by a system of white lines. **EDIBLE.** (Hall)

A *Tuber melanosporum* (Périgord black truffle) weighing about 250 g. **EDIBLE.** (Hall)

The surface ornamentation of *Tuber melanosporum* (Périgord black truffle) is not sufficient to distinguish it from some Asiatic truffles. **EDIBLE.** (Hall)

Some Asian truffles are so similar in appearance to the Périgord black truffle that they are difficult to distinguish without using a high-powered microscope. Because Asian truffles have either a poor taste and smell or none at all, in China they fetch only a few dollars per kilogram. However, opportunists in Europe mix them with the Périgord black truffle or sprinkle them with artificial black truffle essence to give them some flavor and then market them as the real thing. The marketing of these truffles as true Périgord black truffles has the potential to degrade the industry in France, Italy, and Spain (Chevalier and Riousset 1995, Courvoisier 1995). Some people also fear that these Asian truffles will eventually find their way into European truffières and begin to displace the native species.

The Burgundy truffle (*Tuber uncinatum*), which is easily distinguished by its coffee-colored interior and the network of ridges that covers the surface of its spores, is widely consumed in Italy and parts of France (Chevalier and Frochot 1997), and was popular in Victorian England. It is also canned and bottled by companies like Urbani in Italy, and the preserved products are readily available in retail stores throughout Europe. However, the smell and flavor of this truffle are not as powerful as those of the Périgord black truffle and the Italian white truffle. The winter truffle (*T. brumale*) is often found in the same truffières as the Périgord black truffle, and though its flavor is not as powerful, the two species are often sold mixed together.

Tuber magnatum (Italian White Truffle) and Other *Tuber* Species

Italian white truffles are only white when very young. At maturity they are usually cream to light brown and have a suedelike surface, quite unlike the faceted surface of the Périgord black truffle. They typically range from the size of a golf ball to that of a tennis ball, although most people are only likely to see two or three white truffles about 10 mm in diameter preserved in a small bottle in a delicatessen. The inside of an Italian white truffle is light brown to coffee-colored and crisscrossed by a system of white lines. When ripe, Italian white truffles have a strong garlic-like smell that is quite distinct from the smell of the Périgord black truffle.

The Italian white truffle is found in northern and central Italy, Istria in Croatia, southeastern France, and southern Switzerland (Lawrynowicz 1993, Zambonelli and Di Munno 1992) from late summer to early winter. Mycorrhizal host plants include oaks (*Quercus*), poplars (*Populus*), willows (*Salix*), and limes (*Tilia*) (Hall,

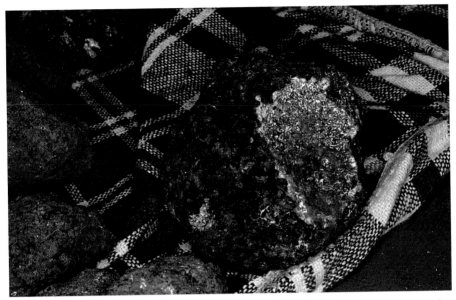

Tuber uncinatum (Burgundy truffles) coated in soil, which adds to the weight. Note the tan interior. **EDIBLE.** (Hall)

Immature *Tuber sinense*, a Chinese truffle. When mature this species can easily be mistaken for *Tuber melanosporum* (Périgord black truffle). **EDIBLE.** (Wang)

A dish of Italian white truffles (*Tuber magnatum*), the most expensive mushrooms in the world. **EDIBLE.** (Squires)

Zambonelli et al. 1998). The soils in which the white truffle is found are extremely soft and porous and contain large amounts of limestone. Fresh soil and plant materials are often naturally incorporated into such soils—for example, on the banks of streams or where the soil is cultivated (Hall, Zambonelli et al. 1998).

The aroma of the Italian white truffle is easily lost when cooked. As a result, white truffles are usually shaved over salads or over hot dishes just before serving—giving Italian chefs plenty of opportunities to show their skill and panache. There is little competition in the marketplace between the Italian white truffle and the Périgord black truffle, due to their different smells, uses, and harvesting times. Over the past few years the price of the Italian white truffle has rocketed, reaching $13,200 per kilogram at the annual Alba truffle festival in November 2000 (Johnston 2000). Even modest specimens retailed for $9000 per kilogram, and the market annually is worth several hundred million dollars (Hall, Zambonelli et al. 1998).

A number of other species of truffles are superficially similar to the Italian white truffle. These include *Tuber borchii*, *T. dryophilum*, and *T. maculatum*. The Oregon white truffle (*T. gibbosum*) is found under

A natural *Tuber magnatum* (Italian white truffle) truffière in central Italy. (Zambonelli)

Tuber borchii (bianchetto), sometimes mistaken for *Tuber magnatum* (Italian white truffle). **EDIBLE.** (Hall)

Tuber maculatum, another truffle mistaken for *Tuber magnatum*. **EDIBLE.** (Hall)

Terfezia claveryi, a desert truffle, fruiting in the rooting zone of a rock rose (*Helianthemum*), its mycorrhizal host plant. **EDIBLE.** (Honrubia)

Douglas fir (*Pseudotsuga menziesii*) and other hosts in the Pacific Northwest region of North America and is said by some to be as good as the Italian white truffle. It is consumed in small quantities not only by keen trufflers (Evans and Evans 1987) but also by small mammals, some of which have an exclusive diet of truffles (Malajczuk et al. 1987, Maser et al. 1978). While toxic mushrooms in the genus *Scleroderma* are quite different from *T. magnatum*, they are not infrequently assumed to be white truffles, and many specimens have been sent in error to specialists for identification either before or after someone has eaten them.

The Italian white truffle has been successfully cultivated only within the last decade (Giovanetti 1990, Giovanetti et al. 1994). Although the techniques used commercially to produce plants infected with this truffle have not been published, it is likely that variations on Talon's technique are used by some. As such, sterile seedlings are grown in the rooting zone of a mother plant already infected with the fungus. Unfortunately, some plants that are claimed to be infected with the Italian white truffle may actually be infected with other species. A comprehensive scientific review of the Italian white truffle has been published (Hall, Zambonelli et al. 1998).

Terfezia and *Tirmania* Species (Desert Truffles)

The desert truffles (*Terfezia* and *Tirmania*) are found throughout the Middle East and northern Africa in areas between the desert proper and adjacent wetter areas. Desert truffles are associated with small shrubs such as rock rose (*Cistus* and *Helianthemum*) and are among the largest truffles in the world, sometimes weighing 1 kg or more. These truffles have a relatively mild taste and flavor, particularly when cooked with spicy Middle Eastern and northern African dishes. Like the Périgord black truffle, they are reputed to have aphrodisiac qualities (M. Zaptia, personal communication).

Bovista nigrescens, Bovista plumbea, and *Vascellum pratense* (Common Puffballs)

Bovista nigrescens, *B. plumbea*, and *Vascellum pratense*, collectively known as the common puffballs, are 2–4 cm in diameter (sometimes as much as 6 cm) and are often found in lawns and other grassy areas. These are edible in the immature stage before the interior of the fruiting body changes from white to brown, which indicates spore formation.

Bovista plumbea, a common puffball. **EDIBLE.** (Hall)

It is essential to distinguish between small puffballs and other, sometimes poisonous fungi that may appear rather similar. Examples of the latter include *Scleroderma*, immature specimens of *Geastrum* of unknown edibility, and immature fruiting bodies of the death cap (*Amanita phalloides*). It is always important to check the interior of a puffball to ensure that it is white throughout and that there are no developing gills or caps. This is particularly important if what appear to be puffballs have been collected near ectomycorrhizal trees, in which case the mushrooms in question may be immature fruiting bodies of poisonous species of *Amanita*. Even so it is still possible to confuse very young specimens of *Scleroderma* with puffballs, so it is important to section older specimens to see if there is any blackening of the interior, which is characteristic of mature *Scleroderma*.

Calvatia cyathiformis (Purple-Spored Puffball)

Though not as large as those of the giant puffball, the fruiting bodies of *Calvatia cyathiformis* can be as much as 20 cm in diameter. Usually nearly round to somewhat oval when young, fruiting bodies tend to become more pear-shaped or top-shaped as they mature. The purple-

Calvatia cyathiformis (purple-spored puffball). **EDIBLE.** (Johnson)

Calvatia excipuliformis (long-stemmed puffball). **EDIBLE.** (Hall)

spored puffball is most common in pastures, lawns, and other grassy areas. The spore mass is at first white, then yellow, finally turning a dull purple to purple-brown at maturity. The purple color of the spore mass distinguishes *C. cyathiformis* from all other species of *Calvatia*. Old weathered fruiting bodies, usually consisting of the sterile base along with remnants of the spore case, often persist for several months and can be found during the winter or even early spring. *Calvatia cyathiformis* is edible until the flesh begins to turn light tan. *Calvatia excipuliformis* (long-stemmed puffball) can be found in grasslands and forests.

Calvatia gigantea (Giant Puffball)

A modest football-sized giant puffball would be impossible to confuse with any other mushroom, and this would be doubly true for a larger specimen. However, smaller specimens of the giant puffball might be confused with the unopened fruiting bodies of much less edible mushrooms, such as poisonous species of *Amanita*. *Calvatia gigantea*, also known as *Langermannia gigantea*, is usually found growing on bare soil or in grassy areas in places where there is

Calvatia gigantea (giant puffball). The larger puffball has had a slice removed to show the firm, edible interior. The smaller, more mature puffball, which is well beyond the edible stage, displays the small stalk at its base that attached it to the mycelium in the soil. **EDIBLE.** (Hall)

A fruiting body of *Calvatia gigantea* (giant puffball) that has split while growing. **EDIBLE.** (Hall)

considerable organic matter in the soil. It is commonly found in well-manured pastures, gardens, and around silage pits in autumn. The base of the puffball is attached to the mycelium in the soil by a thick central stalk. While fruiting bodies are normally more or less spherical, if growth is very rapid they can split like overwatered cherries and become irregularly shaped.

To determine if a giant puffball is ready for eating, tap the outside. A sound similar to that of tapping an inflated football is a good indication that it can be consumed. Next, try to push a finger gently into the surface. If this leaves a depression, as it would with risen dough, the puffball has probably started to produce spores and is no longer in an edible condition. Giant puffballs appear to rapidly pass into the inedible spore-producing stage after being exposed to a day or so of sunshine. This developmental stage is associated with a change in the color of the interior of the fruiting body from white to pale yellow and then to greenish or brownish gray, by which time the contents will have become powdery and the puffball will have split open, allowing the spores to spill out. It may then become detached from the soil and perhaps roll around in the wind.

One of the easiest ways to prepare the giant puffball is to simply slice it and fry the pieces in butter, although finding a large enough frying pan may be a challenge. The very largest specimens of the giant puffball ever reported were more than 150 cm in diameter, 45 cm high, and would have weighed more than 100 kg when fresh (*Guinness Book of Records* 2000).

Lycoperdon perlatum (Gem-Studded Puffball) and *Lycoperdon pyriforme* (Pear-Shaped Puffball)

Species of *Lycoperdon* produce a fruiting body with an approximately spherical head (as the upper portion of a puffball is often called) supported by a broad stalk. When mature the head becomes filled with light to dark brown spores, which are released through a pore that develops at the top of the fruiting body. While the edibility of some species of *Lycoperdon* has not been determined, and while *L. marginatum* (peeling puffball) and *L. mixtecorum* contain hallucinogens (Benjamin 1995), *L. perlatum* (gem-studded puffball) and *L. pyriforme* (pear-shaped puffball) are edible provided they are picked when young and the contents of the head are still white and firm. Moreover, the spore mass of a number of different species of *Lycoperdon* has been used in traditional medicine to help stop the

Lycoperdon perlatum (gem-studded puffball). **EDIBLE.** (Hall)

Lycoperdon pyriforme (pear-shaped puffball). **EDIBLE.** (Johnson)

flow of blood from open wounds and to relieve the pain of burns (Walleyn and Rammeloo 1994).

Lycoperdon perlatum is very widely distributed and is probably the single most common woodland puffball in North America. It can be found from midsummer to autumn as solitary, scattered, or clustered fruitings on the ground in both coniferous and hardwood forests. The fruiting bodies are pear-shaped to nearly round with a narrowed base, 2.5–6.5 cm wide, and 2.5–8 cm tall. The surface of the upper portion of the fruiting body is covered with short, cone-shaped white spines, which leave pockmarks when they fall off.

Lycoperdon pyriforme is a widespread, rather common puffball. The fruiting bodies are similar in shape to those of *L. perlatum* but lack the covering of conelike spines on the upper surface and are usually smaller, 1.5–4.5 cm in diameter and 2–5 cm high. However, the most important difference is that fruiting bodies of the pear-shaped puffball occur on decaying wood instead of the ground, though sometimes fruiting bodies growing on buried wood or wood debris may appear to be on the soil surface. This species is found during autumn and often occurs in dense clusters on old decaying logs and stumps.

Melanogaster ambiguus (false truffle). **EDIBLE.** (Hall)

Melanogaster Species

The fruiting bodies of species of *Melanogaster* superficially resemble those of truffles and are also very strong smelling. When people find these mushrooms they often jump to the conclusion that they have found a true truffle. However, the contents of a *Melanogaster* fruiting body are spongy, and though they may be black, sometimes with white flecks, they always lack the distinct network of white lines found in true truffles. *Melanogaster* can be eaten (Evans and Evans 1987), but the very pungent smell might be off-putting. *Melanogaster ambiguus* is a false truffle that fruits below the soil surface.

Rhizopogon rubescens (Shoro)

While shoro (literally "dew of the pine") can be found fruiting at the soil surface, this mushroom, like the truffle, is also found below ground. Fruiting bodies are typically spherical and 1–7 cm in diameter. They are white with pinkish or reddish blotches when young, turning light to mid brown with age. When conditions are dry, the surface of the fruiting body may crack, exposing the lighter-colored

Rhizopogon rubescens (shoro). **EDIBLE.** (Hall)

interior. When young, the interior of the fruiting body is pale, spongy, and edible. However, as it matures the contents become darker and unpalatable. Eventually the whole fruiting body turns into a light brown, gelatinous mass. Occasionally shoro is found growing with *Rhizopogon luteolus*, which is not as palatable.

During the nineteenth century, shoro was consumed in large quantities in Japan, particularly in the Osaka and Kyoto districts. However, the mushroom is now rare and many Japanese chefs are unsure how to cook it. Although shoro has little flavor of its own, the spongelike texture of the fruiting body allows it to absorb the flavors of the food with which it is cooked. Its crisp texture is referred to by the Japanese as having a "good tooth touch," which adds to its appeal. Shoro is also found in North America under pines (*Pinus*) and in April 2001 was cultivated on Monterey pine (*P. radiata*) in New Zealand.

Scleroderma Species (Earthballs)

The earthballs, belonging to the genus *Scleroderma*, occur as ecto-mycorrhizal associates of a wide range of trees, including oaks (*Quercus*) and eucalypts (*Eucalyptus*). Fruiting bodies are formed at the surface of the soil or just below it, and their more or less spherical shape makes it easy to confuse them with the often edible puffballs and truffles. *Scleroderma verrucosum*, for example, is sometimes mistaken for a truffle. Earthballs can be distinguished from puffballs and truffles by cutting their fruiting body in half with a sharp knife. Immature earthballs have an off-white, spongy interior; but as they mature, brown spores form inside, giving the contents a purple-brown to black color. This dense, dark tissue is surrounded by a tough white or light brown covering. Some species also have a stalk at the bottom of the fruiting body. Earthballs do not have the network of pale lines characteristic of truffles. Puffballs, in contrast, are white inside until the spores mature and gradually turn yellowish, eventually becoming brown and powdery.

Although earthballs sometimes smell like field mushrooms, at least four species—*Scleroderma albidum*, *S. areolatum*, *S. cepa*, and *S. citrinum*—are poisonous. Symptoms can occur within an hour of eating and include loss of consciousness, nausea, severe abdominal pains, vomiting, perspiration, generalized tingling sensations, spasms, cramps, paralysis, and anaphylactic shock (Benjamin 1995, Bresinsky and Besl 1990, Southcott 1997).

Scleroderma verrucosum. **POISONOUS.** (Hall)

As they mature, the contents of *Scleroderma* species turn black and spongy. **POISONOUS.** (Hall)

Daldinia concentrica (Carbon Balls)

Daldinia concentrica belongs to a large and diverse group of ascomycetes that decay the wood of living and dead broadleaf trees. The irregularly spherical to cushion-like fruiting bodies of this fungus are commonly encountered on dead but not yet decorticated trunks and on branches of such trees as ash (*Fraxinus*), beech (*Fagus*), and oak (*Quercus*). At first red-brown but later becoming black (hence the common name), fruiting bodies are 2–4 cm across and quite hard to the touch. When sectioned, the conspicuous concentric zones present on the interior of the fruiting body are revealed. Nothing about this fungus suggests it might be suitable for the table.

Daldinia concentrica (carbon balls). **EDIBILITY UNKNOWN: AVOID.** (Johnson)

---

13. Mushrooms with fruiting bodies consisting of a simple or branched linear structure growing from decaying wood or arising from an adult or larval insect

---

Cordyceps Species (Vegetable Caterpillar Fungi) and *Claviceps* Species

Vegetable caterpillar fungi typically infect insects or their larvae, though some species infect spiders and other small animals. Once inside, the fungus grows through the tissues, producing a mummy more or less in the shape of the host. Eventually one or more thin spindle-shaped stalks grow upward out of the mass of fungal tissue, and the spores are produced in small flask-shaped structures located at the top of the stalk. Some of the caterpillars infected by *Cordyceps* live in vertical underground burrows, and finding the light to dark brown, twiglike fungal stalks that grow out of these burrows can take some practice. While most species of *Cordyceps* are parasitic on insects, *C. ophioglossoides* and *C. capitata* grow on *Elaphomyces* species.

Several species of *Cordyceps* have been used in traditional medicine for the treatment of such things as liver disorders. Moreover, the

All that can be seen of the vegetable caterpillar fungus (*Cordyceps robertsii*) is a thin twiglike fruiting structure above the soil surface. **MEDICINAL.** (Wang)

Cordyceps robertsii that has been excavated to show the association between the underground infected caterpillar and aboveground fruiting structure. **MEDICINAL.** (Wang)

The parasitic *Cordyceps ophioglossoides* grows on a truffle (*Elaphomyces* sp.). **EDIBILITY UNKNOWN: AVOID.** (Wang)

active agents found in these fungi (probably ophiocordin and various polysaccharides) have been reported to have antitumor, antibiotic, and antifungal properties. In China *C. sinensis* is so revered as a medicine that it sells for up to $2000 per kilogram. Members of the closely related genus *Claviceps* are parasites on cereal grains such as wheat and rye, producing sclerotia in the diseased flowers of the host plant. The sclerotia of *Claviceps purpurea* (wheat ergot) contain several types of toxic alkaloids that can result in death when consumed by humans or livestock. However, these same substances have also been used medicinally to induce labor, to prevent hemorrhaging associated with childbirth, and to ease the pain of migraine headaches (Alexopoulos et al. 1996).

Xylaria polymorpha (Dead Man's Fingers)

The genus *Xylaria* is both large and widely distributed throughout the world. One of the most common species is dead man's fingers (*X. polymorpha*), so called because the fruiting bodies are somewhat finger-like in both shape and size. These are typically 2–8 cm high and 1–3 cm thick, occurring in clusters (though solitary fruiting bodies are occasionally encountered) on logs and stumps of broadleaf trees, especially beech (*Fagus*) and maple (*Acer*). Gray-brown or light brown when young, they become black when mature. Only the crust-like surface of the fruiting body is black, however: the interior is white. This fungus is much too tough to be considered edible.

---

14. Mushrooms with spindle-, coral-, icicle-, or cauliflower-shaped fruiting bodies

Clavaria, *Clavulinopsis*, and *Ramaria* are among the common genera of club and coral mushrooms. Most are found on the ground or on wood, and some form mycorrhizas. *Ramaria formosa* (pink coral mushroom) often forms in large mats, while *Clavulina cavipes* can sometimes be little more than a few small stalks on the soil surface. *Clavulina rugosa* and some species of *Clavaria* and *Clavulinopsis* are edible (Imazeki et al. 1988, Phillips 1981), whereas *R. formosa* and *R. pallida* cause stomach cramps and diarrhea. However, most species are too small and tasteless to be worth collecting for the table.

Xylaria polymorpha (dead man's fingers). **EDIBILITY UNKNOWN: AVOID.** (Izawa)

Ramaria formosa (pink coral mushroom). **POISONOUS.** (Izawa)

Clavulina cavipes, a coral mushroom. **EDIBILITY UNKNOWN: AVOID.** (Hall)

Clavulina cristata (crested coral). **EDIBILITY UNKNOWN: AVOID.** (Johnson)

Clavulina cristata (Crested Coral)

Clavulina cristata is a widely distributed species of coral mushroom often encountered on the ground in hardwood and coniferous forests throughout temperate regions of the Northern Hemisphere. The fruiting body is a white to buff, many-branched structure that is 2.5–8.0 cm high and 2–4 cm wide. The individual branches have toothlike, jagged tips. This mushroom is edible but too tough to be worth considering for the table. *Ramaria stricta* is very similar in appearance to *C. cristata* but has consistently parallel straight branches and, more importantly, occurs on wood.

Sparassis crispa (Cauliflower Fungus)

The cauliflower fungus is a parasite of pines (*Pinus*) and can be found around the bases of infected trees and on wood buried in the ground. It can be up to 50 cm in diameter and is therefore large enough to provide an entire meal. The fruiting body consists of numerous

Sparassis crispa (cauliflower fungus). **EDIBLE.** (Izawa)

Ileodictyon cibarium (basket fungus). **EDIBLE.** (Cole)

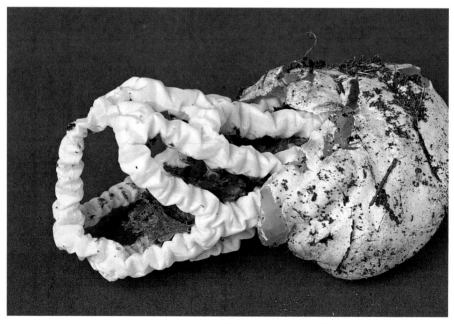

Ileodictyon cibarium (basket fungus) just beyond the edible egg stage. (Cole)

Aseroe rubra hatching from an egg that is tightly wrapped around the base of the stem. **EDIBILITY UNKNOWN: AVOID.** (Squires)

Geastrum saccatum (earthstar). **EDIBILITY UNKNOWN: AVOID.** (Johnson)

flattened, somewhat leaflike branches arising from a short, thick, deeply rooted, central stalklike base. The branches are at first white to buff but darken with age. This widely distributed species is found throughout temperate regions of the Northern Hemisphere. It is considered a choice edible mushroom, but it has to be cleaned of bits of wood, insects, and soil before cooking, and this can be a real chore.

15. Mushrooms with basket-shaped fruiting bodies or fruiting bodies with tentacle-like arms hatching from an egg

Clathrus ruber (Latticed Stinkhorn) and *Ileodictyon cibarium* (Basket Fungus)

Both the latticed stinkhorn and the basket fungus grow from an egg about 5 cm in diameter. The North American species *Clathrus ruber* is probably not edible. *Ileodictyon cibarium* is edible while in the egg stage, but once it opens out into a basket-like structure 10–15 cm in diameter, it begins to produce an unpleasant aroma that attracts flies. At one time the New Zealand Maori ate the basket fungus in the egg stage (Riley 1988).

Clathrus archeri and *Aseroe rubra* (Octopus Stinkhorns)

While octopus stinkhorns are edible in the egg stage before they hatch from the egg (Arora 1986), they eventually open out into star-shaped structures that, though attractive to look at, have awful aromas. These aromas attract flies, which carry the slimy spore masses away on their legs.

---

16. Mushrooms with spherical fruiting bodies that open out into star-shaped structures, with the spores contained in a central ball that discharges dry spores through a small central pore—earthstars

---

Geastrum saccatum (Earthstar)

Geastrum saccatum is closely allied to puffballs. The fruiting bodies are initially spherical but with a two-layered wall. The outer wall splits from the top down, opening out into a star-shaped structure with the spherical inner wall at its center. A pore forms at the top of the central sphere, and through this the dry spores are released.

---

17. Mushrooms with more or less cup-shaped fruiting bodies, with the spores produced inside the cup on a feltlike surface or within small egglike structures

---

Aleuria aurantia (Orange-Peel Mushroom)

The shallow cup-shaped fruiting body of *Aleuria aurantia* somewhat resembles a discarded piece of orange peel, which accounts for the common name of this mushroom. Usually occurring on areas of disturbed soil such as those found along roads and paths, orange-peel mushroom is widely distributed throughout the world. Fruiting bodies are commonly 2–10 cm in diameter, occur in clusters, and lack

Aleuria aurantia (orange-peel mushroom). **EDIBLE.** (Johnson)

a stalk. The upper (inner) surface is bright orange to reddish orange or orange-yellow, with the lower (outer) surface noticeably lighter and slightly downy. Though thin and rather brittle, the fruiting bodies are edible and have been consumed either raw or cooked. The latter, of course, is the safer choice.

Peziza, Helvella, Paxina, and *Sarcosphaera* Species

Peziza, Helvella, Paxina, and *Sarcosphaera* are all ascomycetes that produce cup-shaped fruiting bodies, with the spores formed in asci that cover the concave upper surface of the cups. These mushrooms are typically found on the surface of soil. The fruiting bodies of *Peziza vesiculosa* (common dung cap), *Helvella acetabulum* (brown-ribbed elfin cup), and *Paxina leucomelas* (white-footed elfin cup) are poisonous unless cooked well (Phillips 1981), while the similar species *Sarcosphaera crassa* (crown fungus) is considered suspect (Bresinsky and Besl 1990). The edibility of many other species of these genera is unknown.

An ascocarp of *Peziza ammophila* growing in a sand dune. **EDIBILITY UNKNOWN: AVOID.** (Wang)

Peziza species growing on a bark-based potting mix in a garden shop. The green color is the result of an alga growing in the surface layers of the fruiting body. **EDIBILITY UNKNOWN: AVOID.** (Hall)

Cyathus striatus (bird's nest fungus). **EDIBILITY UNKNOWN: AVOID.** (Johnson)

Cyathus striatus and *Crucibulum laeve* (Bird's Nest Fungi)

Most fungi with cup-shaped fruiting bodies are ascomycetes, but a few are basidiomycetes. Such is the case for the bird's nest fungi, so named because the fruiting bodies produced by members of this group resemble miniature bird's nests with eggs inside. What look like eggs are actually peridioles. The "nests" function as splash cups, using the force of falling raindrops to disperse the peridioles. Under ideal conditions, a peridiole can be displaced more than a meter from the fruiting body, where it may land on some type of organic debris subject to being colonized by the mycelium that develops from the spores inside the peridiole. The broadly cup-shaped fruiting bodies of *Cyathus striatus* are commonly 7–15 mm high and 6–8 mm wide at the top, narrowing below. The outer surface of the cup is firm, cinnamon-brown to dark brown, and covered with shaggy, woolly hairs. The inner surface is smooth, shiny, and noticeably grooved. The peridioles are 1–1.5 mm in diameter, somewhat triangular, and dark in color. In *Crucibulum laeve*, another common and widely distributed bird's nest fungus, the peridioles are white to buff. Fruiting bodies of *Cyathus striatus* occur on hardwood debris, twigs, bark, and wood chips throughout North America.

---

18. Mushrooms with cushion-shaped fruiting bodies that are at first outwardly slimy, then rather fragile

---

Fuligo septica (Scrambled-Egg Slime Mold)

All the mushrooms described thus far belong to two major taxonomic classes: the Ascomycetes and the Basidiomycetes. *Fuligo septica* belongs to an entirely different group of organisms: the Myxomycetes, or slime molds. Slime molds have long intrigued and perplexed biologists because they possess characteristics of both fungi and animals. The fruiting bodies they produce resemble those of fungi, but some of their other characteristics, including the capability for locomotion during the feeding stage, are normally associated only with animals. In fact myxomycetes are now considered to be members of the Protozoa, separate from both fungi and animals. For most of its life a slime mold exists as a thin, free-living mass of protoplasm. Sometimes this mass is several centimeters across and, as the name "slime mold" suggests, viscous or slimy to the touch. This mass of protoplasm, called a plasmodium, can change form and creep slowly about, much like a giant amoeba. As it moves along, the plasmodium feeds upon bacteria and bits of organic matter.

Slime mold plasmodia occur in moist, shady places such as within crevices of decaying wood and beneath the partially decayed bark of logs and stumps. After a period of feeding and growth, the plasmodium moves out of its usual habitat and into a drier, more exposed location. Here it transforms into one or more fruiting bodies. Most slime mold fruiting bodies are quite small, often no more than a millimeter or two in height. However, this is not the case for *Fuligo septica*, which produces cushion-shaped fruiting bodies often 10–20 cm wide and 1–3 cm thick. They are red to bright yellow or, less often, white to pale or bright pink. The outer portion of the fruiting body is calcareous and rather fragile. When disrupted, a dark gray or dull black spore mass is revealed. Fruiting bodies typically occur on decaying wood or bark but can also be found on forest floor litter and even bare soil. *Fuligo septica* is one of the few slime molds reported to have been consumed by humans (Stephenson and Stempen 1994).

Fuligo septica (scrambled-egg slime mold). **EDIBLE.** (Izawa)

However, it is the transforming plasmodium and not the mature fruiting body that is eaten. In any case, this mushroom should not be considered an item for the table.

---

19. Mushrooms with leaflike fruiting bodies that are dark green or nearly black and closely appressed to vertical rocky surfaces

---

Umbilicaria esculenta (Iwatake)

Umbilicaria esculenta is a lichen—a "composite" organism formed by a fungus and an alga. It is considered a delicacy in China and Japan, where it has been collected and eaten for centuries. It is usually found on exposed, rocky, mountainous, vertical faces, which is why it is commonly known as *iwatake* ("rocky fungus") in Japan and as *shier* and *yaner* ("rocky ear") in China. Intrepid collectors, often hanging suspended on a rope, pluck iwatake from the rock surfaces upon which it occurs, and later dry it before offering it for sale. Iwatake is often incorporated into soups or stir fry dishes with meats. Before cooking with it, however, the lichen is soaked in warm water and soil and other debris are removed. In China iwatake is used in traditional medicine to treat coughs (Hu et al. 1980).

Umbilicaria esculenta (iwatake). **EDIBLE.** (Hall)

CONVERSION CHART

inches	centimeters
⅛	0.3
¼	0.6
⅓	0.8
½	1.25
⅔	1.7
¾	1.9
1	2.5
1¼	3.1
1⅓	3.3
1½	3.75
1¾	4.4
2	5.0
3	7.5
4	10
5	12.5
6	15
7	17.5
8	20
9	22.5
10	25
2	30
5	37.5
8	45
20	50
24	60
30	75
36	90

feet	meters
¼	0.08
⅓	0.1
½	0.15
1	0.3
1½	0.5
2	0.6
2½	0.8
3	0.9
4	1.2
5	1.5
6	1.8
7	2.1
8	2.4
9	2.7
10	3.0
15	4.5
20	6.0
25	7.5
30	9.0
35	10.5
40	12
45	13.5
50	15

$$°C = \tfrac{5}{9} \times (°F - 32)$$

$$°F = (\tfrac{9}{5} \times °C) + 32$$

1 hectare = 2.47 acres

1 acre = 0.405 hectare

CHINESE NAMES OF MUSHROOMS

Chinese common names, scientific names, and English common names of edible and medicinal mushrooms known from China. Some of the mushrooms listed are not mentioned in the text because of their relatively minor importance outside of China. Additional information is provided in the text for many of the more important examples. English common names are given only for those species for which they are available.

† Species known or suspected to be mycorrhizal. ^C Cultivated species.
* Name formulated by Wang Yun.

Chinese common name	Pinyin	Scientific name	English common name
白柄乳牛肝菌	baibing runiuganjun	*Suillus albivelatus* A. H. Sm., Thiers et O. K. Mill.[†]	
白草菇	baicaogu*	*Volvariella diplasia* (Berk. et Broome) Singer[C]	straw mushroom
白侧耳	baiceer*	*Pleurotus opuntiae* (Durieu et Lév.) Sacc.[C]	white oyster mushroom
白冬块菌	baidongkuaijun*	*Tuber hiemalbum* Chatin[†]	white winter truffle
白黄侧耳	baihuangceer	*Pleurotus cornucopiae* (Paulet) Rolland[C]	yellow oyster mushroom
白鸡油菌	baijiyoujun*	*Cantharellus subalbidus* A. H. Sm. et Morse[†]	white chanterelle
白块菌	baikuaijun*	*Tuber borchii* Vittad.[†]	bianchetto
白蜡伞	bailansan	*Hygrophorus eburneus* (Fr.) Fr.[†]	ivory waxy cap

Chinese common name	Pinyin	Scientific name	English common name
白林地菇	bailindigu	*Agaricus sylvicola* (Vittad.) Peck[C]	woodland agaricus
白香蘑	baixiangmo	*Lepista caespitosa* (Bres.) Singer	
白鲜菇	baixiangu	*Agaricus bernardii* Quél.	salt-loving agaricus
白猪块菌	baizhukuaijun*	*Choiromyces meandriformis* Vittad.[†]	white truffle
棒柄杯伞	bangbing beisan	*Clitocybe clavipes* (Pers.: Fr.) P. Kumm.	club-foot clitocybe
棒地菇	bangdigu*	*Terfezia claveryi* Chatin[†]	desert truffle
半开羊肚菌	bankai yangdujun	*Morchella semilibera* DC.: Fr.	half-free morel
鲍鱼侧耳	baoyuceer	*Pleurotus abalonus* Y. H. Han, K. M. Chen et S. Cheng[C]	abalone mushroom
巴西蘑菇	baxi mogu	*Agaricus blazei* Murrill	almond portobello
贝形拟侧耳	beixing nicer*	*Pleurocybella porrigens* (Pers: Fr.) Singer	angel's wings
杯形秃马勃	beixing tumabo	*Calvatia cyathiformis* (Bosc) Morgan	purple-spored puffball
变黑离褶伞	bianhei lizhesan	*Lyophyllum sykosporum* Hongo et Clémençon	
变绿红菇	bianlu honggu	*Russula virescens* (Schaeff.) Fr.[†]	quilted green russula
变盔孢伞	bianquibaosan	*Kuehneromyces mutabilis* (Schaeff.: Fr.) Singer et A. H. Sm.[C]	changeable pholiota
波甘地块菌	bogandi kuaijun*	*Tuber uncinatum* Chatin[†]	Burgundy truffle
伯格诺利块菌	bogenuoli kuaijun*	*Tuber mesentericum* Vittad.[†]	bagnoli truffle
波缘多孔菌	boyuan duokongjun	*Albatrellus confluens* (A. et S.: Fr.) Kotl. et Pouz.[†]	
彩色豆马勃	caise doumabo	*Pisolithus tinctorius* (P. Micheli ex Pers.: Pers.) Coker et Couch	dye-maker's false puffball
草地拱顶菌	caodi gongdingjun	*Camarophyllus pratensis* (Pers: Fr.) P. Kumm.[†]	meadow waxy cap
草菇	caogu	*Volvariella volvacea* (Bull.: Fr.) Singer[C]	straw mushroom
草莓菌	caomeijun*	*Cyttaria gunnii* Berk.	beech strawberry

Chinese common name	Pinyin	Scientific name	English common name
草原侧耳	caoyuan ceer*	*Pleurotus eryngii* (DC.: Fr.) Quél.[c]	king oyster mushroom
长根小奥德蘑	changgen xiaoaodemo*	*Oudemansiella radicata* (Relhan: Fr.) Singer	rooting oudemansiella
蝉花	chanhuan	*Cordyceps sobolifera* (Berk.) Berk.	
茶烟白齿菌	chayanbaichijun*	*Bankera fuligineoalba* (J. C. Schmidt: Fr.) Coker et Beers ex Pouzar[†]	
茶银耳	chayiner	*Tremella foliacea* Pers.: Fr.	
橙盖鹅膏	chenggai egao	*Amanita caesarea* (Scop.: Fr.) Pers.[†]	Caesar's mushroom
橙红乳菇	chenghongrugu	*Lactarius akahatsu* Tanaka[†]	
橙网孢盘菌	chengwang baopanjun	*Aleuria aurantia* (Pers.: Fr.) Fuckel[c]	orange-peel mushroom
赤褐鹅膏	chihe egao	*Amanita fulva* (Schaeff.) Fr.[†]	tawny grisette
虫草	chongcao	*Cordyceps sinensis* (Berk.) Sacc.	Chinese caterpillar fungus
垂幕菇	chuimugu	*Psathyrella candolleana* (Fr.: Fr.) Maire	common psathyrella
刺拟小齿伞	cinixiaochisan*	*Mycoleptodonoides aitchisonii* (Berk.) Maas Geest.	
刺托竹荪	cituo zhusun	*Dictyophora echinovolvata* M. Zang, D. R. Zheng et Z. X. Hu[c]	
粗鳞大环柄菇	culin dahuanbinggu	*Macrolepiota rachodes* (Vittad.) Singer	shaggy parasol
粗腿羊肚菌	cutui yangdujun	*Morchella crassipes* (Vent.: Fr.) Pers.	thick-footed morel
粗网柄牛肝菌	cuwangbingniuganjun	*Boletus ornatipes* Peck[†]	ornate-stalked bolete
粗壮口蘑	cuzhuangkoumo	*Tricholoma robustum* (Alb. et Schwein.: Fr.) Ricken (sensu Imazeki)[†]	
大孢菇	dabaogu*	*Agaricus macrosporus* (F. H. Møller et Jul. Schäff.) Pilát	

Chinese common name	Pinyin	Scientific name	English common name
大肥菇	dafeigu	*Agaricus bitorquis* (Quél.) Sacc.[C]	button mushroom
大马勃	damabo	*Calvatia gigantea* (Batsch: Pers.) Lloyd	giant puffball
大乳头蘑	darutoumo*	*Catathelasma imperiale* (Fr.) Singer[†]	imperial cap
大团囊虫草	datuannang chongcao	*Cordyceps ophioglossoides* (Ehrenb.: Fr.) Link	
大紫菇	dazigu	*Agaricus augustus* Fr.	the prince
点柄乳牛肝菌	dianbing runiuganjun	*Suillus granulatus* (L.: Fr.) Roussel[†]	dotted-stalk suillus
冬块菌	dongkuaijun	*Tuber brumale* Vittad.[†]	winter truffle
短柄乳牛肝菌	duanbing runiuganjun	*Suillus brevipes* (Peck) Kuntze[†]	short-stalked suillus
短裙竹荪	duanqun zhusun	*Dictyophora duplicata* (Bosc) E. Fisch.[C]	netted stinkhorn
盾蚁巢伞	dunyichaosan*	*Termitomyces clypeatus* R. Heim	termite mushroom
多汁鳞伞	duozhi linsan	*Pholiota adiposa* (Batsch: Fr.) P. Kumm.	fat pholiota
多汁乳菇	duozhi rugu	*Lactarius volemus* (Fr.: Fr.) Fr.[†]	weeping milky cap
俄勒冈白块菌	elegang baikuaijun*	*Tuber gibbosum* Harkn.[†]	Oregon white truffle
发光蜜环菌	faguang mihuangjun	*Armillaria tabescens* (Scop.) Emel	ringless honey mushroom
绯红蜡菇	feihong lagu*	*Hygrocybe coccinea* (Schaeff.: Fr.) P. Kumm.[†]	scarlet waxy cup
非洲地蘑	feizhou dimo*	*Tirmania africana* Chatin[†]	desert truffle
粉侧耳	fenceer*	*Pleurotus djamor* (Rumph. ex Fr.: Fr.) Boedijn[C]	pink oyster mushroom
凤尾菇	fengwuigu	*Pleurotus pulmonarius* (Fr.: Fr.) Quél.[C]	phoenix mushroom
粉状绒盖牛肝菌	fenzhuang ronggainiuganjun	*Xerocomus pulverulentus* (Opat.) J. E. Gilbert[†]	
粉紫香蘑	fenzixiangmo	*Lepista personata* (Fr.: Fr.) Cooke[† C]	field blewit

Chinese common name	Pinyin	Scientific name	English common name
浮雕马勃	fudiao mabo	*Calvatia caelata* (Bull.) Morg.	
茯苓	fuling	*Wolfiporia cocos* (F. A. Wolf) Ryvarden et Gilb.	fuling
肝色牛排菌	ganse niupaijun	*Fistulina hepatica* (Schaeff.: Fr.) With.	beefsteak fungus
干小皮伞	ganxiaopisan	*Marasmius siccus* (Schwein.: Fr.) Fr.	orange pinwheel
高大环柄菇	gaodahuanbinggu	*Macrolepiota procera* (Scop.: Fr.) Singer[†]	parasol mushroom
高丝膜菌	gaosimojun	*Cortinarius elatior* Fr.[†]	
高羊肚菌	gaoyangdujun	*Morchella elata* Fr.: Fr.	black morel
革质红菇	gezhi honggu	*Russula alutacea* (Pers.: Fr.) Fr.[†]	
格状猴头菌	gezhuang houtoujun	*Hericium clathroides* (Pall.: Fr.) Pers.	fungus icicles
冠锁瑚菌	guan suohujun	*Clavulina cristata* (Holmsk.: Fr.) J. Schröt.	crested coral
光孢环枝瑚菌	guangbao huangzhihujun	*Ramaria obtusissima* (Peck) Corner[†]	
光滑鳞伞	guanghua lingsan*	*Pholiota lubrica* (Pers.: Fr.) Singer	
管形鸡油菌	guangxing jiyoujun	*Cantharellus tubaeformis* (Bull.: Fr.) Fr.	autumn chanterelle
鬼笔	guibi	*Phallus impudicus* L.: Pers.[†]	common stinkhorn
古尼虫草	guni congcao	*Cordyceps gunnii* (Berk.) Berk.	vegetable caterpillar fungus
古氏地空菌	gushi dikongjun	*Geopora cooperi* Harkn.[†]	fuzzy truffle
含糊黑腹菌	hanhu heifujun	*Melanogaster ambiguus* (Vittad.) Tul. et C. Tul.	black-veined false truffle
好哈吐虫草	hauhatu chongcao*	*Cordyceps robertsii* (Hook.) Berk.	vegetable caterpillar fungus
好吐鲁虫草	hautulu chongcao*	*Cordyceps hauturu* Dingley	vegetable caterpillar fungus
褐环乳牛肝菌	hehuan runiuganjun	*Suillus luteus* (L.: Fr.) Roussel[†]	slippery jack

Chinese common name	Pinyin	Scientific name	English common name
黑孢块菌	heibao kuaijun	*Tuber melanosporum* Vittad.[†]	Périgord black truffle
黑地荤	heidixun*	*Picoa carthusiana* Tul.	
黑蚁巢伞	heiyichaosan*	*Termitomyces fuliginosus* R. Heim	termite mushroom
褐圆孢牛肝菌	henyuanbaoniuganjun	*Gyroporus castaneus* (Bull.: Fr.) Quél.[†]	chestnut bolete
褐绒盖牛肝菌	heronggainiuganjun	*Xerocomus badius* (Fr.: Fr.) Kühner[†]	bay bolete
合生离褶伞	hesheng lizhesan*	*Lyophyllum connatum* (Schumach.: Fr.) Singer	
荷叶离褶伞	heye lizhesan	*Lyophyllum decastes* (Fr.: Fr.) Singer[†]	hatakeshimeji
褐疣柄牛肝菌	heyoubingniuganjun	*Leccinum scabrum* (Bull.: Fr.) Gray[†]	brown birch bolete
红盾赤褶菇	hongdun chizhegu	*Rhodophyllus clypeatus* (L.: Fr.) Quél.[†]	Roman shield entoloma
红盖鹅膏	honggai egao*	*Amanita hemibapha* (Berk. et Broome) Sacc.[†]	slender Caesar's mushroom
红菇蜡伞	honggu lasan	*Hygrophorus russula* (Schaeff.: Fr.) Quél.[†]	russula-like waxy cap
红鸡油菌	hongjiyoujun	*Cantharellus cinnabarinus* (Schwein.: Fr.) Schwein.[†]	red chanterelle
红绒盖牛肝菌	hongronggainiugangjun	*Xerocomus chrysenteron* (Bull.) Quél.[†]	red-cracked bolete
红须腹菌	hongxufujun	*Rhizopogon rubescens* (Tul. et C. Tul.) Tul. et C. Tul.[†]	shoro
红汁乳菇	hongzhi rugu	*Lactarius hatsudake* Tanaka[†]	hatsudake
厚环乳牛肝菌	houhuan runiuganjun	*Suillus grevillei* (Klotzsch) Singer[†]	larch bolete
厚鳞多孔菌	houlin duokongjun*	*Pachyma hoelen* Rumph. ex Fr.: Fr.	hoelen
猴头	houtou	*Hericium erinaceus* (Bull.: Fr.) Pers.[c]	lion's mane mushroom
桦澳洲牛干菌	hua aozhouniuganju*	*Austroboletus betula* (Schweinitz) E. Horak	shaggy-stalked bolete

Chinese common name	Pinyin	Scientific name	English common name
滑菇	huagu	*Pholiota nameko* (T. Ito) S. Ito et S. Imai[c]	nameko
花脸香蘑	hualian xiangmo	*Lepista sordida* (Schumach.: Fr.) Singer	
华美牛肝菌	huamei niuganjun	*Boletus speciosus* Frost[†]	
黄孢红菇	huangbao honggu	*Russula xerampelina* (Schaeff.) Fr.[†]	shrimp russula
黄地蘑	huangdimo*	*Tirmania pinoyi* (Maire) Malençon[†]	
黄金耳	huangjiner	*Tremella mesenterica* Retz.: Fr.[c]	witch's butter
黄鸡油菌	huangjyoujun*	*Cantharellus luteocomus* H. E. Bigelow[†]	
黄丝膜菌	huangsimojun	*Cortinarius claricolor* (Fr.) Fr. var. *turmalis* (Fr.) M. M. Moser[†]	
灰鹅膏	huiegao	*Amanita vaginata* (Bull.: Fr.) Lam.[†]	grisette
灰盖鬼伞	huigai guisan	*Coprinus cinereus* (Schaeff.: Fr.) Gray[c]	shaggy dung coprinus
灰光柄菇	huiguangbinggu	*Pluteus atricapillus* (Batsch) Fayod[†]	deer mushroom
灰褐香蘑	huihexiangmo	*Lepista luscina* (Fr.: Fr.) Singer	
灰口蘑	huikoumo	*Tricholoma portentosum* (Fr.: Fr.) Quél.[†]	streaked tricholoma
灰离褶伞	huilizhesan*	*Lyophyllum fumosum* (Pers.: Fr.) P. D. Orton	ashy tricholoma
灰色锁瑚菌	huisesuohujun	*Clavulina cinerea* (Bull.: Fr.) J. Schröt.	gray coral
灰树花	huishuhua	*Grifola frondosa* (Dicks.: Fr.) Gray	hen of the woods
虎皮小牛肝菌	hupi xiaoniuganjun	*Suillus pictus* (Peck) Kuntze[†]	painted suillus
假猴头	jiahoutou	*Hericium ramosum* (Bull.) Letell.[c]	comb tooth mushroom

Chinese common name	Pinyin	Scientific name	English common name
尖羊肚菌	jianyangdujun	*Morchella conica* Pers.: Fr. var. *deliciosa* (Fr.: Fr.) Cetto	black morel
胶玉蘑	jiaoyumo*	*Hypsizygus marmoreus* (Peck) H. E. Bigelow[c]	shimeji
加州块菌	jiazhou kuaijun*	*Tuber californicum* Harkn.[†]	California truffle
洁丽香菇	jieli xianggu	*Lentinus suffrutescens* (Brot.: Fr.) Fr.	train-wrecker
金耳	jiner	*Tremella aurantia* Schwein.: Fr.	golden ear
晶粒鬼伞	jingli guisan	*Coprinus micaceus* (Bull.: Fr.) Fr.	mica cap
金褐伞	jinhesan	*Phaeolepiota aurea* (Matt.: Fr.) Maire	
金毛多汁鳞伞	jinmao lingsan	*Pholiota aurivella* (Batsch.: Fr.) P. Kumm.	golden pholiota
金针菇	jinzhengu	*Flammulina velutipes* (Curtis: Fr.) Singer[c]	enokitake
寄生田头菇	jisheng tiantougu*	*Agrocybe parasitica* Stevenson	poplar mushroom
鸡油菌	jiyoujun	*Cantharellus cibarius* Fr.: Fr.[†]	chanterelle
卷缘齿菌	juanyan chijun	*Hydnum repandum* L.: Fr.[†]	hedgehog mushroom
菌核侧耳	junhe ceer	*Pleurotus tuber-regium* (Rumph. ex Fr.: Fr.) Singer[c]	sclerotia-producing pleurotus
空柄小牛肝菌	kongbing xiaoniuganjun	*Suillus cavipes* (Opat.) A. H. Sm. et Thiers[†]	hollow-stalked boletus
口蘑	koumo	*Tricholoma mongolicum* S. Imai	
喇叭菌	labajun	*Craterellus cornucopioides* (L.: Fr.) Pers.[†]	horn of plenty
兰黄红菇	lanhuang honggu	*Russula cyanoxantha* (Schaeff.) Fr.[†]	blue russula
兰绿乳菇	lanlu rugu	*Lactarius indigo* (Schwein.: Fr.) Fr.[†]	indigo milky
兰圆孢牛肝菌	lanyuanbaoniuganjun	*Gyroporus cyanescens* (Bull.: Fr.) Quél.[†]	bluing bolete
肋脉羊肚菌	leimai yangdujun	*Morchella costata* (Vent.) Pers.	morel

Chinese common name	Pinyin	Scientific name	English common name
雷蘑	leimo	*Leucopaxillus giganteus* (Sibth.: Fr.) Singer[†]	giant clitocybe
裂褶菌	liezhejun	*Schizophyllum commune* Fr.: Fr.	common split gill
鳞多孔菌	lin duokongjun	*Polyporus squamosus* (Huds.: Fr.) Fr.	dryad's saddle
林地蘑菇	lindi mogu	*Agaricus sylvaticus* Schaeff.	forest mushroom
棱柄马鞍菌	lingbing maanjun	*Helvella lacunosa* Afzel.: Fr.[†]	elfin sandle
柄条孢牛肝菌棱	lingbing tiaobaoniuganjun	*Boletellus russellii* (Frost) J. E. Gilbert[†]	jagged-stalked bolete
菱红菇	linghonggu	*Russula vesca* Fr.[†]	edible russula
灵芝	lingzhi	*Ganoderma* aff. *lucidum* (W. Curt.) P. Karst.[c]	reishi
栗牛肝菌	liniugajun*	*Boletus aestivalis* (Paulet) Fr.[†]	white-cap bolete
硫磺菌	liuhuangjun	*Laetiporus sulphureus* (Bull.: Fr.) Murrill	chicken of the woods
梨形灰孢	lixing huibao	*Lycoperdon pyriforme* Schaeff.: Pers.[†]	pear-shaped puffball
隆纹黑蛋巢菌	longwei heidanchaojun	*Cyathus striatus* (Huds.: Pers.) Willd.	bird's nest fungus
漏斗鸡油菌	loudou jiyoujun	*Cantharellus infundibuliformis* (Scop.) Fr.[†]	funnel-shaped chanterelle
鹿花菌	luhuajun	*Gyromitra esculenta* (Pers.) Fr.[†]	false morel
雷丸	luiwan	*Laccocephalum mylittae* (Cook et Massee) Núñez et Ryvarden	native bread
铆钉菇	maodinggu	*Chroogomphus rutilus* (Schaeff.: Fr.) O. K. Mill.	viscid gomphidius
毛木耳	maomuer	*Auricularia polytricha* (Mont.) Sacc.[c]	wood ear
毛头鬼伞	maotou guisan	*Coprinus comatus* (Müll.: Fr.) Pers.[c]	shaggy ink cap
美味牛肝菌	meiwei niuganjun	*Boletus edulis* Bull.: Fr.[†]	porcini
美味红菇	meiwui honggu	*Russula delica* Fr.[†]	milk-white russula
美味乳菇	meiwui rugu	*Lactarius deliciosus* (L.: Fr.) Gray[†]	saffron milk cap

Chinese common name	Pinyin	Scientific name	English common name
美洲松茸	meizhou songrong	*Tricholoma magnivelare* (Peck) Redhead[†]	white matsutake
蜜环丝膜菌	mihuan simojun	*Cortinarius armillatus* (Fr.: Fr.) Fr.[†]	bracelet cortinarius
摩冬块菌	modongkuaijun*	*Tuber brumale* Vittad. var. *moschatum* Ferry[†]	
蘑菇	mogu	*Agaricus campestris* L.: Fr.	field mushroom
墨汁鬼伞	mozhi guisan	*Coprinus atramentarius* (Bull.: Fr.) Fr.	common ink cap
木耳	muer	*Auricularia auricula* (Pers.: Fr.) Fuckel[C]	wood ear
南非地菇	nanfi digu*	*Terfezia pfeilii* Henn.[†]	
囊侧耳	nangceer*	*Pleurotus cystidiosus* O. K. Mill.[C]	abalone mushroom
囊马勃	nangmabao*	*Vascellum pratense* (Pers.: Pers.) Kreisel	common puffball
粘柄丝膜菌	nianbing simojun	*Cortinarius collinitus* (Sow.: Fr.) Fr.[†]	
粘小奥德蘑	nianxiaoaodemo	*Oudemansiella mucida* (Schrad.: Fr.) Höhn.[C]	porcelain fungus
鸟褐地菌	niaohedijun*	*Phaeangium lefebvrei* Pat.[†]	desert truffle
拟兰紫丝膜菌	nilanzisimojun*	*Cortinarius pseudosalor* J. E. Lange[†]	
柠檬蜡伞	ningmeng lasan*	*Hygrophorus lucorum* Kalchbr.[†]	
牛舌菌	niushejun	*Fistulina hepatica* (Schaeff.: Fr.) With. var. *antarctica* (Speg.) J. E. Wright	chestnut tongue
拟四陷块菌	niwaxian kuaijun	*Tuber pseudoexcavatum* Y. Wang, G. Moreno, Riousset, Manjón et G. Riousset[†]	Chinese truffle
浓香乳菇	nongxiang rugu	*Lactarius camphoratus* (Fr.: Fr.) Fr.[†]	aromatic milky
欧洲松茸	ouzhou songrong	*Tricholoma caligatum* (Viv.) Ricken[†]	European matsutake

Chinese common name	Pinyin	Scientific name	English common name
平菇	pinggu	*Pleurotus ostreatus* (Jacq.: Fr.) P. Kumm.[c]	oyster mushroom
葡萄状枝瑚菌	putaozhuang zhihujun	*Ramaria botrytis* (Pers.: Fr.) Ricken[†]	purple-tipped coral fungus
捕蝇口蘑	puying koumo*	*Tricholoma muscarium* Kawam. ex Hongo[†]	
漆蜡蘑	qi lamo	*Laccaria laccata* (Scop.: Fr.) Berk. et Br.[†]	the deceiver
翘鳞伞	qiaolingsan	*Pholiota squarrosa* (Oeder: Fr.) P. Kumm.	scaly pholiota
球杯伞	qiubeisan*	*Clitocybe gibba* (Pers.: Fr.) P. Kumm.	common funnel cap
日本口蘑	ribenkoumo*	*Tricholoma japonica* Kawam.[†]	
绒盖条孢牛肝菌	ronggai tiaobaoniuganjun	*Boletus mirabilis* Murrill[†]	admirable bolete
绒红铆钉菇	ronghongmaodinggu	*Chroogomphus tomentosus* (Murrill) O. K. Mill.	woolly gomphidius
绒木耳	rongmuer*	*Auricularia fuscosuccinea* (Mont.) Henn.[c]	black jelly fungus
肉色杯伞	rouse beisan	*Clitocybe geotropa* (Bull. ex DC.) Quél.	
肉色香蘑	rouse xiangmo	*Lepista irina* (Fr.) H. E. Bigelow	
乳牛肝菌	runiugangjun	*Suillus bovinus* (L.: Fr.) Kuntze[†]	Jersey cow bolete
稍厚赤褶菇	shaohou chizhegu	*Rhodophyllus crassipes* (Imazeki et Toki) Imazeki et Hongo[†]	
沙生地菇	shasheng digu*	*Terfezia arenaria* (Moris) Trappe[†]	desert truffle
傻松茸	shasongrong	*Tricholoma bakamatsutake* Hongo[†]	bakamatsutake
石耳	shier	*Umbilicaria esculenta* (Miyoshi) Minks	iwatake
双孢蘑菇	shuangbao mogu	*Agaricus bisporus* (J. E. Lange) Imbach[c]	button mushroom
树状蜡伞	shuzhuang lansan	*Hygrophorus arbustivus* Fr.[†]	

Chinese common name	Pinyin	Scientific name	English common name
丝盖口蘑	sigai koumo	*Tricholoma sejunctum* (Sowerby: Fr.) Quél.[†]	separating tricholoma
丝盖小包脚菇	sigai xiaobaojiaogu	*Volvariella bombycina* (Schaeff.: Fr.) Singer[c]	silky volvaria
松茸	song rong	*Tricholoma matsutake* (S. Ito et S. Imai) Singer[†]	matsutake
松牛肝菌	songniuganjun*	*Boletus pinicola* (Vittad.) A. Venturi[†]	cep
桃红牛肝菌	taohongniuganjun	*Boletus regius* Krombh.[†]	butter bolete
田头菇	tiantougu	*Agrocybe praecox* (Pers.: Fr.) Fayod	spring agrocybe
铁杉灵芝	tieshan lingzhi	*Ganoderma tsugae* Murrill[c]	hemlock polypore
铜绿红菇	tongluhonggu	*Russula aeruginea* Lindblad ex Fr.	green russula
铜色牛肝菌	tongse niuganjun	*Boletus aereus* Bull.: Fr.[†]	cep
土褐牛肝菌	tuheniuganjun	*Boletus pallidus* Frost[†]	
陀螺菌	tuoluojun	*Gomphus clavatus* (Pers.: Fr.) Gray[†]	short-stalked chanterelle
网柄牛肝菌	wangbing niuganjun*	*Boletus reticulatus* Schaeff.[†]	cep
网兜菌	wangdoujun*	*Ileodictyon cibarium* Tul. et C. Tul.	basket fungus
网纹灰孢	wangwen huibao	*Lycoperdon perlatum* Pers.: Pers.[†]	gem-studded puffball
凹陷块菌	waxian kuaijun	*Tuber excavatum* Vittad.[†]	hollowed truffle
纹环球盖菇	wenhuan qiugaigu*	*Stropharia rugosoannulata* Farl. ex Murrill[c]	wine-cap stropharia
纹褶小奥德蘑	wenzhe xiaoaodemo*	*Oudemansiella venosolamellata* (Imazeki et Toki) Imazeki et Hongo	
污褐牛肝菌	wuheniuganjun	*Boletus variipes* Peck[†]	
夏块菌	xiakuaijun	*Tuber aestivum* Vittad.[†]	summer truffle
线柄松塔牛肝	xianbing songtaniugang	*Strobilomyces floccopus* (Vahl: Fr.) P. Karst.[†]	old man of the woods
香杯伞	xiangbeisan	*Clitocybe odora* (Fr.) P. Kumm.	anise-scented clitocybe

Chinese common name	Pinyin	Scientific name	English common name
香菇	xianggu	*Lentinula edodes* (Berk.) Pegler	shiitake
香肉齿菌	xiangrouchijun	*Sarcodon aspratus* (Berk.) S. Ito[†]	
香信口蘑	xiangxing koumo	*Calocybe gambosa* (Fr.: Fr.) Singer	St. George's mushroom
小牛肝菌	xiaoniuganjun	*Fuscoboletinus paluster* (Peck) Pomerleau[†]	
小蚁巢伞	xiaoyichaosan*	*Termitomyces microcarpus* (Berk. et Broome) R. Heim	termite mushroom
细柄丝膜菌	xibing simojun*	*Cortinarius tenuipes* (Hongo) Hongo[†]	
斜盖伞	xiegaisan	*Clitopilus prunulus* (Scop.: Fr.) P. Kumm.	sweet bread mushroom
新西兰榛蘑	xinxilan zhenmo*	*Armillaria novaezelandiae* (Stevenson) Herink	bootlace mushroom
绣球菌	xiuqiujun	*Sparassis crispa* (Wulfen: Fr.) Fr.[c]	cauliflower fungus
血红乳菇	xuehong rugu	*Lactarius sanguifluus* (Paulet) Fr.[†]	red-juice milk cap
羊肚菌	yangdujun	*Morchella esculenta* Pers.: Fr.	yellow morel
羊肚菌	yangdujun	*Morchella esculenta* var. *rigida* Krombh.	yellow morel
羊肚菌	yangdujun	*Morchella esculenta* var. *rotunda* Pers.: Fr.	yellow morel
羊肚菌	yangdujun	*Morchella esculenta* var. *umbrina* (Boud.) S. Imai	yellow morel
羊肚菌	yangdujun	*Morchella esculenta* var. *vulgaris* Pers.: Fr.	yellow morel
艳乳菇	yanrugu*	*Lactarius laeticolor* (S. Imai) Imaz.[†]	
烟云杯伞	yanyun beisan	*Clitocybe nebularis* (Batsch.: Fr.) P. Kumm.	clouded clitocybe
药用层孔菌	yaoyong cengkongjun	*Fomitopsis officinalis* (Batsch: Fr.) Bondartsev et Singer	purging agaric
亚香棒虫草	yaxiangbang chongcao	*Cordyceps hawkesii* G. R. Grey	

Chinese common name	Pinyin	Scientific name	English common name
亚砖红沿丝伞	yazhuanhong yansisan	*Naematoloma sublateritium* (Fr.) P. Karst.	brick caps
野蘑菇	yemogu	*Agaricus arvensis* Schaeff.	horse mushroom
蚁巢伞	yichaosan	*Termitomyces albuminosa* (Berk.) R. Heim	termite mushroom
意大利白块菌	yidali baikuijun*	*Tuber magnatum* Picco[†]	Italian white truffle
印度块菌	yindu kuaijun	*Tuber indicum* Cooke et Massee[†]	Indian truffle
银耳	yiner	*Tremella fuciformis* Berk.[c]	white jelly fungus
硬柄皮伞	yingbing pisan	*Marasmius oreades* (Bolton: Fr.) Fr.[c]	fairy ring mushroom
蛹虫草	yong chongcao	*Cordyceps militaris* (L.: Fr.) Link	scarlet caterpillar fungus
油口蘑	youkoumo	*Tricholoma flavovirens* (Pers.: Fr.) S. Lundell[†]	canary tricholoma
油味乳菇	youwei rugu	*Lactarius quietus* (Fr.: Fr.) Fr.[†]	southern milk cap
远东疣柄牛肝菌	yuandong liubingniugangjun	*Leccinum extremiorientale* (Lar. N. Vassiljeva) Singer[†]	
元蘑	yuanmo	*Hohenbuehelia serotina* (Pers.: Fr.) Singer[c]	mukitake
缘纹丝膜菌	yuanwen simojun	*Cortinarius praestans* (Corda) Gillet[†]	
榆耳	yuer	*Gloeostereum incarnatum* S. Ito et Imai	
榆黄蘑	yuhuangmo	*Pleurotus cornucopiae* (Paulet) Rolland var. *citrinopileatus* (Singer) Ohira	golden oyster mushroom
云芝	yunzhi	*Trametes versicolor* (L.: Fr.) Pilát	many-colored polypore
玉髯	yuran	*Hericium coralloides* (Scop.: Fr.) Gray[c]	coral tooth mushroom
玉草离褶伞	yuxun lizhesan*	*Lyophyllum shimeji* (Kawam.) Hongo[†]	honshimeji
皂腻口蘑	zaoni koumo	*Tricholoma saponaceum* (Fr.: Fr.) P. Kumm.[†]	soap-scented tricholoma

Chinese common name	Pinyin	Scientific name	English common name
杂色黑腹菌	zase heifujun	*Melanogaster variegatus* (Vittad.) Tul. et C. Tul.	black-veined false truffle
赭盖鹅膏	zhegai egao	*Amanita rubescens* Pers.: Fr.[†]	the blusher
榛蘑	zhenmo	*Armillaria mellea* (Vahl: Fr.) P. Kumm.	honey mushroom
中非议巢伞	zhongfei yichaosan*	*Termitomyces schimperi* (Pat.) R. Helm	termite mushroom
中华块菌	zhonghua kuaijun	*Tuber sinense* K. Tao et B. Liu[†]	Chinese truffle
轴灰包	zhou huibao	*Podaxis pistillaris* (L.: Pers.) Morse	stalked puffball
皱盖罗鳞伞	zhougai luolinsan	*Rozites caperatus* (Pers.: Fr.) P. Karst[†]	gypsy mushroom
猪苓	zhuling	*Grifola umbellata* (Pers.: Fr.) Pilát.	umbellate polyporus
竹荪	zhusun	*Dictyophora indusiata* (Vent.: Pers.) Desv.[c]	bamboo mushroom
柱状田头菇	zhuzhuang tiantougu	*Agrocybe cylindracea* (DC.) Maire[c]	southern poplar mushroom
紫晶腊蘑	zijing lamo	*Laccaria amethystea* Cooke[†]	amethyst laccaria
紫牛肝菌	ziniuganjun	*Boletus violaceofuscus* W. F. Chiu[†]	
紫绒丝膜菌	zirongsimojun	*Cortinarius violaceus* (L.: Fr.) Fr.[†]	violet cortinarius
紫色马勃	zise mabo	*Calvatia lilacina* (Mont. et Berk.) Henn.	puffball
紫色丝膜菌	zisesimojun	*Cortinarius purpurascens* (Fr.) Fr.[†]	
紫珊瑚菌	zishanhujun	*Clavaria purpurea* O. F. Müll.: Fr.	purple fairy club
紫香蘑	zixiangmo	*Lepista nuda* (Bull.: Fr.) Cooke[†c]	wood blewit
棕红块菌	zonghong kuaijun	*Tuber rufum* Picco[†]	cinnamon truffle

HELPFUL ADDRESSES

Australasian Mycological Society
c/o Cheryl Grgurinovic
Australian Biological Resources Study
G.P.O. Box 787
Canberra, A.C.T. 2601, Australia

Australian Truffle Association
c/o Australian Truffle Industries
P.O. Box 93
Bombala, New South Wales 2632, Australia

British Mycological Society
Joseph Banks Building
Royal Botanic Gardens, Kew
Richmond Surrey, TW9 3AB, United Kingdom

Danish Mycological Society
Foreningen til Svampekundskabens Fremme
Søndermarken 75
3060 Espergærde, Denmark

German Mycological Society
Deutsche Gesellschaft für Mykologie
c/o Wolfgang Thrun
Postfach 700447
D-81304 München, Germany

Italian Mycological Society
Unione Mycologica Italiana
c/o Gilberto Govi
Centro di Micologia
Università di Bologna
Via Filippone 8
1-40126 Bologna, Italy

Korean Society of Mycology
c/o Department of Applied Biology
College of Biological Resources Science
Dongguk University
Seoul 100-715, Republic of Korea

Mycological Society of Finland
Suomen Sieniseura Ry
Unioninkatu 44
SF 00170 Helsinki 17, Finland

Mycological Society of Japan
c/o Business Center for Academic Societies Japan
5-16-9 Honkomagome
Bunkyo-ku, Tokyo 113-8622, Japan

Mycological Society of the Republic of China
c/o Wen-Hsui Hsieh
Department of Plant Pathology
National Chung Hsing University
Taichung, Taiwan, Republic of China

Netherlands Mycological Society
c/o Centraalbureau voor Schimmelcultures
Postbus 85167
3508 AD Utrecht, Netherlands

New Zealand Truffle Association
c/o New Zealand Institute for Crop and Food Research
Invermay Agricultural Centre
Private Bag 50034
Mosgiel, New Zealand

North American Mycological Association
c/o Judy Roger, Executive Secretary
6615 Tudor Court
Gladstone, Oregon 97027-1032, United States

North American Truffling Society
P.O. Box 296
Corvallis, Oregon 97339, United States

Norwegian Mycological Society
Norsk Soppforening
Postboks 2828 Tøyen
N-0655 Oslo, Norway

Swedish Mycological Society
Sveriges Mykologisk Förening
c/o Arne Ryberg
Boafallsvägen 10
293 72 Jämshög, Sweden

Tartufomania
25 Via Zena
40065 Bologna, Italy

Le Trufficulteur Français
B.P. 7065
rue de Jardin Public
24007 Périgeaux, France

WEB SITES

American Mushroom Institute (AMI).
http://www.americanmushroom.org/

Bad Bug Book. Foodborne pathogenic microorganisms and natural toxins handbook. U.S. Food and Drug Administration, Center for Food Safety and Applied Nutrition.
http://www.cfsan.fda.gov/~mow/chap40.html

British Mycological Society (BMS).
http://www.ulst.ac.uk/faculty/science/bms/

Canadian Poison Control Centers. A list created by the Children's Safety Association of Canada. http://www.safekid.org/

Centers for Disease Control and Prevention (CDC).
http://www.cdc.gov

Economic Fungi of China.
http://www.has-china.com/new_page_1.htm

Fungi Images on the Net. http://www.in2.dk/fungi/

Fungi of California. http://www.mykoweb.com/CAF/index.html

Fungi Perfecti. www.fungi.com

George Barron's Web Site on Mushrooms and Other Fungi. University of Guelph. Guelph, Ontario.
http://www.uoguelph.ca/~gbarron/

Introduction to the Fungi. University of California, Berkeley.
http://www.ucmp.berkeley.edu/fungi/fungi.html

Malawi Fungi. http://www.malawifungi.org/

Mushroom Council. http://www.mushroomcouncil.com/

Mushroom Toxins. vm.cfsan.fda.gov/~mow/chap40

Mycorrhiza Information Exchange. http://mycorrhiza.ag.utk.edu/

Myxo Web: A Virtual Field Guide to the Myxomycetes.
http://www.wvonline.com/myxo/

National Capital Poison Center (United States).
http://www.poison.org/

National Poisons Information Service (United Kingdom). http://www.npis.org/

Northwest Fungus Group. http://www.fungus.org.uk/nwfg.htm

Penn State University Mushroom Industry Short Course. http://conferences.cas.psu.edu/

Poison Center Directory. http://www.aapcc.org/director2.htm

Psylocybe Fanaticus. http://www.fanaticus.com/

Sacred Mushrooms: The Vaults of Erowid. http://www.erowid.org/plants/mushrooms/

Tom Volk's Fungi. Department of Biology. University of Wisconsin, La Crosse. http://www.botit.botany.wisc.edu/toms_fungi/

Truffle.org: The New Smell of Truffles. http://www.truffle.org/

Wild Mushrooms from Tokyo. http://www.ne.jp/asahi/mushroom/tokyo/right

WWW Virtual Library of Mycology. Cornell University. http://www.mycology.cornell.edu

GLOSSARY

For other mycological terms and names see *Elsevier's Dictionary of Edible Mushrooms* (Chandra 1989) and *Ainsworth and Bisby's Dictionary of the Fungi* (Kirk et al. 2001).

Actinomycete. Usually filamentous, gram-positive bacteria (for example, *Streptomyces*) that superficially resemble filamentous fungi.

Aerobic. Living and growing only in the presence of oxygen.

Arbuscules. Microscopic treelike structures that form in vesicular-arbuscular mycorrhizas and help transfer nutrients between the host plant and fungus.

Ascocarp. A cup-shaped structure formed by some ascomycetes, on which asci develop.

Ascomycetes. The largest class of fungi, containing more than thirty-two thousand species. Members are referred to as ascomycetes.

Ascospore. A sexual spore produced by ascomycetes and usually borne in an ascus.

Ascus (pl. asci). A saclike structure produced by ascomycetes in which ascospores are produced.

Autoclave. An oven used to sterilize media and equipment using steam typically at 121°C.

Bagasse. The dry pulp (as of sugar cane, for example) left after extracting juice from plant material.

Basidiomycetes. A class of fungi containing more than thirty thousand species, including the rusts, smuts, and most fungi that produce what are commonly called "mushrooms." Members are referred to as basidiomycetes.

Biological efficiency rating. The fresh weight of mushrooms expressed as a fraction of the dry weight of the substrate.

Bioluminescent. Producing light through a biological process.

Biomass. A quantity of biological material.

Block. A substrate formed into a more or less rectangular slab.

Brûlé. The bare area around truffle-infected trees, said to indicate the start of truffle production.

Button stage. The stage of a young mushroom before the cap has expanded and opened out.

Cap. The fertile, usually upper section of a mushroom. Also called the pileus.

Carbon-nitrogen ratio. The organic carbon present in a soil, expressed as a fraction of total nitrogen.

Casing. A mixture of moistened peat, top soil, and lime spread over mushroom compost.

Cellulose. A carbohydrate composed of very long chains of glucose molecules. Cellulose is the major structural component in the cell walls of higher plants.

Cortina. A network of delicate weblike material that covers the gills in some mushrooms.

Culture. The cultivation of an organism on a suitable medium, as with nutrient agar grown in a petri dish.

Cyclopeptides. Amino acids arranged in a ring.

Ectomycorrhiza. A mycorrhizal fungus that usually forms a mantle.

Gasteromycetales. An artificial group of about twelve hundred species that do not actively discharge their spores, placed in the Basidiomycetes.

Gills. The vertical plates on the underside of the caps of certain mushrooms, on which spores are formed. Also called the lamellae.

Hartig net. A hyphal network formed by ectomycorrhizal fungi that extends from the inner surface of the mantle into the root of a host plant.

Head. The name generally given to the upper expanded portion of stinkhorns and puffballs.

Heavy metal. A generally toxic metal, such as chromium, lead, and mercury.

Herbarium. A systematically arranged collection of dried plant or fungal specimens.

Hypha (pl. **hyphae**). One of the filaments of a fungal mycelium.

Infect. To contaminate, as when a fungus invades a plant.

Indigenous. Native to a particular area.

Inoculate. To place a culture of something—for example, a fungus—on a culture medium or potential host plant.

Lamina flow cabinet. A sterile chamber that allows an operator to manipulate bacterial and fungal cultures.

Little brown mushrooms (LBMs). A category of mushrooms, some of which are poisonous and all of which are difficult to identify without the use of a microscope.

Macroscopic. Large enough to be seen by the naked eye.

Mantle. The layer of fungal material covering the fine roots of an ectomycorrhizal host plant.

Membranous. Very thin.

Microscopic. Too small to be seen by the naked eye.

Mycelium. A mass of fungal hyphae.

Mycorrhiza. The close symbiotic association of a fungus and a host plant.

Niche. A habitat that supplies the appropriate set of conditions needed for a species to grow and thrive.

Parasite. An organism that gains its nutrients from a host organism with or without causing damage to the host.

Pasteurization. A process that involves heating a substance in order to free it of objectionable organisms.

Pathogen. An organism that causes disease.

Peridioles. Small egglike packages containing spores; characteristic of the bird's nest fungi.

pH. A measure of soil acidity and alkalinity. A value of 7 indicates neutrality, a value higher than 7 indicates alkalinity, and a value lower than 7 indicates acidity.

Plasmodium (pl. **plasmodia**). The irregular, amoebic structure formed by slime molds.

Polysaccharide. A chain of sugar molecules.

Primordium (pl. **primordia**). An organ, such as a fruiting body, in the early stages of development.

Quarantine. A period of isolation imposed on animals or plants that have arrived from elsewhere or that may have been exposed to an infectious disease.

Radioisotope. A radioactive isotope.

Ring. A ringlike structure on the stalk of some mushrooms that represents the remains of the partial veil. Also called the annulus.

Saprobe. An organism that gains its nutrients from animal or plant remains.

Sclerotium (pl. **sclerotia**). A mass of fungal tissue most often appearing underground.

Shiro. The underground fungal colony formed by *Tricholoma* species.

Spawn. A culture of a fungus used to inoculate the substrate.

Specialty mushroom. Any cultivated mushroom other than *Agaricus bisporus* and *A. bitorquis*.

Spines. The vertical projections on the underside of the caps of certain mushrooms, such as species of *Hydnum* and *Sarcodon*, on which spores are formed.

Spore. A general term for a typically small reproductive structure in bacteria, bryophytes, ferns, fungi, lichens, and slime molds.

Stalk. The section of a mushroom between the substrate and the cap. Also called the stipe or stem.

Sterilize. To completely free of living organisms.

Strain. A clonal culture of an organism.

Substrate. The material on which a fungus or bacterium grows.

Symbiosis. A close physical relationship between dissimilar organisms in which both partners generally benefit.

Toadstool. A mushroom with an umbrella-shaped cap. The word is a corruption of the German *Todesstuhl* ("death's stool"), which has no scientific meaning.

Toxin. A poison produced by a living organism.

Truffle. The underground fruiting body of fungi in the Tuberales, such as species of *Tuber*.

Truffière. A natural area or artificial plantation where truffles are found.

Tubes. The vertical pores on the underside of the caps of certain mushrooms, such as *Boletus* and *Suillus* species, in which spores are formed.

Veil. A membrane that covers the gills on certain mushrooms.

Vesicles. Swollen cells at the end of hyphae that form in vesicular-arbuscular mycorrhizas and function as small storage organs.

Vesicular-arbuscular mycorrhiza (VAM). A mycorrhiza formed by the vast majority of higher plants in association with fungi in the family Endogonaceae.

Volva. The cup at the base of the stalk, especially of species of *Amanita*.

REFERENCES AND FURTHER READING

In addition to references cited, we have included information about useful Asian, Australasian, and Western field guides and books on the cultivation of saprobic, mycorrhizal, and medicinal mushrooms.

Abate, D. 1996. Cultivation of the oyster mushroom in traditional brick pots. *Mycologist* 9: 179–181.

Alexopoulos, C. J., C. W. Mims, and M. Blackwell. 1996. *Introductory Mycology*. 4th ed. New York: John Wiley and Sons.

Allen, J. W., M. D. Merlin, and K. L. R. Jansen. 1991. An ethnomycological review of psychoactive agarics in Australia and New Zealand. *Journal of Psychoactive Drugs* 23: 39–69.

Anonymous. 1997. Cultivating morels. *The Mushroom Growers' Newsletter* 5 (12): 2–5.

Anonymous. 2000a. U.S. wholesale market prices. *The Mushroom Growers' Newsletter* 9 (5): 4.

Anonymous. 2000b. Truffle kerfuffle. *Divine Food and Wine* 23: 6–12.

Arora, D. 1986. *Mushrooms Demystified: A Comprehensive Guide to the Fleshy Fungi*. 2nd ed. Berkeley, California: Ten Speed Press. Western field guide.

Arora, D. 1991. *All That the Rain Promises and More: A Hip Pocket Guide to Western Mushrooms*. Berkeley, California: Ten Speed Press. Western field guide.

Astier, J. 1998. *Truffes Blanches et Noires* (Tuberaceae and Terfeziaceae). La Penne sur Huveaune, France: Joseph Astier. Western field guide.

Baker, H. 1989. Fungal styptics. *Mycologist* 3: 19–20

Baker, H. 1997. Gourmet mushrooms for all. *New Scientist* 153: 2066.

Barnhart, H. 2000. Reciprocity law failure fixed? *Mushroom: The Journal of Wild Mushrooming* 69 (4): 22.

Beauséjour, T. M. 2000. Morel cultivation for the adventurous and observant. *Mushroom: The Journal of Wild Mushrooming* 18 (3): 21–24.

Becker, P. 1983. Ectomycorrhizae on *Shorea* (Dipterocarpaceae) seedlings in a lowland Malaysian rainforest. *Malaysian Forester* 46: 146–170.

Bencivenga, M., and G. Vignozzi. 1989. *I tartufo in Toscana*. Firenze, Italy: Il vantaggio edizioni. Guide to cultivation of mycorrhizal mushrooms.

Benjamin, D. R. 1995. *Mushrooms: Poisons and Panaceas*. New York: W. H. Freeman.

Bessette, A. E., A. R. Bessette, and D. W. Fischer. 1997. *Mushrooms of Northeastern North America*. Syracuse, New York: Syracuse University Press. Western field guide.

Bessette, A. E., O. K. Miller, Jr., A. R. Bessette, and H. H. Miller. 1995. *Mushrooms of North America in Color*. Syracuse, New York: Syracuse University Press. Western field guide.

Bessette, A. E., W. C. Roody, and A. R. Bessette. 2000. *North American Boletes: A Color Guide to the Fleshy Pored Mushrooms*. Syracuse, New York: Syracuse University Press. Western field guide.

Beug, M. 1999. Your behaviour—just having a home and a lawn—could get you into trouble. *Mushroom: The Journal of Wild Mushrooming* 17 (4): 13–14.

Both, E. E. 1993. *The Boletes of North America*. Buffalo, New York: Buffalo Museum of Science. Western field guide.

Bougher, N. L., and K. Syme. 1998. *Fungi of Southern Australia*. Nedlands, Western Australia: University of Western Australia Press. Australasian field guide.

Branzanti, B., and A. Zambonelli. 1987. Effetti della micorrizazione sullo sviluppo di semenzali di *Pinus pinaster*. *Micologia Italiana* 16: 53–57. Guide to cultivation of mycorrhizal mushrooms.

Brasier, C. 1992. A champion thallus. *Nature* 356: 382–383.

Breitenbach, J., and F. Kränzlin. 1984–1995. *Fungi of Switzerland*. 5 vols. Lucerne, Switzerland: Verlag Mykologia. Western field guide.

Bresinsky, A., and H. Besl. 1990. *A Colour Atlas of Poisonous Fungi*. London: Wolfe.

Brightwell, S. 1993. Feasting on fungi. *New Zealand Geographic* 18 (April–June): 35–58. Australasian field guide.

Buchanan, P. K. 1995. Recent mushroom poisonings in New Zealand. *Australasian Mycological Newsletter* 14 (4): 57–60.

Buchanan, P. K. 1996. The mushroom cultivation industry in New Zealand. In *Proceedings of the Annual Meeting of the Mushroom Technology Society of Japan*. Chiba, Japan. 18–22.

Buchanan, P. K., R. S. Hseu, and J. M. Moncalvo, eds. 1995. *Ganoderma*: systematics, phytopathology, and pharmacology. In *Proceedings of Contributed Symposium 59 A, B, Fifth International*

Mycological Congress, 14–21 August 1994. Vancouver, British Columbia. Guide to medicinal mushrooms.

Buscot, F., and I. Kotte. 1990. The association of *Morchella rotunda* (Pers.) Boudier with roots of *Picea abies* (L.) Karst. *New Phytologist* 116: 425–430.

CBC Newsworld. 1996. Poison mushrooms kill 92 in Ukraine. Retrieved 1997 from http://newsworld.cbc.ca/archive/html/1996/10/01/poisonmushrooms

Centers for Disease Control and Prevention (CDC). 1997. *Amanita phalloides* mushroom poisoning—northern California, January 1997. Morbidity and Mortality Weekly Report 46 (22): 489–492. Retrieved 1997 from http://www.cdc.gov/epo/mmwr/preview/mmwrhtml/00047808.htm

Ceruti, A., M. Tozzi, and G. Reitano. 1988. Micorrize di sintesi tra *Boletus edulis*, *Pinus silvestris*, e *Picea excelsa*. *Allionia* 28: 117–124. Guide to cultivation of mycorrhizal mushrooms.

Cetto, B. 1989–1992. *I Funghi dal Vero*. 7 vols. Trento, Italy: Saturnia. Western field guide.

Chandra, A. 1989. *Elsevier's Dictionary of Edible Mushrooms: Botanical and Common Names in Various Languages of the World*. Amsterdam: Elsevier Science.

Chang, S. T. 1991. Mushroom biology and mushroom production. *Mushroom Journal for the Tropics* 11: 45–52. Guide to cultivation of saprobic mushrooms.

Chang, S. T. 1999. World production of cultivated edible and medicinal mushrooms in 1997 with emphasis on *Lentinus edodes* (Berk.) Sing. in China. *International Journal of Medicinal Mushrooms* 1: 291–300.

Chang, S. T., J. A. Buswell, and S. W. Chiu, eds. 1993. *Mushroom Biology and Mushroom Products*. Hong Kong: Chinese University Press. Guide to medicinal mushrooms and cultivation of saprobic mushrooms.

Chang, S. T., J. A. Buswell, and P. G. Miles. 1993. *Genetics and Breeding of Edible Mushrooms*. Chemin de la Sallaz, Switzerland: Gordon and Breach. Guide to medicinal mushrooms and cultivation of saprobic mushrooms.

Chang, S. T, and W. A. Hayes, eds. 1978. *The Biology and Cultivation of Edible Mushrooms*. New York: Academic Press. Guide to medicinal mushrooms and cultivation of saprobic mushrooms.

Chang, S. T., and P. G. Miles. 1989. *Edible Mushrooms and Their Cultivation*. Boca Raton, Florida: CRC Press. Guide to medicinal mushrooms and cultivation of saprobic mushrooms.

Chang, S. T., and P. G. Miles. 1992. Mushroom biology—a new discipline. *Mycologist* 6: 64–65. Guide to medicinal mushrooms and cultivation of saprobic mushrooms.

Chang, S. T., and T. H. Quimio. 1989. *Tropical Mushrooms: Biological Nature and Cultivation Methods*. Hong Kong: Chinese University Press. Guide to medicinal mushrooms and cultivation of saprobic mushrooms.

Chauvin, J. E., and G. Salesses. 1988. Quelques aspects de la culture in vitro chez le chataignier (*Castanea* sp.). In *Septieme colloque sur les recherches fruitières, 23 Decembre 1987, Pont de la Maye*. Bordeaux, France: CTIFL/INRA. 147–160. Guide to cultivation of mycorrhizal mushrooms.

Chen, A. W. 1997. Topical use of *Ganoderma* mushrooms. *The Mushroom Growers' Newsletter* 5 (11): 2–3. Guide to medicinal mushrooms.

Chen, A. W. 2001. A practical guide to the production of *Agaricus blazei*: a mushroom of culinary and biomedical importance. *The Mushroom Growers' Newsletter* 9 (9): 3–7. Guide to cultivation of saprobic mushrooms.

Chen, A. W., and N. L. Huang. 2001. Production of tuber-like sclerotia of medicinal value by *Pleurotus tuber-regium* (Fr.) Singer. *The Mushroom Growers' Newsletter* 10 (3): 2–7. Guide to cultivation of saprobic mushrooms.

Chen, A. W., P. Stamets, and N. L. Huang. 1999. Compost-substrate fermentation and alternatives for successful production of *Agaricus blazei*. In *Proceedings of the Third International Conference on Mushroom Biology and Mushroom Products and AMGA's Twenty-Sixth National Mushroom Industry Conference, October, 1999*. Two CD-ROMs. Eds. A. J. Broderick and N. G. Nair. Hawkesbury, Sydney, Australia: University of Western Sydney. Guide to cultivation of saprobic mushrooms.

Cherfas, J. 1991. Disappearing mushrooms: another mass extinction? *Science* 254: 1458.

Chevalier, G. 1998. The truffle cultivation in France: assessment of the situation after twenty-five years of intensive use of mycorrhizal seedlings. In *Proceedings of the First International Meeting on Ecology, Physiology, and Cultivation of Edible Mycorrhizal Mushrooms*. Uppsala, Sweden.

Chevalier, G., and C. Desmas. 1975. Synthèse axenique des mycorhizes de *Tuber melanosporum*, *Tuber uncinatum*, et *Tuber rufum* sur *Pinus sylvestris* a partir de cultures pures du champignon. *Annales de Phytopathologie* 7: 338. Guide to cultivation of mycorrhizal mushrooms.

Chevalier, G., and C. Dupré. 1990. Recherche et experimentation sur la truffe et la trufficulture en France. In *Atti del Secondo Congresso Internazionale sul Tartufo, 24–27 Novembre 1988.* Eds. M. Bencivenga and B. Granetti. Spoleto, Italy. 157–166. Guide to cultivation of mycorrhizal mushrooms.

Chevalier, G., and H. Frochot. 1997. La Truffe de Bourgogne, *Tuber uncinatum* Chatin. Levallois-Perret, France: Pétrarque. Guide to cultivation and ecology of mycorrhizal mushrooms.

Chevalier, G., and G. Riousset. 1995. Truffes de Chine. Quelle truffe? *Tuber himalayense* ou *T. indicum. Le Trufficulteur Français* 11: 13–14.

Chinese Association of Edible Fungi. 2000. Production of edible mushrooms in China. *Edible Fungi of China* 19 (2): 6.

Ciani, A., B. Granetti, and D. Vincenti. 1992. Il tartufo in Italia e nel mondo: aree di produzione, mercato e prezzi. *Liinformatore Agrario* 47: 51–62.

Cole, F. M. 1993. *Amanita phalloides* in Victoria. *Medical Journal of Australia* 158: 849–850.

Cole, M. 1994. Edible and poisonous fungi in southern Australia—cases of mistaken identity. *Mycologist* 8: 35–36.

Colinas, C., J. A. Bonet, and C. Fischer. 1999. Truffle cultivation: an alternative to agricultural subsidies. In *Proceedings, Fifth International Congress on the Science and Cultivation of Truffles.* Aix-en-Provence, France. (Abstract)

Cooke, R. C. 1980. *Fungi, Man, and His Environment.* 2nd ed. London: Longman Group.

Coombs, D. H. 1994. Cultivated morels are promised but—. *Mushroom: The Journal of Wild Mushrooming* 12 (4): 7.

Courtecuisse, R., and B. Duhem. 1995. *Mushrooms and Toadstools of Britain and Europe.* London: Collins. Western field guide.

Courvoisier, M. 1995. Les importations de truffes fraîches en provenance de Chine. *Le Trufficulteur Français* 11: 10–11.

Craddock, J. 1994. Mycorrhizal association between *Corylus heterophylla* and *Tuber melanosporum. ISHS Acta Horticulturae* 351: 291–298.

Craw, C. J. 1995. *Poisonous Plants and Fungi of New Zealand.* Whangarei, New Zealand: Northland Regional Council.

Cribb, A. 1987. Mushrooms and toadstools. In *Toxic Plants and Animals: A Guide for Australia*. Eds. J. Covacevich, P. Davie, and J. Pearn. Brisbane, Australia: Queensland Museum. 22–31.

Crowe, A. 1983. *A Field Guide to the Native Edible Plants of New Zealand*. Auckland, New Zealand: Collins. Australasian field guide.

Danell, E. 1994. *Cantharellus cibarius*: mycorrhiza formation and ecology. Acta Universitatis Upsaliensis. Comprehensive summaries of Uppsala dissertations from the Faculty of Science and Technology 35. Uppsala, Sweden. Guide to ecology of mycorrhizal mushrooms. http://www.mykopat.slu.se/mycorrhiza/kantarellfiler/texter/rtf.htm

Danell, E., and F. J. Camacho. 1997. Successful cultivation of the golden chanterelle. *Nature* 385: 303. Guide to cultivation of mycorrhizal mushrooms.

Dauncey, E. A., ed. 2000. *Poisonous Plants and Fungi in Britain and Ireland: Interactive Identification Systems on CD-ROM*. Kew, England: Royal Botanic Gardens. Western field guide.

Dhabolt, J. 1993. Mushroom poisons and poisonous mushrooms. *The Puffball: Newsletter of the Willamette Valley Mushroom Society* 16 (3). http://www.mv.com/ipusers/dhabolt/dad/mushroom/puffball/puffball4/poisonous.html

Dickinson, C., and J. Lucas. 1979. *The Encyclopedia of Mushrooms*. London: Orbis. Western field guide.

Duc-Maugé, B., and B. Duplessy. 1997. *Le Livre de la Truffe*. Aix-en-Provence, France: Édisud. Guide to cultivation of mycorrhizal mushrooms.

Eastman Kodak. 1988. *Photography through the Microscope*. 9th ed. Rochester, New York: Professional Photography Division.

Economic Research Service (ERS). 2002. Vegetables and Melons Outlook. U.S. Department of Agriculture, Washington, D.C. http://www.ers.usda.gov/publications/vgs/

Ecoplanning. 1992. Norme pratiche per la coltivazione del tartufo. Città di Castello, Italy: Ministero Dell'Agricoltura e Delle Foreste. Guide to cultivation of mycorrhizal mushrooms.

Eicker, A. 1990. Commercial mushroom production in South Africa. Bulletin 418. Pretoria, South Africa: Department of Agricultural Development.

Eto, S. 1990. Cultivation of the pine seedlings infected with *Tricholoma matsutake* by use of in vitro mycorrhizal synthesis. Bulletin of the Hiroshima Prefectural Forestry Experiment Station

24: 1–6. Guide to cultivation of mycorrhizal mushrooms (in Japanese).

Evans, F., and K. Evans. 1987. *The Cookbook of North American Truffles*. Corvallis, Oregon: The North American Truffling Society.

Evans, S. 1996. Reaction to *Laetiporus sulphureus*. *Mycologist* 10: 87.

Fauconnet, C., and G. Delher. 1998. Infuence des facteurs climatiques sur la production des truffes en Quercy. *Le Trufficulteur Français* 24 (3): 19–21. Guide to cultivation of mycorrhizal mushrooms.

Fischer, D. W., and A. E. Bessette. 1992. *Edible Wild Mushrooms of North America: A Field-to-Kitchen Guide*. Austin, Texas: University of Texas Press.

Flegg, P. B., D. M. Spencer, and D. A. Wood, eds. 1985. *The Biology and Technology of the Cultivated Mushroom*. Chichester, England: John Wiley and Sons. Guide to cultivation of saprobic mushrooms.

Fletcher, J. T., P. F. White, and R. H. Gaze. 1989. *Mushrooms: Pests and Disease Control*. Newcastle upon Tyne, England: Intercept. Guide to cultivation of saprobic mushrooms.

Flück, M. 1995. *Welcher Pilz Ist Das?* Stuttgart, Germany: Franckh-Kosmos Verlags.

Freedman, B. 1996. Recent *Amanita phalloides* poisonings. *Mushroom: The Journal of Wild Mushrooming* 14 (3): 9–11.

Fuhrer, B. 1985. *A Field Companion to Australian Fungi*. Hawthorn, Australia: Five Mile Press. Australasian field guide.

Fuhrer, B., and R. Robinson. 1992. *Rainforest Fungi of Tasmania and South-east Australia*. Melbourne, Australia: CSIRO. Australasian field guide.

Fujita, H, T. Fujita, and T. Ito. 1990. Study on cultivation technique of *Lyophyllum shimeji* using infected tree seedling. Annual Report of the Forestry Experimental Station, Kyoto Prefecture, Japan. (In Japanese)

Gamundí, I. J. 1991. Review of recent advances in the knowledge of the Cyttariales. *Systema Ascomycetum* 1 (2): 69–77.

Gamundí, I. J., and E. Horak. 1995. *Fungi of the Andean-Patagonian Forests*. Buenos Aires: Vazquez Mazzini Editores.

Garcia-Falces, R. S., and A. M. De Miguel Velasco. 1995a. Situación actual de la truficultura en Navarra. *Navarra Agraria* 89: 31–36.

Garcia-Falces, R. S., and A. M. De Miguel Velasco. 1995b. *Guia Practica de Truficultura*. Universidad de Navarra. Guide to cultivation of mycorrhizal mushrooms.

Garnweidner, E. 1990. *Pilze*. Munich: Gräfe und Unzer. Western field guide.

Genders, R. 1990. *Mushroom Growing for Everyone*. London: Faber and Faber. Guide to cultivation of saprobic mushrooms.

Gilbertson, R. L. 1980. Wood-rotting fungi of North America. *Mycologia* 72: 1–49.

Giovanetti, G. 1990. Prima produzione di carpofori di *Tuber magnatum* Pico da piante micorrizate fornite da vivai specializzati. In *Atti del Secondo Congresso Internazionale sul Tartufo, 24–27 Novembre 1988*. Eds. M. Bencivenga and B. Granetti. Spoleto, Italy. 297–302. Guide to cultivation of mycorrhizal mushrooms.

Giovanetti, G., and A. Fontana. 1982. Mycorrhizal synthesis between Cistaceae and Tuberaceae. *New Phytologist* 92: 533–537. Guide to cultivation of mycorrhizal mushrooms.

Giovanetti, G., N. Roth-Bejerano, E. Zanini, and V. Kagan-Zur, eds. 1994. Truffles and their cultivation. *Horticultural Reviews* 16: 71–107. Guide to cultivation of mycorrhizal mushrooms.

Gregori, G. L., and R. Ciappelloni. 1990. Contronto dell'intensita di micorrizazione fra *Corylus avellana* L. di tipo selvatico e da frutto con *Tuber magnatum* Pico. In *Atti del Secondo Congresso Internazionale sul Tartufo, 24–27 Novembre 1988*. Eds. M. Bencivenga and B. Granetti. Spoleto, Italy. 185–190. Guide to cultivation of mycorrhizal mushrooms.

Grgurinovic, C., and K. Mallett, eds. 1996. *Fungi of Australia*. Vols. 1A and 1B, Introduction: Fungi in the Environment. Canberra, Australia: Australian Biological Resources Study. Australasian field guide.

Guinberteau, J., J. M. Olivier, and M. R. Bordaberry. 1989. Données récentes sur la culture des "pieds bleus" (*Lepista* sp.). P. H. M., *Revue Horticole* 298: 17–22.

Guinberteau, J., G. Salesses, J. M. Olivier, and N. Poitou. 1990. Mycorization de vitroplants de noisetiers clones. In *Atti del Secondo Congresso Internazionale sul Tartufo, 24–27 Novembre 1988*. Eds. M. Bencivenga and B. Granetti. Spoleto, Italy. 205–210. Guide to cultivation of mycorrhizal mushrooms.

Guinness Book of Records. 2000. Stamford, Connecticut: Guinness.

Gutierrez Reyes, R. 2000. Indoor cultivation of paddy straw mushroom, *Volvariella volvacea*, in crates. *Mycologist* 14: 174–176.

Guzmán, G., and R. Watling. 1978. Studies in Australian agarics and boletes, 1: some species of *Psilocybe*. *Notes from the Royal Botanic Garden Edinburgh* 36: 199–210. Australasian field guide.

Haard, R., and K. Haard. 1980. *Poisonous and Hallucinogenic Mushrooms*. Seattle, Washington: Homestead. Western field guide.

Hall, I. R. 1988. Potential for exploiting vesicular-arbuscular mycorrhizas in agriculture. In *Biotechnology in Agriculture*. Vol. 9, Advances in Biotechnological Processes. Ed. A. Mizrahi. New York: Alan R. Liss. 141–174.

Hall, I. R., G. Brown, and J. Byars. 1994. *The Black Truffle: Its History, Uses, and Cultivation*. 2nd ed. Christchurch, New Zealand: New Zealand Institute for Crop and Food Research. Guide to cultivation of mycorrhizal mushrooms.

Hall, I. R., A. J. E. Lyon, Y. Wang, and L. Sinclair. 1998. Ectomycorrhizal fungi with edible fruiting bodies. 2. *Boletus edulis. Economic Botany* 52: 44–56. Guide to cultivation and ecology of mycorrhizal mushrooms.

Hall, I. R., and Y. Wang. 1996. Edible fungi—supplementary crops to wood production in plantation forests. In *Proceedings of the New Zealand Institute of Forestry Conference*. Invercargill, New Zealand. 77–82.

Hall, I. R., and Y. Wang. 2000. Edible mushrooms as secondary crops in forests. *Quarterly Journal of Forestry* 94: 299–304.

Hall, I. R., A. Zambonelli, and F. Primavera. 1998. Ectomycorrhizal fungi with edible fruiting bodies. 3. *Tuber magnatum. Economic Botany* 52: 192–200. Guide to cultivation and ecology of mycorrhizal mushrooms.

Hamlyn, P. F. 1996. Mycologist's guide to the internet. *Mycologist* 9: 165–167.

Hamlyn, P. F. 1997a. Mycological resources on the internet. *Mycologist* 10: 7.

Hamlyn, P. F. 1997b. Creating a mycological site on the internet. *Mycologist* 11: 23–26.

Harding, P., T. Lyon, and G. Tomblin. 1996. *How to Identify Edible Mushrooms*. London: Harper Collins. Western field guide.

Harris, B. 1993. *Growing Shiitake Commercially*. Summertown, Tennessee: Second Foundation Publications. Guide to cultivation of saprobic mushrooms.

Hayes, W. A. 1987. Edible mushrooms. In *Food and Beverage Mycology*, 2nd ed. Ed. L. R. Beuchat. New York: AVI. 355–390. Guide to cultivation of saprobic mushrooms.   •

Heckman, D. S., D. M. Geiser, B. R. Eidell, R. L. Stauffer, N. L. Kardos, and S. B. Hedges. 2001. Molecular evidence for the early colonization of land by fungi and plants. *Science* 293: 1129–1133.

Hobbs, C. 1995. *Medicinal Mushrooms*. Santa Cruz, California: Botanica Press. Guide to medicinal mushrooms.

Holmberg, P., and H. Marklund. 1996. *Nya Svampboken*. Stockholm, Sweden: Prisma. Western field guide.

Holmgren, P. K., N. H. Holmgren, and L. C. Barnett, eds. 1990. *Index Herbariorum, Part 1: The Herbaria of the World*. 8th ed. Regnum Vegetabile 120. Bronx, New York: New York Botanical Garden.

Hongo, T., T. Ueda, and M. Izawa. 1994. *Fungi: Field Book Number 10*. Toyko: Yama-kei. Asian field guide (in Japanese).

Hood, I. A. 1992. *An Illustrated Guide to Fungi on Wood in New Zealand*. Auckland, New Zealand: Auckland University Press.

Hopple, J. S., and R. Vilgalys. 1994. Phylogenetic relationships among coprinoid taxa and allies based on data from restriction site mapping of nuclear rDNA. *Mycologia* 86: 96–107.

Hu, S. Y., Y. C. Kong, and P. P. H. But. 1980. *An Enumeration of the Chinese Materia Medica*. Hong Kong: Chinese University Press. Guide to medicinal mushrooms.

Hudler, G. W. 1998. *Magical Mushrooms, Mischievous Molds*. Princeton, New Jersey: Princeton University Press.

Imazeki, R., Y. Otani, T. Hongo, M. Izawa, and N. Mizuno. 1988. *Coloured Illustrations of Mushrooms of Japan*. Tokyo: Yama-kei. Asian field guide (in Japanese).

Iwase, K., T. Ito, H. Fujita, S. Matsui, T. Tanigichi, and A. Obayashi. 1988. Acceleration of fruit-body formation under environmental control in an area with shiro of *Tricholoma matsutake*. *Transactions of the Mycological Society of Japan* 29: 97–105.

Jacab, C. 1993. *Mushrooms and Other Fungi*. Auckland, New Zealand: Pye Anderson. Western field guide (for children).

Japan External Trade Organization (JETRO). 2000a. Japanese Market Report: Mushrooms. Shares of Imports in the Japanese Market. http://www.jetro.go.jp/ec/e/market/jmr/044/1-DE.html#1-D

Japan External Trade Organization (JETRO). 2000b. Japanese
    Market Report: Mushrooms. Trends in Domestic Production.
    http://www.jetro.go.jp/ec/e/market/jmr/044/1-B.html

Johnson, P. 1977. Mycorrhizal endogonaceae in a New Zealand
    forest. *New Phytologist* 78: 161–170.

Johnston, B. 2000. Gold not worth its weight in truffles. *The Daily
    Telegraph*, 14 November. United Kingdom.

Johnston, P. R., and P. K. Buchanan. 1995. The genus *Psilocybe*
    (Agaricales) in New Zealand. *New Zealand Journal of Botany*
    33: 379–388. Australasian field guide.

Johnston, P. R., and P. K. Buchanan. 1997. Invasive exotic fungi in
    New Zealand's indigenous forests—you can help. *New Zealand
    Botanical Society Newsletter* 47: 8–10.

Jones, K. 1995. *Shiitake: The Healing Mushroom*. Rochester, New
    York: Healing Arts Press. Guide to medicinal mushrooms.

Jordan, M. 1996. Evidence of severe allergic reaction to *Laetiporus
    sulphureus*. *Mycologist* 9: 157–158.

Jordan, P., and S. Wheeler. 1995. *The Ultimate Mushroom Book*.
    London: Anness. Western field guide.

Kagan-Zur, V., E. Raveh, S. Lischinsky, and N. Roth-Bejerano. 1994.
    Initial association between *Helianthemum* and *Terfezia* is
    enhanced by low iron in the growth medium. *New Phytologist*
    127: 567–570. Guide to cultivation of mycorrhizal mushrooms.

Kalotas, A. C. 1997. Aboriginal knowledge and use of fungi. In
    Fungi of Australia. Vol. 1B, Introduction: Fungi in the Environ-
    ment. Eds. C. Grgurinovic and K. Mallett. Canberra, Australia:
    Australian Biological Resources Study. Australasian field guide.

Kidcheck. 2002. Mushrooms. *Kidcheck: An Interactive Guide to
    Children's Health*. http://www.kidcheck.org/wildlife/
    wildlife3.html

Kirk, P. M., P. F. Cannon, J. C. David, and J. A. Staplers, eds. 2001.
    Ainsworth and Bisby's Dictionary of the Fungi. 9th ed. Walling-
    ford, England: CABI.

Kozikowski, G. R. 1996. Foray report from Skye. *Mycologist* 10:
    183–184.

Læssøe, T., and A. Del Conte. 1996. *The Mushroom Book*. London:
    Dorling Kindersley. Western field guide.

Læssøe, T., and B. Spooner. 1994. The uses of gasteromycetes.
    Mycologist 8: 154–159. Guide to medicinal mushrooms.

Largent, D. L. 1986. *How to Identify Mushrooms to Genus*. Vol. 1,
    Macroscopic Features. Eureka, California: Mad River Press.

Lawrynowicz, M. 1993. Distributional limits of truffles in Northern Europe. *Micologia e Vegetazione Mediterranea* 7 (1): 31–38.

Lefevre, C., and I. R. Hall. 2001. The global status of truffle cultivation. In *Fifth International Congress on Hazelnuts*, August 2000. Corvallis, Oregon: Acta Horticulturae.

Legg, A. 1990. Your top twenty fungi: the final list. *Mycologist* 4: 23–24.

Lincoff, G. H., and D. H. Mitchel. 1977. *Toxic and Hallucinogenic Mushroom Poisoning: A Handbook for Physicians and Mushroom Hunters*. New York: Van Nostrand Reinhold.

Lincoff, G. H., and C. Nehring. 1995. *The Audubon Society Field Guide to North American Mushrooms*. New York: Alfred A. Knopf.

Luo, X. C., and M. Zang, ed. 1995. The biology and technology of *Lentinula* mushroom. In *Proceedings of the International Symposium on Production and Products of Lentinula Mushroom*. 2 vols. Qingyuan, China: China Agricultural Scientech Press. Guide to cultivation of saprobic mushrooms.

Malajczuk, N., J. M. Trappe, and R. Molina. 1987. Interrelationships among some ectomycorrhizal trees, hypogeous fungi, and small mammals: Western Australia and northwestern American parallels. *Australian Journal of Ecology* 12: 53–55.

Marais, L. J., and J. M. Kotzé. 1977. Notes on ectotrophic mycorrhizae of *Pinus patula* in South Africa. *South African Forestry Journal* 100: 61–71.

Marchand, A. 1971–1986. *Champignons du Nord et du Midi*. 9 vols. Perpignan, France: Société Mycologique des Pyrénées Méditerranéennes. Western field guide.

Maser, C., J. M. Trappe, and R. A. Nussbaum. 1978. Fungal–small mammal interrelationships with emphasis on Oregon coniferous forests. *Ecology* 59: 799–809.

May, T. W., and A. E. Wood. 1997. *Fungi of Australia*. Vol. 2A, Catalogue and Bibliography of Australian Macrofungi. 1. Basidiomycota p.p. Canberra, Australia: Australian Biological Resources Study. Australasian field guide.

Mendaza Rincón De Acuña, R., and G. Díaz Montoya. 1994. *Las Setas en la Naturaleza*. Madrid: Iberdrola. Western field guide.

Miller, O. K., Jr. 1981. *Mushrooms of North America*. New York: Chanticleer Press.

Miller, O. K., Jr., and D. F. Farr. 1975. *An Index of the Common Fungi of North America: Synonymy and Common Names*. Bibliotheca Mycologica 44. Vaduz, Germany: J. Cramer.

Ministry of Agriculture and Fisheries. 1945. *Edible and Poisonous Fungi.* Bulletin 23. London: Her Majesty's Stationery Office.

Mirabella, A., F. Primavera, and L. Gardin. 1992. Formation dynamics and characterization of clay minerals in a natural truffle bed of *Tuber magnatum* Pico on Pliocene sediments in Tuscany. *Agricoltura Mediterranea* 122: 275–281. Guide to cultivation of mycorrhizal mushrooms.

Mischiati, P., and A. Fontana. 1993. In vitro culture of *Tuber magnatum* isolated from mycorrhizae. *Mycological Research* 97: 40–44. Guide to cultivation of mycorrhizal mushrooms.

Mizuno, T., ed. 1995. Mushrooms: the versatile fungus—food and medicinal properties. *Food Reviews International* 11 (1): 1–236. Guide to medicinal mushrooms.

Monnier, G, and R. Courtecuisse. 1993. *Guide de Poche des Champignons.* Lausanne, Switzerland: Delachaux et Niestle. Western field guide.

Montecchi, A., and G. Lazzari. 1993. *Atlante Fotografico di Funghi Ipogei.* Vicenza, Italy: Associazione Micologica Bresadola, Centro Studi Micologici. Western field guide.

Mycology section. 1988. *Poisonous Mushrooms.* Mycology Section of the Institute of Microbiology, Academia Sinica. Beijing: Science Publishing House. Asian field guide (in Chinese).

Mycorrhiza Information Exchange. 2002. http://mycorrhiza.ag. utk.edu/

National Agricultural Statistics Service (NASS). 2000. Mushrooms: record high levels continue for volume and value of sales of all mushrooms. U.S. Department of Agriculture, Washington, D.C., 18 August. http://usda.mannlib.cornell.edu/reports/nassr/ other/zmu-bb/mush0800.txt·

Neuhaus, V., and K. Neuhaus. 1947. *Pilze.* Iserlohn, Germany: Holzwarth-Verlag.

Nicholls, D. W., B. E. B. Hyne, and P. Buchanan. 1995. Death cap mushroom poisoning. *New Zealand Medical Journal*, 14 June.

Oei, P. 1996. *Mushroom Cultivation with Special Emphasis on Appropriate Techniques for Developing Countries.* Leiden, Netherlands: Tool Publications. Guide to cultivation of saprobic mushrooms.

Ogawa, M. 1977. Microbial ecology of shiro in *Tricholoma matsutake* (Ito et Imai) Sing. and its allied species. V. *Tricholoma matsutake* in *Tsuga sieboldii* forests. *Transactions of the Mycological Society of Japan* 18: 34–46. (In Japanese)

Ogawa, M., and S. Ito. 1989. *Is It Possible to Cultivate Matsutake?* Tokyo: Sou Shin Press. (In Japanese)

Ohara, A., and M. Hamada. 1967. Disappearance of bacteria from the zone of active mycorrhizas in *Tricholoma matsutake* (S. Ito et Imai) Singer. *Nature* 217: 528–29.

Ohenoja, E., and S. Lahti. 1978. Food from the Finnish forests. In *Proceedings of the Eighth World Forestry Congress, 16–28 October 1978*. Vol. 3, Forestry for Food. Jakarta. 1013–1021.

Ohta, A. 1994. Production of fruit-bodies of a mycorrhizal fungus, *Lyophyllum shimeji*, in pure culture. *Mycoscience* 35: 147–151.

Olivier, J. M. 2000. Progress in the cultivation of truffles. In *Mushroom Science XV: Science and Cultivation of Edible Fungi*. Vol. 2. Ed. L. J. L. D. Van Griensven. Rotterdam, Netherlands: Balkema. 937–942.

Olivier, J. M., J. C. Savignac, and P. Sourzat. 1996. *Truffe et Trufficulture*. Perigueux, France: Fanlac. Guide to cultivation of mycorrhizal mushrooms.

Ortega, A., J. Piqueras, and P. Amate. 1996. *Setas: Identificatión, Toxicidad, Gastromicología*. Granada, Spain: Proyecto Sur. Western field guide.

Oss, O. T., and O. N. Oeric. 1976. *Psilocybin: Magic Mushroom Growers' Guide*. Berkeley, California: And/Or Press. Western field guide.

Ower, G. L. 1988. Cultivation of *Morchella*. U.S. patent number 4866878.

Pacioni, G., and O. Comandini. 2000. *Tuber*. In *Ectomycorrhizal Fungi: Key Genera in Profile*. Eds. J. W. G. Cairney and S. M. Chambers. New York: Springer-Verlag. 163–186.

Palm, M. E., and I. H. Chapela, eds. 1997. *Mycology in Sustainable Development: Expanding Concepts, Vanishing Borders*. Boone, North Carolina: Parkway.

Pegler, D. N. 2000. Useful fungi of the world: some uses of bracket fungi. *Mycologist* 14: 6–7. Guide to medicinal mushrooms.

Pegler, D. N., T. Læssøe, and B. M. Spooner. 1995. *British Puffballs, Earthstars, and Stinkhorns*. Kew, England: Royal Botanic Gardens. Western field guide.

Pegler, D. N., and B. M. Spooner. 1997. *The Mushroom Identifier*. London: Grange. Western field guide.

Pegler, D. N., B. M. Spooner, and T. W. K. Young. 1993. *British Truffles: A Revision of British Hypogeous Fungi*. Kew, England: Royal Botanic Gardens. Western field guide.

Penn State Mushroom Laboratory. 2002. http://mushroomspawn. cas.psu.edu/

Percudani, R., A. Zambonelli, and S. Ottonello. 1996. Computer-assisted recognition of truffles. Abstracts of the First International Conference on Mycorrhizae, 4–9 August: 96. University of California, Berkeley.

Phillips, R. 1981. *Mushrooms and Other Fungi of Great Britain and Europe*. London: Pan. Western field guide.

Phillips, R. 1991. *Mushrooms of North America*. Boston: Little, Brown. Western field guide.

Picart, F. 1980. *Truffle: The Black Diamond*. Santa Rosa, California: Agri-Truffe.

Pilz, D., J. Smith, M. P. Amaranthus, S. Alexander, R. Molina, and D. Luoma. 1999. Mushrooms and timber: managing commercial harvesting in the Oregon Cascades. *Journal of Forestry* 97 (3) 4–11.

Pirazzi, R. 1990. Micorrizazione artificiale con miceli isolati "in vitro" di *Tuber melanosporum* Vitt. e *T. magnatum* Pico. In *Atti del Secondo Congresso Internazionale sul Tartufo, 24–27 Novembre 1988*. Eds. M. Bencivenga and B. Granetti. Spoleto, Italy. 173–190. Guide to cultivation of mycorrhizal mushrooms.

Poitou, N., M. Mamoun, M. Ducamp, J. Guinberteau, and J. M. Olivier. 1989. Mycorrhization controlée et culture expérimentale du champ de *Boletus* (=*Suillus*) *granulatus* et *Lactarius deliciosus*. In *Proceedings of the Twelfth International Congress on the Science and Cultivation of Edible Fungi, 1987*. Brunswick, Germany. 551–563. Guide to cultivation of mycorrhizal mushrooms.

Primavera, F. 1995. La coltivazione del tartufo "secondo natura." *Terra e Vita* 45: 57–59.

Przybylowicz, P., and J. Donoghue. 1988. *Shiitake Growers' Handbook*. Dubuque, Iowa: Kendall/Hunt.

Quack, W., T. Anke, F. Oberwinkler, B. M. Giannetti, and W. Steglich. 1978. Antibiotics from basidiomycetes, 5. Merulidial, a new antibiotic from the basidiomycete *Merulius tremellosus* Fr. *Journal of Antibiotics* 31: 737–741.

Rammeloo, J., and R. Walleyn. 1993. *Scripta Botanica Belgica*. Vol. 5, The Edible Fungi of Africa South of the Sahara: A Literature Survey. Meise: National Botanic Garden of Belgium.

Reddish, D. 1995. Delicious radiata! *New Zealand Pine International* (January–February): 27.

Redecker, D., R. Kodner, and L. E. Graham. 2000. Glomalean fungi from the Ordovician. *Science* 289: 1920–1921.

Reid, D. A. 1980. A monograph of the Australian species of *Amanita* Pers. ex Hook. (Fungi). *Australian Journal of Botany, Supplementary Series* 8: 1–96. Australasian field guide.

Renaud, Y. 1989. Controle des champignons sauvages effectué au Marché Central, rapport d'activité. Service des Marchés, Ville de Nancy, France.

Reyna Domenech, S. 1992. *La Trufa*. Madrid: Agrogías mundi-prensa. Guide to cultivation of mycorrhizal mushrooms.

Reynolds, J. E. F., and K. Parfitt. 1996. *Martindale: The Extra Pharmacopoeia*. London: Royal Pharmaceutical Society.

Riley, M. 1988. *Maori Vegetable Cooking*. Paraparaumu, New Zealand: Viking Sevenseas.

Riley, M. 1994. *Maori Healing and Herbal*. Paraparaumu, New Zealand: Viking Sevenseas.

Riousset, G., G. Chevalier, and M. C. Bardet. 2001. *Truffes d'Europe et de Chine*. Paris: CTIFL/INRA. Western field guide.

Rowe, R. F. 1997. The commercial harvesting of wild edible mushrooms in the United States. *Mycologist* 11: 10–15.

Samuels, C. B. 2002. *Discover Mushrooms*. Computer database. www.mushroom.cc/discover.htm

Sanders, R. 2000. New fossil find pushes age of terrestrial fungi back 60 million years, to the same era when green plants pulled themselves onto land. *Campus News*, 14 September. University of California, Berkeley. http://www.berkeley.edu/news/media/releases/2000/09/14_funghi.html

Scates, K. 1995. *Diagnosis and Treatment of Mushroom Poisoning on the Basis of Symptoms and Mushrooms*. Portland, Oregon: Fungal Cave Books. Wall chart.

Schlosser, W. E., and K. A. Blatner. 1995. The wild edible mushroom industry of Washington, Oregon, and Idaho. *Journal of Forestry* (March): 31–36.

Scrase, R. 1996. Cultivating mushrooms: making composted and non-composted substrates. *Mycologist* 10: 52–55. Guide to cultivation of saprobic mushrooms.

Segedin, B. P. 1987. An annotated checklist of agarics and boleti recorded from New Zealand. *New Zealand Journal of Botany* 25: 185–215.

Segedin, B. P., and S. R. Pennycook. 2001. A nomenclatural checklist of agarics, boletes, and related secotioid and gasteromycetous fungi recorded from New Zealand. *New Zealand Journal of Botany* 39: 285–348.

Shepherd, C. J., and C. J. Totterdell. 1988. *Mushrooms and Toadstools of Australia*. Melbourne, Australia: Inkata Press. Australasian field guide.

Simons, D. M. 1987. Poisonous mushrooms. In *Food and Beverage Mycology*. Ed. L. R. Beuchat. New York: AVI. 391–433. Western field guide.

Singer, R. 1986. *The Agaricales in Modern Taxonomy*. 4th ed. Koenigstein, Germany: Koeltz Scientific Books. Western field guide.

Slater, N. 2000. Down to earth. *The Observer*, 10 September. London.

Smith, R. F. 1990. *Microscopy and Photomicroscopy: A Working Tool*. Boston: CRC Press.

Smith, S. E., and D. J. Read. 1997. *Mycorrhizal Symbiosis*. London: Academic Press.

Sourzat, P. 1994. *Guide pratique de trufficulture*. Station d'experimentations sur la truffe. Lycée professionnel agricole Cahors-Le Montat, Le Montat.

Southcott, R. V. 1974. Notes on some poisonings and other clinical effects following ingestion of Australian fungi. *South Australian Clinics* 6: 441–478.

Southcott, R. V. 1997. Mechanisms of macrofungal poisoning in humans. In *Fungi of Australia*. Vol. 1B, Introduction: Fungi in the Environment. Eds. C. Grgurinovic and K. Mallett. Canberra, Australia: Australian Biological Resources Study. 297–313. Australasian field guide.

Spoerke, D. G., and B. H. Rumack, eds. 1994. *Handbook of Mushroom Poisoning: Diagnosis and Treatment*. Boca Raton, Florida: CRC Press.

Stamets, P. 1993. Cultivating morels. *Mushroom: The Journal of Wild Mushrooming* 11 (4): 9–15.

Stamets, P. 1996. *Psilocybin Mushrooms of the World: An Identification Guide*. Berkeley, California: Ten Speed Press.

Stamets, P. 2000. *Growing Gourmet and Medicinal Mushrooms*. Berkeley, California: Ten Speed Press. Guide to cultivation of saprobic mushrooms.

States, J. S. 1990. *Mushrooms and truffles of the Southwest*. Tucson, Arizona: University of Arizona Press. Western field guide.

Stephenson, S. L., and H. Stempen. 1994. *Myxomycetes: A Handbook of Slime Molds*. Portland, Oregon: Timber Press.

Stevenson, G. 1994. *New Zealand Fungi: An Illustrated Guide*. Christchurch, New Zealand: Canterbury University Press. Australasian field guide.

Sun, W. S., and J. Y. Xu. 1999. Cultivation of edible fungi has become one of the backbone industries in the rural economy of China. *Edible Fungi of China* 18 (2): 5–6.

Taylor, M. 1983. Some common fungi of Auckland city. *Tane* 29: 133–142. Australasian field guide.

Taylor, M. 1991. *Mushrooms and Toadstools*. Wellington, New Zealand: Reed. Australasian field guide.

Thomas, M. G., and D. R. Schumann. 1993. Income opportunities in special forest products: self-help suggestions for rural entrepreneurs. Agriculture Information Bulletin 666. Washington, D.C.: United States Department of Agriculture.

Thomson, D. J., and S. Bradbury. 1987. *An Introduction to Photomicrography*. Oxford: Oxford University Press.

Tocci, A, G. Gregori, and G. Chevalier. 1985. Produzione di piantine tartufigene (*Tuber magnatum* Pico) sinitesi micorrizica col sistema dell' "innesta" radicale. *L'Italia Forestale e Montana* 3: 143–152. Guide to cultivation of mycorrhizal mushrooms.

Toleman, E. E. 1985. *Mushrooms*. Information Services Aglink. 4 vols, HPP 317–320. Wellington, New Zealand: Ministry of Agriculture and Fisheries. Guide to cultivation of saprobic mushrooms.

Tominaga, Y. 1975. Studies on the tunnel cultivation, the so-called Hiroshima method of *Tricholoma matsutake* (Ito et Imai) Sing., I: On the forcing culture of *Tricholoma matsutake* in the year 1974. Bulletin of the Hiroshima Agricultural College 5: 165–80. (In Japanese)

Tominaga, Y., and S. Komeyama. 1987. *Practice of Matsutake Cultivation*. Tokyo: Youken. (In Japanese)

Trappe, J. M. 1979. The orders, families, and genera of hypogeous Ascomycotina (truffles and their relatives). *Mycotaxon* 9: 297–340.

Ueda, T., M. Uchida, S. Oogi, S. Miyauchi, and Y. Yamada. 1992. The best 100 wild mushrooms. Kinoko 1. *Yume Shizen* (September): 35–67. Asian field guide (in Japanese).

Urbani, G. 1995. La tartuficoltura razionale: analisi di un investimento. *L'informatore Agrario* 31: 29–32.

Van der Westhuizen, G. C. A. 1983. Mushrooms and toadstools: a guide to the common edible, inedible, and poisonous South African species. South African Department of Agriculture Bulletin 396.

Van Griensven, L. J. L. D., ed. 2000. Science and cultivation of edible fungi. In *Proceedings of the Fifteenth International Congress, Maastricht, Netherlands, 15–19 May 2000*. Rotterdam, Netherlands: A. A. Balkema. Guide to cultivation of saprobic mushrooms.

Vitroplant. 1994. Propone piante di qualità con micorrizazione garantita. Gambettola, Italy: Vitroplant. Guide to cultivation of mycorrhizal mushrooms.

Walleyn, R., and J. Rammeloo. 1994. *Scripta Botanica Belgica*. Vol. 10, The Poisonous and Useful Fungi of Africa South of the Sahara: A Literature Survey. Meise: National Botanic Garden of Belgium.

Wang, Y. 1995. *Tricholoma matsutake*. Ph.D. Thesis, University of Otago, Dunedin, New Zealand. Guide to cultivation of mycorrhizal mushrooms.

Wang, Y., I. R. Hall, and L. Evans. 1997. Ectomycorrhizal fungi with edible fruiting bodies. 1. *Tricholoma matsutake* and allied fungi. *Economic Botany* 51: 311–327. Guide to cultivation and ecology of mycorrhizal mushrooms.

Wang, Y., I. R. Hall, L. Sinclair, and A. L. J. Cole. 1995. *Botetus edulis* sensu lato: a new record for New Zealand. *New Zealand Journal of Crop and Horticultural Science* 23: 227–231.

Wasser, S. P., and A. L. Weis. 1999. Medicinal properties of substances occurring in higher basidiomycetes: current perspectives (review). *International Journal of Medicinal Mushrooms* 1: 31–62. Guide to medicinal mushrooms.

Wood, T. G., and R. J. Thomas. 1989. The mutualistic association between Macrotermitinae and *Termitomyces*. In *Insect-Fungus Interactions*. Eds. N. Wilding, N. M. Collins, P. M. Hammond, and J. F. Webber. London: Academic Press. 69–92.

Wuest, P. J., D. Levanon, and Y. Hadar, eds. 1994. Spent mushroom substrate symposium 1994. In *Proceedings of the Spent Mushroom Substrate Symposium*. Philadelphia.

Wuest, P. J., D. J. Royce, and R. B. Beelman, eds. 1987. Cultivating edible fungi. Developments in crop science 10. In *Proceedings of the International Symposium on Science and Technical Aspects of Cultivating Edible Fungi*. Amsterdam: Elsevier Science. Guide to cultivation of saprobic mushrooms.

Ying, J. Z., X. L. Mao, Q. M. Ma, L. W. Yu, and Y. C. Zong. 1988. *Edible Mushrooms*. Beijing: Science Publishing House. Asian field guide (in Chinese).

Ying, J. Z., X. L. Mao, Q. M. Ma, Y. C. Zong, and H. A. Wen. 1987. *Icones of Medicinal Fungi from China*. Beijing: Science Press. Guide to medicinal mushrooms.

Young, T. 1982. *Common Australian Fungi*. Kensington, Australia: New South Wales University Press. Australasian field guide.

Zambonelli, A., and R. Di Munno. 1992. Indagine sulla possibilità di diffusione dei rimboschimenti con specie tartufigene: aspetti tecnico-colturali ed economici. Ministero dell'Agricoltura e delle Foreste. Citta di Castello, Italy.

Zambonelli, A., G. Govi, and A. Previati. 1989. Micorrizazione in vitro di piantine micropropagate di *Populus alba* con micelio di *Tuber albidum* in coltura pura. *Micologia Italiana* 3: 105–111. Guide to cultivation of mycorrhizal mushrooms.

Zuccherelli, G. 1988. Prime esperienze sulla produzione di piante forestali micorrizate con *Boletus edulis*. *Monti e Boschi* 39: 11–14. Guide to cultivation of mycorrhizal mushrooms.

ABOUT THE AUTHORS

Photo by Jack Squires.

Ian Hall was awarded a Ph.D. in botany (mycology) from Otago University, New Zealand, for his research on the effects of vesicular-arbuscular mycorrhizas on native plants, carried out under the direction of Professor Geoff Baylis. He has worked at Illinois University with Dr. Jim Gerdemann and at the Ministry of Agriculture and Fisheries at Invermay Agricultural Centre near Dunedin, where he studied the pathology of grasses oversown into native grasslands and the beneficial effects of vesicular-arbuscular mycorrhizas on pasture species. In 1985 he shifted his attention to ectomycorrhizal fungi and some of the edible mushrooms they produce. He is now a scientist with Crop and Food Research at Invermay, specializing in edible mushrooms and mycorrhizas.

Photo by Barbara Stephenson.

Steve Stephenson received a Ph.D. in botany (plant ecology) from Virginia Polytechnic Institute and State University in the United States. He is a professor of biology at Fairmont State College, West Virginia, and author of *Myxomycetes: A Handbook of Slime Molds*. He has collected and studied mushrooms and other fungi on six continents, from the tropics to the polar regions of both hemispheres.

Photo by Martin Heffer.

Peter Buchanan was awarded a Ph.D. in fungal taxonomy from the University of Auckland, New Zealand. He has worked as a mycologist at the Mt. Albert Research Centre, Auckland, since 1977. His early research focused on microfungi of grasses but has since extended to wood-decay fungi, especially the identification, classification, and ecology of polypores. Publications include taxonomic treatments of polypores, corticioid (crust) fungi, and mushrooms. A research interest in the cultivation of edible and medicinal mushrooms has led to several trips to Asia to study mushroom cultivation and to trials in Auckland to grow new kinds of mushrooms for New Zealand consumers.

Photo by Jack Squires.

Wang Yun earned degrees from Northwest Agricultural University and Academia Sinica in China and received a Ph.D. in botany (mycology) from Otago University in New Zealand. He has worked as a scientist at the Forestry Sciences Laboratory in Corvallis, Oregon, and as professor and director of the Department of Botany at the Institute of Applied Ecology, Academia Sinica. Since 1990 he has worked as a mycologist at Invermay Agricultural Centre, specializing in the beneficial effects of ectomycorrhizas, edible mushrooms, and silviculture.

Photo by M. J. Walters.

Tony Cole received an M.S. in mycology from the University of Nottingham, England, and a Ph.D. in plant pathology from the University of London. After spending one year at Cornell University as a research associate, he returned to England in 1968 as a lecturer in microbiology at the University of Hull. Since 1973 he has been at the University of Canterbury. His teaching and research interests are mainly mycological, with a special interest in biologically active compounds from fungi.

INDEX

Numbers in bold refer to figures.